# WAR FOR ETERNITY

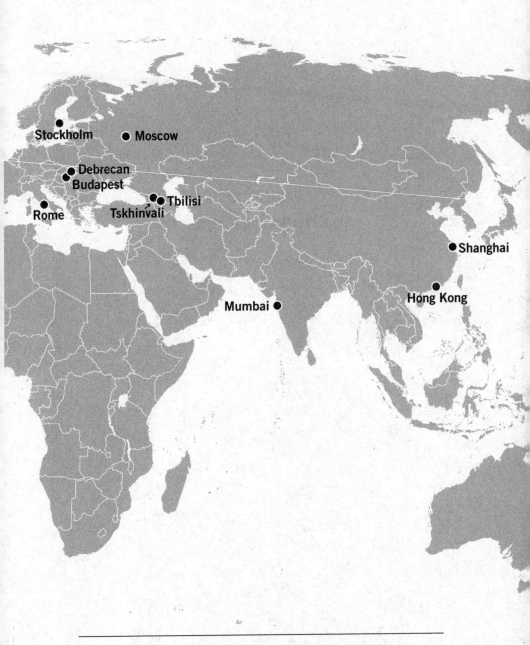

KEY PLACES IN *WAR FOR ETERNITY*

**ALSO BY BENJAMIN R. TEITELBAUM**

*Lions of the North:*
*Sounds of the New Nordic Radical Nationalism*

# WAR FOR ETERNITY

INSIDE BANNON'S FAR-RIGHT CIRCLE

OF GLOBAL POWER BROKERS

## Benjamin R. Teitelbaum

**DEY ST.**
*An Imprint of* WILLIAM MORROW

Excerpt from *Voluspa* in *The Poetic Edda: Stories of the Norse Gods and Heroes* by Jackson Crawford. © 2015 Hackett Publishing Company.

FIRST EDITION

*Designed by Michelle Crowe*

*Map designed by Michelle Crowe. Map background adapted from Peter Hermes Furian/Shuttershock, Inc.*

Library of Congress Cataloging-in-Publication Data has been applied for.

ISBN 978-0-06-297845-5

20 21 22 23 24  LSC  10 9 8 7 6 5 4 3 2 1

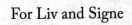

For Liv and Signe

A man encountered a tiger in the forest. Unable to flee or subdue the animal by force, he chose a third option, and leapt on the tiger's back. The man knew that if he was careful and patient he could ride the tiger until it was old and weak. Then he could clutch its neck and begin to squeeze.

—East Asian parable

# CONTENTS

# AUTHOR'S NOTE

I AM BY TRADE AN ETHNOGRAPHER, NOT A JOURNALIST. I am trained in a method of academic research where scholars observe, interact with, and sometimes live among the people they study for extended periods of time, a central goal being one of empathy: to understand and interpret the ways they see the world. Ethnography has often involved the study of the poor and disenfranchised by the powerful. There are ideological and practical reasons for this. Scholars have tended to see political virtue in empathizing with and giving voice to the marginalized, and the same people are often more accessible to—alternately, less able to resist—study. Ethnography isn't the best tool for producing impassioned criticism of its subjects. Its use in the study of powerful elites is rare.

This book is not a proper ethnography, but rests instead in the blurred space between that method and investigative journalism. It is based primarily on firsthand accounts and interviews, most conducted between June 2018 and September 2019, including over twenty hours of on-the-record interviews with Stephen K. Bannon. My writing also draws from informal time I spent with and around the book's main characters or in the ideological and social worlds they inhabit. As a scholar, my instinct is to relate the stories and events I encountered to academic discussions. However, because of the timeliness and broad relevance of the book's content, I have limited academic commentary and placed most in endnotes.

Virtually all of the exchanges and statements I write about were recorded as part of on-the-record interviews. In cases where a recording device was not present, I have contacted participants afterward to confirm transcriptions made from my memory of a verbal exchange. My ability to perform these and similar tasks varied, because I had differing levels of access to those I studied. With Steve Bannon, John Morgan, and Jason Jorjani, I was able to have not only extended visits and observations but also rich dialogues about my analyses and lingering questions. My relationship with them has been much closer to that I am accustomed to as a scholar. With others, notably Aleksandr Dugin and Olavo de Carvalho, interactions were more limited and formalized, consisting to a large degree of interview time and little else.

This becomes challenging when tracing interactions between those I engaged with closely and those I did not, as well as re-creating conversations and actions I did not witness. Key instances of this are the prologue and chapters 2, 4, 8, 10, and 12. I advise readers that reported spoken and inner dialogues in these chapters come from interviews I conducted later—months later in the case of chapter 12, years later in the others. I have made an editorial decision to recontextualize those statements based on my understanding of past events, and in the case of chapter 12, based on an informal review of the text by one of the participants (Bannon) but not the other (Dugin). At best, I will have captured the dialogue and events that once took place; at worst, I will have decontextualized thoughts and expressions. Readers can trust, nonetheless, that extended quotations and substantive inner dialogues are statements that were made to me by the figures in question in on-the-record interviews or verified afterward. Note that though Steve Bannon and I reviewed informally sections from the prologue and chapters 2 and 12, he has not formally reviewed these quoted materials nor any others, and this despite intentions to do so on his part and considerable effort from me (circa fifty text messages or emails to him and his handlers sent from October through November 2019, plus one meeting in D.C. and one trip to New York City with a canceled meeting). Note also that I have lightly edited the grammar of verbal statements by non-English speakers. Note also that I have changed the names of certain secondary individuals.

# PROLOGUE

HIS CAR ROLLS SLOWLY ATOP THE COBBLESTONES OF Via del Babuino, toward the Piazza del Popolo—the People's Square—where crowds swirl round a two-thousand-year-old Egyptian obelisk before the gazes of stone lions, demons, and dogs. It's a warm Rome morning in November 2018, and Russian philosopher and political activist Aleksandr Dugin is headed to one of the city's most exclusive addresses for a meeting he has sworn never to speak of.

He steps out onto the street just shy of the piazza and walks in among the white arches of the opulent Hotel de Russie. Glancing through the lobby and its rear windows, he sees the terraced gardens framing the courtyard and the outdoor Stravinskij Bar behind it, lush even in fall with palm trees, poplars, sculpted vines, and shrubs. Dugin doesn't linger. He passes through the lobby and turns up the stairs, where he is greeted by a handler who walks him onward, down a hall, through another set of doors, and into a suite and the outstretched arms of Stephen K. Bannon.

They exchange smiles and pleasantries while Bannon looks

Dugin over, studying the Russian's marble-blue eyes and his signature long grizzled beard—an emblem of another place and another time. "Incredible," Bannon says, "Can you imagine what Washington would think?"

Good question. Dugin was banned from traveling to the United States and Canada in 2015 after allegedly calling for a genocide in Ukraine. His international reputation, justified or not, as the mad mastermind of Vladimir Putin's geopolitical agenda makes him particularly poisonous for someone like Bannon. Back in the States, Donald Trump's successful presidential campaign has been under criminal investigation for over a year and a half amid allegations it coordinated and colluded with the Russian government during the 2016 election. Bannon managed that campaign, and although those who worked under and around him are falling to the investigation as it churns on—three high-profile figures have pled guilty in the past weeks alone—he himself remained untouched. Now he is standing face-to-face with Russia's most notorious ideologue, an inspiration not only to Putin's geopolitics but to the Russian leader's radicalism as well.

They are in one of the hotel's private rooms and will remain there all day, hidden from the white-clad clerks, concierges, and bellhops below; from the bustle of the piazza outside; from the metastasizing hunt for Russian influence in the U.S. government that rages across the Atlantic. Risks abound, but this couldn't wait any longer. Both men want to influence each other, and for Bannon, this entails bringing Dugin to his side, and Russia to America's. How? By leveraging a bond between him and his guest that few know about, and even fewer would understand.

ABOUT EIGHT HOURS LATER, they emerge from the room, shaking hands and promising to meet again.

"You are a very different kind of person, Mr. Bannon."

"You, too, brother."

Reverent, irreverent till the end. Bannon's handlers start to brief him on his dinner plans. Dugin turns back down the stairs, moving through the hotel lobby and out into the dark Rome night, where his car is waiting. For all the time they have spent together, there is still much left unsaid. In truth, Dugin regards Bannon as more than simply "different," more in fact than a mere person. This American emerged from a wasteland, a society forged in modernism with no connection to its soil, no connection to history, and no sacred roots. To be American is to be without Tradition, which has made Bannon's rise all the more spectacular. For there, among the ruins of modernity and materialism—in the midnight kingdom, at the midnight hour—a sudden blast of light. The Russian sees Bannon's rise to power as the beginning of a successful revolt against the modern world, one foretold by ancient mystics and detailed in the writings of underground twentieth-century spiritualists. Bannon isn't a person; he's an eschatological sign.

They may disagree about geopolitics, and their careers may have had ups and downs. It doesn't matter. They are differentiated men, men of the spirit, men against time—part of the same transcendental unity. *We are Traditionalists,* Dugin thinks to himself, *and it is our time.*

# 1

## PILLARS OF TRADITION

I TURNED ON MY RECORDER. "SO MY FIRST—MY MAIN question is, are you a Traditionalist?"

Steve Bannon pondered this question as he sat down at the table across from me, framed by windows opening onto the skyline of Manhattan's Upper East Side. It was June 2018 and we were in one of the most exclusive hotels in the neighborhood. I had given Bannon's code name to the reception desk. Soon uniformed staff whisked me up to his luxurious penthouse apartment, in the middle of which he presided, swarmed by assistants meeting his every request. *He looks better in person,* I thought, fresh out of the shower with his hair slicked back and face shaved. Tossed onto the couch behind him, however, was his signature green and brown barn jacket—ratty, worn, unbecoming on any body, and particularly on Bannon's when he was at his most rumpled and ruddy. The jacket had itself become an object of caricature and ridicule in pop culture, an emblem of the ugliness many saw in the man himself and his ideas; ugliness that had been the preoccupation of exasperated and outraged liberals throughout Europe and North America who were struggling to make sense of his many contradictions and the possibility that he still wielded influence in their societies and beyond.

He took a sip of his black coffee. "It depends what you mean. And this is off the record today. Later, we can see."

*Click.*

Only a few seconds had passed since I had turned my recorder on, then off, but what Steve said during the interval was richly revealing. My question caused him to hesitate and retreat; I doubt he would have done this had I asked about the sensational labels he is so often described with these days, like *white supremacist, white nationalist,* or *neo-Nazi.* His caution indicated that he knew exactly what I meant by Traditionalism, that he took the question seriously, and that he knew certain answers could be damning. It meant that the effort on my part—a year of emails and text messages, false alarm trips to the airport, and a flight to New York City across two time zones on little more than a hunch—had been worth it.

By Traditionalism—with a capital T—we were referring to an underground philosophical and spiritual school with an eclectic if minuscule following throughout the past hundred years. When combined with anti-immigrant nationalism, however, it was often a sign of a rare and profound ideological radicalism, and that is why I follow it. I am a junior professor and scholar from Colorado specializing in the contemporary far right. For nearly a decade I have devoted myself to studying its personalities, life stories, ideologies, and cultural expressions, preferably through in-person observations and direct interactions. It's complicated work—technically, intellectually, ethically—and it has resulted in a steady stream of speculations and suspicions among my friends and those who know me personally as to how I could persist with, even enjoy, what I do. Indeed, my interest in the subject has various roots, including fear and alarm but also the thrill of discovery and the lessons brought by the unearthing of deeper complexities in places I expected only to find brutal dullness. The timeliness of the subject became an unexpected incentive as well. To study the contemporary radical right is to study the most transformative political movement of the early twenty-first century. It is to witness history.

For years I regarded Traditionalism as the curious prerogative of the most marginalized members of an already marginalized cause—the hallmark of a handful of intellectuals in the radical right disinclined toward skinhead street gangs or populist party politics. Few people knew much about it, not even some expert scholars and journalists, because it just didn't seem consequential. I would introduce it in my classrooms to show students that the people I studied could be not just scary but weird, too. Amid startling political gains for nationalist, anti-immigrant forces in the twenty-first century, Traditionalists on the right appeared to be carrying on with a fantasy role-playing game—like Dungeons & Dragons for racists, as a student once put it. It was the sort of thing that "serious," practical-minded activists on the radical right fled from as they charged toward burgeoning political opportunities and the chance to brand themselves as viable leaders.

That's why I was shocked when media reports surfaced around the 2016 U.S. presidential election that Steve Bannon, then chief strategist to President Trump and the purported mastermind of Trump's campaign, had been recorded name-dropping Traditionalism's key figures. That an individual with such remarkable power and influence even knew about them was almost more than I could believe. How had he come in contact with Traditionalism? What did it say about him, his visions for the United States and the world? And who else was he speaking to about it?

I asked myself whether it was crazy to think he might speak to *me* about it, too. I'm not a political scientist or a journalist—my main department at the university was ethnomusicology, and that was more likely to confuse than impress. But I had rare insight into the fusion of Traditionalism and right-wing politics, as well as a network of insider contacts years in the making to help me study it. It was enough to prompt me to try, though not enough to make me feel as though I belonged as I sat there in front of him; a man who, for a period of time at least, had been one of the most powerful people on the planet, and whom I had managed to freeze with a single query.

But let me back up first and explain what both Steve and I knew when we met.

IT MAY SOUND simple and familiar: Traditionalism. It is anything but.

In casual conversation, we use the word *traditionalist* to describe a person who prefers doing things the old-fashioned way, who believes that life used to be better and is critical of new trends. The kind of Traditionalism I'm talking about may incidentally overlap with that, but it is far more complicated and bizarre. To introduce ourselves to the way Traditionalists think, we'll do best to start by looking at what they reject, for that is far easier to understand than what they champion. They claim to oppose modernity, another concept that sounds deceptively familiar. While we tend to think of *modern* as meaning something that is new or updated, they speak about modernity the way a historian or a social scientist would, as both a method for organizing social life and a period of time when that method came to predominate Europe and the Europeanized world, which is to say generally the 1800s and forward. Modernization, to paint in broad strokes, involves the retreat of public religion in favor of reason. Corresponding to this, it entails a weakening of the symbolic in favor of the literal, and a declining interest in things that aren't easily mathematicized and quantified—spirit, emotions, the supernatural—in favor of those that are, namely material things. Modernization also involves the organization of greater and greater masses of people for the sake of more powerful political mobilization (nations and colonialism) or industrial production and consumption of goods. This leads to attempts to standardize social life so that mass populations may more easily be created. Finally, modernization centers on the belief that through human innovation we can gain a better world than the one we have. A faith in progress, in other words, which in the realm of Western politics has tended to show itself in calls for greater freedom and equality.

Traditionalists aspire to be everything modernity is not—to commune with what they believe are timeless, transcendent truths and lifestyles rather than to pursue "progress." Some Traditionalists work their values into a system of thought far beyond the pale of what counts as modern left or right politics: some even say that it is beyond fascism. Consequently, to the extent that it has infused the thinking of right-wing anti-immigrant, populist, and nationalist actors, it has done so awkwardly. It is anti-capitalist, for instance, and can be anti-Christian. It condemns the nation-state as a modernist construct and celebrates aspects of Islam and the Eastern world more generally. Sound right-wing?

Indeed, the patriarch of Traditionalism was a Muslim convert from France named René Guénon. Tall and thin, with the daintiest of mustaches, he died in 1951 in Cairo, having traded his Western suits for white robes and a turban and having changed his name to Abd al-Wahid Yahya. He embraced Islam while also recognizing it as only one of multiple valid paths toward a greater end. Guénon and his followers believed there once was a religion—the Tradition, the core, or the perennial Tradition—that has been lost, its values and concepts surviving today only in fragments across different faith practices. Like the occurrence of a similar physical trait in separate species, commonalities among different belief systems testify to a common ancestor—namely, the original core religion. And for many Traditionalists, inter-religious agreement is most apparent among the so-called Indo-European religions, notably Hinduism, Zoroastrianism, and the pre-Christian pagan religions of Europe.

Some believed that Catholicism also covertly preserved pre-Christian Indo-European truths. Guénon disagreed, although he thought that Sufi Islam had performed such a task. He aspired to live as a Muslim, regarding investment in a single living Tradition a virtue. But though he avoided religious syncretism in his own daily practice, his writings and those of his followers sought to fuse the wisdom of the various faiths and thereby illuminate the pillars of the Tradition.

So what is *it*—the Tradition? What are the beliefs and values it channels, and how should they be implemented? You'll seldom hear anyone offer details; Traditionalists often speak in broad generalizations. Nonetheless, their thinking tends to be framed by a peculiar understanding of time and society. Let's start with time. Even if we think of our own lives as having a beginning, a middle, and an end, Traditionalists follow Hinduism in believing that human history has always cycled through four distinct ages: from a gold age to silver to bronze and then to dark before moving back to gold and starting the cycle over again. *Gold*, of course, refers to virtue, and *dark* to depravity, meaning that Traditionalists offer a view of history that is both fatalistic and pessimistic. As time passes, the human condition and the universe at large worsen until a cataclysmic moment when utmost darkness explodes into utmost gold and decay begins anew. It is this cyclicality, and with it the belief that the only way for society to improve is to plunge forward into degeneration, that separates Traditionalism from casual conservativism and skepticism toward change. Further, cyclicality ascribes an unusual importance to history, for here, our past is nothing to overcome or escape; it is as well our future.

Thus far I haven't mentioned what Traditionalists consider to be good and bad, what it is that makes the golden age golden and the dark age dark. To understand that, we need to shift our focus from time to people. Traditionalists—especially those in the radical right—think that each age belongs to a different type of people, a different caste. And these castes are ordered in a hierarchy descending from a priest caste to warriors to merchants and finally to slaves. Traditionalists call the upper two castes spiritual and the lower two materialistic. Priests and warriors live their lives striving toward higher, immaterial ideals—in the case of priests, pure spirituality; in the case of warriors, earthly notions of honor. Merchants, on the other hand, value goods or money—physical stuff, the more the better—and slaves take that a step further by trafficking in the most immediate and basic material they can find: bodies and bodily gratification.

Traditionalism's social hierarchy thus opposes the abstract and the concrete, the spirit and the body, quality and quantity. It also maps onto the ages of the time cycle, showing us in the process what it is that Traditionalists consider to be righteous and how it decays. The golden age is the priestly era, the silver belongs to warriors, the bronze to merchants, and the dark age to slaves. And in each age, the caste that predominates dictates its vision of culture and politics to the rest of society. For instance, during the golden age, the government would be a theocracy and religious authority and devotional art would be prized above all else, while subsequent eras would witness the rise of a military state, plutocracy and the rule of the wealthy, and finally a dark age in which a reign of quantity gives political power to the masses in the form of either democracy or communism. How long is each four-age cycle? Hinduism typically says it takes millions and millions of years to complete. Traditionalists often see it playing out on a shorter time span, though all tend to agree as to which age we live in today: the dark age—the Kali Yuga, in Sanskrit. They condemn the present, accordingly, trusting that time will make their societies great again.

Those are the basics, the points upon which most Traditionalists on the right agree. But to grasp this is only to scratch the surface of their thought.

A complicated successor to René Guénon, Italian baron Julius Evola, would add considerably to Traditionalist thought and carry the school into right-wing politics. Born in Rome in 1889, Evola was less inclined to see Westerners turn East in search of spiritual transcendence. Traditionalism for him would become a tool for championing what he saw as the native European. In addition to a hierarchy with spirituality on top and materialism at the bottom, Evola proposed that race also ordered human beings, with whiter, Aryan people constituting a historical ideal atop those with darker skin—Semites, Africans, and other non-Aryans. Other hierarchies he honored included those placing masculinity above femininity, geographical northernness over the global south, even one ordering people's body postures and gazes, with those looking upward and worshiping the sun being more virtuous than those oriented toward the ground.

And like Guénon, Evola also thought that the hierarchy itself was a variable in this scheme. As he wrote regarding Traditional societies of the golden age, "the underlying principle [. . .] in such societies [. . .] is that there does not exist one, simple universal way of living one's life, but several distinct spiritual ways." As the time cycle advances, differentiation and diversity recede as the caste that reigned in one age disintegrates during the next. With time, priests and warriors simply disappear, or become costumed versions of the dominant caste—people dressing and acting like priests and warriors but with the values and attitude of merchants and slaves. Time, in other words, levels humanity into a mass community based on its lowest common denominator, and hierarchy and human differentiation can return only after the turning of the dark age. Thus we can name an additional hierarchy, one with differentiated social order at the top and mass homogenization at the bottom.

Ponder the potential synergies and interactions between these hierarchies and you will have begun to grasp Traditionalism as most on the radical right relate to it. In the version I've presented here, spirituality, antiquity, Aryan or white race, masculinity, the northern hemisphere, sun worship, and social hierarchy are all intertwined. Having an authentic relationship to any one of these items entails embracing them all. This informed part of Evola's understanding of history: he believed that Aryans were descended from a patriarchal society of ethereal, ghostly beings who lived in the Arctic and whose virtue declined as they migrated south and became incarnate. Alternately, he and others saw in modernity the rise of a dark age where democracy and communism proceeded from widespread contempt for the past and a corresponding faith in progress; where politics focused on economics, where the global population was darkening due to northward migration from the global south, and where feminism and secularism forged a culture that celebrates sexual hedonism and chaotic disregard for boundaries of all kinds.

Thus what Traditionalism offers is an account of history and society that treats a wide range of modern ideals and movements as interrelated and equally contemptible. One cannot celebrate capitalism while opposing a similarly mass-ified and materialistic communism, or endorse a Christian worldview that treats the past as a sin and the future as salvation, claims all are equal before God, and advocates a separation of church and state while also condemning a modern feminism that channels similar ideals. The Traditionalist is obliged to resist it all to the extent he (most are men) can. That's why its political incarnation seems so radical, and also why it is so hard to imagine Traditionalism ever operating *within* the institutions of contemporary democratic politics.

BANNON AND I had been speaking for nearly an hour and a half when the door to his apartment opened and his next guest, early bitcoin investor Jeffrey Wernick, entered the room. I took my leave, rode the elevator down to the hotel lobby, passed the dapper bar to the right, and wended my way out to the street.

How surreal it all was. Bannon was well-read and quick-thinking. Brilliant, even. And yet our conversation also left me curious and unnerved. An obscure and exceptionally radical way of thinking had somehow moved from shrouded religious sects and ultraconservative intellectual circles into the White House and beyond. Bannon wasn't just aware of Traditionalism, as some media had reported; it shaped his fundamental understanding of the world and of himself.

I didn't yet have time to ponder it all, because immediately after leaving Bannon's hotel, I had another meeting to attend to. In haste I walked to Fifth Avenue and turned left, heading down the eastern edge of Central Park before turning right on 59th Street and entering the Plaza Hotel and the glimmering Palm Court restaurant in its center. Margarita in hand, a slight young man named Jason Reza Jorjani was waiting for me at the bar, a smile on his face. Jason wasn't new to me. He was the type of person I was more accustomed to studying: the former editor of the leading English-language publisher of far-right intellectualism and Traditionalism, Arktos, and a former associate of notorious white nationalist activists like Daniel Friberg in Sweden and Richard B. Spencer in the United States.

An hour or so later, as I was leaving the bar, he handed me a copy of his book *Prometheus and Atlas*. "If you get a chance, would you give this to Steve?" he asked. I hesitated, replying that I couldn't count on getting another interview. Jason understood, but insisted nonetheless. We shook hands and I walked out to see Central Park aglow in a warm sunset. I glanced at the cover of the book in my hand, which depicted the two Greek mythological namesakes, and remembered that Prometheus and Atlas were each immortalized as statues in Rockefeller Center just blocks south of me. I flipped to the back cover and read that the book aims, among other things, "to deconstruct the nihilistic materialism and rootless rationalism of the modern West." It sounded Traditionalist. *My mind is too full for more of this right now,* I thought to myself as I put the book in my bag and charted my path across the street and into the park, hopefully to find a secluded space to process and take some notes. I don't know why, but I decided to look at the book one more time. I opened it, skipped to the title page, where I found a handwritten message.

*Dear Steve,*

   *Sorry for the trouble. The* NYT *and* Newsweek *took my words way out of context. But I hardly need to explain to you how fake news works. Thank you for all your efforts to Make America Great Again! Best wishes, Jason*

   *P.S. In case you'd ever like to have the meeting that Jellyfish planned to set up, call me . . .*

*That's odd. Why would Jason give Steve this book? Why would the two meet? And who was Jellyfish?* I looked around. Jason was gone. And something was up.

In that moment, I found myself on the inside—observing an

attempt to open a private line of communication based on Steve Bannon's eccentric philosophical interests. What I didn't know then was that other exchanges of this kind were already taking place, and they would soon involve some of the most influential ideologues on earth. With time, I would work my way inside those communications, too, and explaining what I learned in the process is the purpose of this book.

What follows is a story about hidden ideas and partnerships operating in the global far-right populist revolt. It is a story about an extraordinary way of looking at people and history that moved suddenly, secretly, and almost simultaneously from the margins of society into positions of power throughout the world, wielded by actors seeking to create a political order unlike anything we've seen before. It is about the birth of multiple geopolitical campaigns, as well as a stranger-than-fiction scramble in the underground right-wing intelligentsia to exploit the situation.

During the year and a half that followed my first meeting with Steve Bannon, I would learn how Traditionalism propelled his ongoing efforts to elevate Donald J. Trump, to align the United States and Russia, as well as his campaigns to bolster nationalist parties worldwide while targeting the European Union and the Communist Party of China. Traditionalism was likewise inspiring Brazil's populist leaders to distance their country from China and embrace the United States and, paradoxically, Russia's disinclination to pursue new partnerships with the West. And when exploring the social worlds where Traditionalist ideas grow, I encountered white Aryan nationalists who make pilgrimages to Hare Krishna ashrams in India; frequenters of metaphysical bookstores who claim that multiculturalism can be stopped with mysticism; Caucasian warlords; exiled Chinese kingpins; and lobbyists laundering money for Mexican drug cartels in order to fund anti-immigration projects. Combining to make an outlandish cast of characters, they illustrated the fact that what is taking place today is an exchange between ascendant political elites and intellectual lepers. Their activities are riveting to follow but also startling. For seldom have we seen such an eccentric and incendiary worldview infuse the thinking of such powerful actors, and inspire such a radical reinterpretation of geopolitics, history, and humanity.

By August 2018, I had started visiting Steve Bannon roughly once a month, then for on-the-record interviews, some stretching for hours and hours. I'm not sure why he was so willing to talk to me, and why—more remarkably—he was so candid. Maybe it was the opportunity to converse with someone else with a deep knowledge of politics and Traditionalism. I would like to think that my demeanor had something to do with it: my curiosity was real, as was my will to grapple with his thoughts as they actually are. Or maybe he saw me as a means to spread his messages.

Regardless of his motivations, I had an agenda and priorities of my own. During my first on-the-record conversation, in the same room at the same hotel as last time, I explained that I wanted to know more about the roots of his interest in esotericism and in Traditionalism. Why start there? Because the writings of Julius Evola and René Guénon are so rare in the West. You won't find them on the shelves of just any bookstore, or hear them mentioned in a standard philosophy, religion, or politics course in college. They circulate instead through marginal channels, often of either the obscure occultist or the radical rightwing variant (or both). If I can find out when, where, and how he first came across this literature, it will tell me more about him—about the venues in which he seeks direction and intellectual sustenance as well as the social circles he has moved in.

The problem is, he couldn't tell me when he first encountered Traditionalism—perhaps because he didn't want to, but maybe because he honestly couldn't remember. It was decades ago, he assured me, and it could have occurred in any number of different settings and occasions. Could he tell me one, a possible occasion?

Yes, he replied. There was one time in Hong Kong, forty years ago.

# 2

## POLLYWOG GONE NATIVE

*January 1980. Hong Kong.*

STEVE BANNON HAS A CREW CUT AND A BIG EGO.

He's handsome, too. The twenty-six-year-old glanced at himself in the mirror outside the front heads and straightened his white collar before crossing the deck of his destroyer, the USS *Paul F. Foster*. Sailors were lining up for the short ferry ride from their anchor position to the platform of the Royal Navy piers in Hong Kong. Anticipation was high. It had been a long trip from their home port, but tonight they were free to roam the city and its infamous heart, the Wan Chai district.

The *Foster* had been Steve's home for more than two years, and the address was a point of pride. Most guys who had followed his path ended up on aircraft carriers or in some shitty junior officer job. Minesweepers in Charleston, South Carolina—stuff like that. He got a Spruance-class destroyer based in San Diego, California. It was the elite of the elite, both the crew and the ship. The *Foster*'s standard missions were to protect U.S. aircraft carriers and track Soviet submarines in the Pacific, and Steve had worked on it in a variety of capacities—in surface warfare; as a navigator, a personnel officer, and an engineer. The tasks were mechanical and analytical and he found many of them wearying, but he executed them with rare skill. He had a special ability to focus, he'd tell you—oh, did he have a presence. Promotions were coming his way. Informally, however, he was still considered a novice on the ship, a "pollywog." Whispers were that soon they would be deployed south and cross the equator. That would allow for the uninitiated sailors, Steve among them, to go through an elaborate ceremony—concluding with him kissing the bare belly of a senior comrade—and become a "shellback." The Navy had its own set of myths and rituals.

Now impeccably trimmed and creased, Steve barely resembled himself of just a few years prior. During college at Virginia Tech, he lived in a tent off campus, grew his hair long, listened to the Grateful Dead, and partied hard. That didn't stop him from winning a contentious, mud-slinging election to become president of the Student Government Association during his junior year, or from transitioning to the Navy after graduation. Enlistment had been his plan all along. His folks back in Richmond, Virginia, were working-class Democrats, but they were culturally conservative and had sent him and his brothers to a Catholic military academy. The renegade behavior of his college years was a hiatus, it seemed, rather than a change in direction.

Granted, counterculture still lived beneath his starched and ironed exterior on the destroyer, but few people knew about it. You'd find traces of it tucked away in his duffel bag or under his pillow, in his private routines before bedtime and at dawn. It even made its way into his plans for this evening.

He and his buddies clapped their hands and hooted and hollered as they stepped off the ferry and onto the pier. Bars and brothels awaited the servicemen on these shore leaves, and the mood was electric. Would Steve be joining? Hell yes. He'd never miss a chance to go booming. But he had to take a quick detour, just to run some errands. No, no, no—he didn't need any company, it wouldn't take him long. They should all just head to the bar, to the Pussycat, of course. He'd catch up with them in time for shots.

IN ALMOST EVERY CITY where his destroyer docked, Steve Bannon knew his way to the nearest metaphysical bookstore. He wasn't into incense, crystals, or other New Age tchotchkes, and he wasn't looking to join any clubs. He wanted the serious stuff, books on alternative spirituality. Sometimes he was looking for guides on meditation, other times studies on Eastern religions.

This was part of his private journey, and he didn't know when it all began. Sometimes he thought it was the prominence of Catholicism during his upbringing, though he also wondered if the opposite could be true. The Christian faith had been presented to him as a series of dry moral and ethical edicts, some of which—especially those coming from the Book of Matthew—he wasn't sure he agreed with. Did Christianity today in America have anything to say about the development of his soul, about summoning the mystical and the spiritual here and now?

Not enough. He learned about Transcendental Meditation during college and began reading through the major works of Eastern religion, like the Tao Te Ching and the Hindu Veda texts. Raw intellectual curiosity motivated him, no doubt. But Steve also looked to meditation and spirituality as a set of self–improvement routines—as a complement to his workaholic effort to get ahead in the world, equivalent to academics and his intense regimen of physical exercise. He wanted to be a powerhouse of mind, body, and spirit.

He seldom mentioned any of this to his parents. They might suspect he was straying from his Christian faith, even though he had attended mass semi-regularly throughout college. He was gripped by what he was discovering and found particular inspiration in the methods and practices of spiritualism. Could it be that there was truth to these non-Christian teachings as well, that his own Christianity was only one of many valid paths toward a deeper enlightenment? He knew that it was heresy to fuse faiths. That was called syncretism, and he was no heretic. But what about the possibility that religions have irreconcilable exteriors—"exoteric" forms—but a common inner, esoteric core? Scholars of religion label that idea pluralism, not syncretism, so maybe it's okay. You can belong completely to one faith while taking inspiration from another, right?

It was shortly after enlisting in the Navy that he found the cover he needed to continue: *Zen Catholicism*, a book by an English Benedictine monk named Dom Aelred Graham. It argued that Buddhist meditation could be used to advance the Christian faith, even replenish elements of its ancient spirituality and historic emphasis on practice that had been lost throughout the modern era. For Steve, the message gave him license to forage further, to admit aloud to himself that the Bible as a blueprint for life was incomplete, and that a fuller spirituality even in the Christian tradition would require venturing beyond. At least, that was his tacit justification as he dove into the Upanishads or Aldous Huxley's *Perennial Philosophy*.

And the effort wasn't all about reading, either. Steve renewed his practice of meditation while on the destroyer. The stress of the responsibilities of patrolling the South China Sea was enough to make moments of calm and stillness brought by meditation palliative and essential. His method was basic, a distillation of what he had learned in college: he found a sitting position—nothing fancy—closed his eyes mostly, dropped his chin, relaxed his shoulders, and centered his attention on calming his breaths.

He found a mantra to repeat to himself silently, over and over again. The outcome? For a few minutes, the chaos of his mind was transformed to stillness and order.

He would go through his routines day and night, preferably alone. His roommate occasionally interrupted him or caught sight of an unusual-looking book by his bed. All that came of it was some good-natured razzing, but Steve felt anxious each time it happened. He was fearful of exposure. As a naval officer, especially in this part of the world, you just couldn't be talking about stuff like this. He knew what his superiors would think of him, and had on occasion laid awake at night playing hypothetical conversations in his head. He pictured his superior finding out: "Bannon's doing fucking Zen meditation on a combatant? In the South China Sea? On picket duty? Put a mark in his fitness report. Drop his security clearance. There are nukes on this ship, and we've got a pollywog going native. Bannon's a weirdo!"

That would be devastating—being weird. If you're weird in a wardroom, you'll get a shitty fitness report. You get a shitty fitness report, and you start dropping down the hierarchy. Steve hadn't gotten this far because he was a privileged U.S. Naval Academy grad, like one of those Annapolis ring knockers. He had earned his way on merit and reputation.

AFTER THEY STEPPED OFF the pier, Steve and the other officers went their separate ways. They headed toward the Pussycat club, and he walked deeper into the city: straight south past all the nightlife and almost to the base of the hills, where the roads get crooked. He'd discovered this bookstore during his last shore leave in Hong Kong and suspected he could find his way back. Before long, it came into view. As he crossed a bustling street and approached its doorstep, he stopped and checked all around him. Not a serviceman in sight—he was in the clear, so he went in.

As was true of much of this part of Hong Kong, the bookstore was designed to cater to military personnel from the United States and Great Britain, as well as traveling Western businessmen. In the rest of the city, catering to that clientele meant satisfying male vices. Here it meant English-language books, including a large section on Eastern religion and spirituality.

Steve's interests might have been unorthodox on the ship, but the storekeepers never gave him a second glance when he parked himself in front of their spirituality section. A white Westerner in his twenties who was interested in Buddhism? That was a banality. During the past few decades, Eastern religions had been exploding across Europe and the United States. Some of the growth was from immigration, but the bulk of it came from converts and dabblers—Christians and Jews who felt life in the modern West was meaningless and who thought the ancient East could help them "find themselves" anew. New branches of Buddhism and Hinduism like the Hare Krishna movement emerged with the explicit aim of accommodating newcomers. Yoga and meditation retreats became mainstays from California to New England. And pop culture icons like George Harrison began making pilgrimages to spiritual centers in India.

You could say that Steve was a part of that movement, but he struggled to see himself that way. As early as the turn of the twentieth century, Buddhism, Hinduism, and alternative spirituality outposts served as gathering places for cultural dissidents in white American society—socialists, animal rights activists, polygamists, and feminists—outsiders who nonetheless had the social and economic capital to play with their understandings of life and the universe. The same remained true when Eastern religions surged among young white Americans during the 1960s. Beat poet Gary Snyder famously wrote that he saw morality contained in the dharma as "affirming the widest possible spectrum of non-harmful behavior—defending the right of individuals to smoke hemp, eat peyote, be polygynous, polyandrous, or homosexual. Worlds of behavior and custom long banned by the Judeo-Capitalist-Christian-Marxist West."

Like these others, Steve looked to Buddhism and Hinduism in search of a missing authenticity. He also felt that mainstream American society lacked something, and in that broad sense, perhaps you could call him a dissident, too. But he wasn't especially interested in politics. Like his parents, he identified with the old left—a labor left—primarily because of economic issues. But he was souring on President Jimmy Carter, and the more the left came to be associated with cultural liberalism, the less at home in it he was feeling. And it was that left, the cultural radicals, who were coalescing around alternative spirituality during the 1960s and 1970s.

Maybe Steve was in the wrong place. He was a military guy, a guy's guy. The people flocking to the new ashrams in California may have been from his generation, and most were white, but they otherwise didn't look, act, or talk like him. Then again, maybe it was they who were in the wrong place. Steve knew these ancient writings were steeped in conservative thought practices. Sacred texts like the Bhagavad Gita celebrated militancy, and institutions like the dharma centers were obsessed with hierarchy. Indeed, as Steve was plowing through these texts, Buddhism and Hinduism in the United States were being Americanized—or corrupted, depending on whom you asked—to better align with Western liberal values. These teachings and institutions in their original form were a problem for leftists.

What Steve, the Beats, and Buddhist monks all shared was a belief that human beings were more than just consumers and producers of goods, that what mattered in life were the things we couldn't see with the naked eye or quantify, that hidden wisdom existed not in the latest technology but in some of the oldest religious teaching known to humankind, and that there were virtues to be found by withdrawing oneself from mass society. They argued that much of what the West was calling progress had actually harmed the human condition, that it wouldn't take more innovation and emancipation from the past but rather a return to ancient teachings in order to find a remedy.

Just what ism defined this corrupt mainstream society and its false notions of progress? Was it capitalism, secularism, feminism, Marxism, nationalism, colonialism, urbanization, globalization? Could you find it in its most concentrated forms in consumer society, militaristic jingoism, drug culture, or the sexual hedonism of American flower children? Steve and the other spiritualists might have differing answers to those questions, but their thinking was similar if you zoomed out far enough. Call that what you will.

MINUTES TICKED BY as Steve pored over every book in front of him. Most of these he already owned. The Rigveda. A dozen or so of the Sutra texts. The Tantras. *The Art of War* by Sun Tzu—every dick-face in the military read that one. His eyes stopped on *The Secret Doctrine* by Helena Blavatsky, a brick of over six hundred pages. *What religion is this?* Steve wondered. He opened it up and started surveying the opening pages. "Buddhism" appeared a lot, but so did "Hindu." He turned ahead and continued to read, when a section of a sentence jumped out: "there was a common Aryan religion before the separation of the Aryan race." Aryans?

Just then Steve heard a crash of unidentifiable sounds. He had backed into the shelf behind him and set off a cacophonous chain reaction as small hand cymbals and hanging bells on display banged together. The storekeeper peered around the corner, checking to see if anything had fallen or broken. Steve gave him an apologetic look while the bells continued to reverberate and prisms of light reflecting through a hanging crystal on the shelf danced throughout the room. The storekeeper glared in response and slowly returned to his post at the register.

Steve's focus returned to the book in his hand, and he flipped to the back cover. It said it was the masterwork of Theosophy, containing truths revealed to the author by a set of spiritual masters living in Tibet. He had heard of Theosophy before and thought that it was basically the same thing as the New Age movement. Syncretistic stuff, flimsy. He looked back to the place on the shelf where he found it. He didn't recognize many of the titles. A small gap opened onto a bizarre cover, yellow with the tracing of a face in black—a pointed chin and nose, hollow almond-shaped eyes—and with an arm wrapped awkwardly from behind its head to the front of its face, cradling an orb. A god of some kind? He looked at the spine. *Man and His Becoming According to the Vedanta* by René Guénon.

He was ready to reach out and pick it up when he was interrupted. *Are you going to buy anything?* The storekeeper had lost his patience with the young American. Steve turned away from the shelf and looked back at the book in his hand, the Theosophy text. *I'll go with this one.*

He paid, buried the book deep in his duffel bag, and dashed out the door with a spring in his step. This would make for intense work later, when he's back in his room on the ship. But for now he had to get back to the guys. The Wan Chai night was young. It was time for Steve Bannon to boom.

# 3

# THE JEDI MASTER

BY THE WINTER OF 2018, BANNON AND I HAD SPOKEN four times, and I felt like I was in a routine with him. The last-minute planning and travel. The code words to get to him—you asked for "Alec Guinness" at the hotel reception desk. I still wasn't sure why he continued to speak with me, but I could tell he was enjoying our conversations. I was also getting used to how he speaks.

Bannon can deliver straightforward declarative sentences and stick to a point. I had heard him do it during TV interviews and during debates. Yet for whatever reason, he was abnormally inarticulate during our interviews. His sentences seemed never to end and he could switch topics in the middle of a word. He mispronounced nouns, proper and otherwise. And he had a number of bizarre verbal tics, notably a habit of inserting the word *thingumajig* into empty spaces.

At times, I wondered if his imprecision was due to the topic. Most of our conversations focused on spirituality and metaphysics, and it's hard for anyone to speak concretely about the hyper-abstract. That, or it could also be that I was forcing him to discuss topics that he claimed to know well, but that in reality he had only dabbled in.

Others who encounter his chaotic syntax take it as a sign of phoniness, maintaining that his thinking is shallow and that he uses mouth sounds to compensate. Indeed, his commentary on Traditionalism was consistently inconsistent: he misattributed works and concepts, gave me contradicting stories of his encounters with different authors, and would occasionally glide between discussion of Traditionalism—capital T—and traditionalism as common usage conceives it. Not that he put on airs of being the philosopher genius that some among his detractors and supporters imagine. "I just grab these ideas and kinda make it—so that I can understand it," he told me. "I'm just some fuckin' guy, making it up as I go."

I was coming to disagree with that statement and with critics' claims that his thinking lacked content. A coherent system of thought was beginning to emerge throughout our conversations, though it often required my studying transcripts of our conversations later. But I was still struggling to make sense of his past and to figure out how he had come in contact with the writings of René Guénon and Julius Evola. In the stories he told me of his youth, he represented his younger self as an intellectual and a spiritual seeker, one who didn't rely on institutions to find his way, one who was apt to pursue this journey alone. Though a few other tidbits had come out along the way.

He picked up his narrative from earlier. After leaving the Navy, Steve gradually worked his way into the materialistic lifestyle of the U.S. coastal elites. That began when he moved back to Virginia and, in 1981, took up a new job at the Pentagon in the office of the chief of naval operations while also pursuing a master's degree in national security studies at Georgetown. (I once called the university graduate school to ask for a copy of his master's thesis, and the woman on the phone replied, "You're not the first to ask, and I actually can't say anything to you. Like, not a word." We sat on the phone in silence for about a minute.) He finished in 1983, and, disillusioned with the bureaucracy of the military, immediately entered Harvard Business School.

His heavy academic load cut into his personal reading, but Steve persisted when he could. And he made sure to keep the two worlds separate—his schoolwork and his personal study. That meant that he avoided taking any "gut courses," which I assumed meant humanities and social psychology. He was in school to fill a requirement and receive a certification. He took finance, analytics, everything he would need to work on Wall Street. The other stuff—history, philosophy, and spirituality—he wanted to do on his own. Institutional training could provide him with professional knowledge, but he would supply himself with "content." And was he ever in a place to do that. He reminded me of a grandfather reminiscing of better times as he elaborated: "Harvard Square to me was a revelation. And then the libraries, you know, Widener Library, and the Harvard Business School library. I could go get lost in the stacks . . . I could get lost in the stacks forever . . ."

And maybe he would have, but in 1985, Wall Street called. He graduated and moved straight into a job at the investment banking mega-firm Goldman Sachs, and life began to accelerate. He entrenched himself in the mergers and acquisitions department, quickly gaining a reputation as a fierce workaholic who was competitive as fuck and constantly on the lookout for new ventures. Two years after starting he began to specialize. Goldman moved him out to Los Angeles in order to work on the valuation and acquisition of Hollywood films. By 1990, he would break off on his own to form Bannon & Co., an investment bank in Beverly Hills targeting the same commodities. That unleashed a flurry of new purchases and mergers—he even gained partial rights to a handful of episodes of the hit television comedy sitcom

*Seinfeld.* Before the end of the decade, he had begun production and filmmaking himself.

His personal life was a wreck. By the end of the 1990s, he was a hard drinker and twice divorced with three children. At the same time, however, the remarkable wealth he had amassed and his evolving employment situation afforded new possibilities for his work on himself—his reading and spiritual pursuits in particular. He was making a lot of money, and once that happened, Boom! He was living a totally different life—he wasn't working for the man anymore. He *was* the man, and he could do whatever the fuck he wanted. He'd go to the Bhodi Tree, a spiritualist bookstore on Melrose Avenue in Los Angeles, work the stacks, find a few books, and then spend entire days reading at a café. He'd tell his secretaries not to bother him. And it was all having an impact, for sure. He had mastered the world of business. Now he was ready for "a change of being."

I interjected, breaking his narrative. I knew where the story was going—he would eventually sharpen his right-wing political convictions, strive to produce conservative-friendly films in Hollywood, and begin to collaborate with firebrand Andrew Breitbart, taking over his news outlet in 2012 after the namesake's sudden death. But I wanted Steve to stay in the 1990s with me, during the time when his wealth and security allowed him to return to his spiritual pursuits with greater zeal. Was this when he actually, for sure, encountered the Traditionalists?

Steve began to hesitate again, and we were back to standard banter. "Yeah, no. Guénon—um, 'cause about this time the Traditionalists, with Guénon, and then, um, later Evola. *Man and His Becoming According to the Vedanta* was one of the first, I gotta remember, I gotta think about this . . . whether that was before Gurdjieff."

During the early 1990s, Steve told me, he connected with University of San Francisco philosophy professor Jacob Needleman: a scholar knowledgeable, indeed, of René Guénon, but more a follower of George Gurdjieff—a better-known Armenian mystic whom Steve calls a Traditionalist, though most would not. Born on an unknown date during the second half of the nineteenth century in Gyumri in the southern Caucasus, Gurdjieff was nominally Orthodox Christian, but his spirituality also drew from a range of ancient religious sources. He wasn't especially political. Instead, Gurdjieff concentrated on developing a routine of practices aimed at awakening deeper levels of consciousness and awareness within an individual. His teachings never bled into radical right-wing politics in the way Evola's did, for example, but proved instead more enticing to high-status professional or philosopher types. They attracted people like Needleman, who spent most of his weekends together with others pursuing Gurdjieffian teachings and following Gurdjieff's method—the Work, as it was called—which involved occasional readings and discussions but also dances, many Sufi in origin.

Steve wasn't interested in joining any group. Part of what he liked about some of these teachings was their emphasis on one's ability to transform internally, to live a normal outer life "in the world" while awakening and transforming one's inner self. And conversing with Needleman on these points was revelatory. Steve felt spiritually starved in his current settings. In the investment banking world, the people you were interacting with were just a bunch of highly paid mechanics. Life was soulless. But in Jacob Needleman he had found someone he could talk to about his most private interests and wonders—namely, the alternative spiritualities that he had kept hidden from his partners at Goldman and his military buddies before that. Steve attended a dinner Needleman held for Gurdjieff's son and heir Michel de Salzmann, and later Steve invited Needleman down to his house in Laguna Beach. The two spent four days together, just talking—four days!

The story, really just the geographical reference, sent him in another direction. He still had his library in Laguna Beach. He put notations in his books, so perhaps I could learn something if he would let me peruse them. Could I go down to Laguna and have a look? No, everything was in storage.

I heard the knock on the door and realized my interview for the day was over. I had wanted to ask him about one other piece of information that I thought could relate to Traditionalism from his time in California, about a TV series he wanted to produce called *Those Who Knew*. His former partner Julia Jones described its premise as being that "the greatest ideas are often the oldest ideas, the ancient wisdom." But there would be no chance.

I THANKED STEVE again for his time, left the hotel, and started walking down 63rd Street in the pouring rain toward my decidedly more modest lodging. Were these interviews productive? I still didn't understand exactly how he had come to know about Traditionalism. And each time I asked, he gave me a slightly different, inconclusive reference to the past. So I thought I would return to the earliest piece of hard evidence I had.

I walked into my room, flopped down on the bed, opened up my laptop, and started a video. There he was again on the screen, a younger-looking version of the man I had just been interviewing. It was then late July 2014 and Steve was a little-known figure, the CEO of a right-wing media outlet called Breitbart. He had recently signed on as vice president of a voter data intelligence firm called Cambridge Analytica. He was speaking via video chat to a room full of conservative Christians gathered for a conference in Vatican City.

What he began to describe was a nightmare. He spoke about a crisis in the West, about capitalism and the way it had morphed into two terrifying forms: a state-sponsored crony incarnation that enriched a select few with political connections, and a libertarian form of selfishness that took no care for community. About the secularization of youth. About a rising conflict with a new brand of Islamic extremism emboldened by newfound access to weapons of mass destruction and the messaging power of social media. And about the prospect of violence returning to Europe and North America.

He called for capitalism to be subordinated to spirituality—to Jewish or Christian values in particular—so as to blunt its instinct to treat human beings as commodities. He called for a conservative revolution, not against leftists, but against the conservative establishment in the West, which was peddling elitism and ensuring crony capitalism. A rebellion was bound to happen, he was sure. It would happen in Europe with nationalist parties like the UK Independence Party (UKIP) and National Rally (formerly National Front) in France. It would happen in the United States through the Tea Party—even Latin America and India were likely candidates. It's not all good, he said: some of the movements are attracting racists and anti-Semites, but those elements are likely to disappear as the cause matures.

*What about Putin?* an attendee asked.

Steve responded: "I think it's a little bit more complicated. When Vladimir Putin— When you really look at some of the underpinnings of some of his beliefs today, a lot of those come from what I call Eurasianism; he's got an adviser who hearkens back to Julius Evola and different writers of the early twentieth century who are really the supporters of what's called the Traditionalist movement, which really eventually metastasized into Italian fascism." That was it—the earliest reference I know of confirming his knowledge of Evola and Traditionalism. And he continued: "A lot of people that are Traditionalists are attracted to that. One of the reasons is that they believe that at least Putin is standing up for traditional institutions, and he's trying to do it in a form of nationalism—and I think that people, particularly in certain countries, want to see the sovereignty for their country, they want to see nationalism for their country. They don't believe in this kind of pan-European Union or they don't believe in the centralized government in the United States. They'd rather see more of a states-based entity that the founders originally set up where freedoms were controlled at the local level. [. . .] We, the Judeo-Christian West, really have to look at what he's talking about as far as Traditionalism goes—particularly the sense of where it supports the underpinnings of nationalism—and I happen to think that the individual sovereignty of a country is a good thing and a strong thing."

Putin was a kleptocrat, Steve went on, one bent on expanding Russia's influence globally, and that's not good, no. But given the threats facing the world and the fact that Putin is in tune with the most important values of conservatism, spirituality, and nationalism, an alliance between him and the West may be in order. "I'm not saying we can put it on a back burner," he added, referring to Putin's corruption and imperialism. "But I think we have to deal with first things first."

If only they knew, the people sitting in that room.

I scrolled back to his statements on Evola. His history telling was a bit muddled. He described early Traditionalism as having been a forerunner to fascism. And while it is true that Julius Evola served in Benito Mussolini's government, Evola could hardly have been described as one of its ideological inspirations. Steve knew a bit about that past, but not much. It was not only a slightly inaccurate but also a seemingly unflattering account of early Traditionalism, far from what one would expect to hear from a person who would associate himself with it. Perhaps he didn't identify as a Traditionalist at the time. Perhaps he was covering his tracks. Or perhaps the possibility that Traditionalism aligned itself with fascism didn't bother him.

Steve's words seemed to clarify little. I scrolled back and listened once more, however, and realized that I had missed something. Steve mentioned someone else, an unnamed "adviser" to Vladimir Putin, the person who "hearkens back to Julius Evola," as Steve put it. This was the person connecting Traditionalism to Putin's politics in Steve's mind, who made Russia's actions intelligible as an ideological push for nation-states and against the rise of mass transnational entities. By the time he got to the end of that section, he seemed favorably inclined to it all, both the ideas and the people. So who was this adviser?

I took a deep breath as it dawned on me that I knew exactly whom Steve was referring to. I had even met the man before. And I couldn't believe that any American politician, anyone who ostensibly wanted to promote America's interests, would ever want to have anything to do with him. His relationship to power isn't easily characterized. He has never been Putin's adviser in any direct or formal sense; his means of influence have been more complicated and unstable than that. Traditionalism led him to view the world and history as a series of ongoing large-scale conflicts between civilizations and spiritualities. He was eager to see those conflicts settled through politics and violence, and wasn't afraid to dirty his hands, whether on the street as a protester, in the field alongside soldiers, in the Duma as an adviser, or in the halls of foreign governments as a diplomat of hidden mandate. Throughout, he has shaped the way politicians speak, facilitated unilateral diplomatic agreements, funded militancy, and perhaps laid out a blueprint for Russia's foreign policy.

His background as I have come to know it from study and networking had a major flashpoint about a decade earlier, some years before he and I crossed paths. It came in battlefields at the intersection of West and East, time and eternity. What happened there is the stuff of lore within certain circles. But the story was also thoroughly documented, with photos, eyewitness accounts, and retrospective journalistic investigations galore; the protagonist—the "adviser" Steve Bannon referred to—wouldn't have had it any other way. His name was Aleksandr Dugin.

# 4

# KILLING TIME

*July 2008. Near Tskhinvali.*

HE STRAIGHTENED HIS MILITARY CAP AND PUT ON thick sunglasses, stroking his long beard as he peered out over the ridge toward the south. Two women standing next to him were outfitted with green helmets and Kalashnikovs, sporting black shirts with a bizarre emblem in yellow on the chest—a sort of starlike icon with eight arrows fanning out from the center. Steep tree-covered mountainsides and green plateaus sprouting wild flowers surrounded them, though the entire landscape before them tilted down.

At their backs to the north rose the towering Greater Caucasus mountain range, separating Asia from Europe. It's beautiful. Since antiquity, its snowcapped peaks formed a near-impenetrable boundary, making strangers out of those on either side and prisoners of those who ventured in. But now a deadly force was mobilizing with the means to cross the Caucasus—not by scaling its rocky summits but via tunnels and air. The man with the beard, Aleksandr Dugin, was counting on that force and its capacity for brutality.

Where was he standing? It depends who you ask. Either in the sovereign territory of the Republic of Georgia or in the independent nation of South Ossetia, just across the border with Russia.

An army of separatists had assembled on the mountainside with tanks, mortars, rocket-propelled grenade launchers, sniper rifles, and machine guns. They were Ossetians, the majority ethnic group in the area, and their goal was to break off from Georgia. It was bound to be a messy affair. The Caucasus are the dream and the nightmare of the ethnic separatist, home to a kaleidoscope of groups with differing histories, faiths, and allegiances speaking at times mutually unintelligible languages. Seldom are they neatly siloed from one another, nor is intermingling, secularization, or migration uncommon. Volatility always lays dormant, and it takes a mere drop of domestic antagonism or foreign machination to rouse it to life.

South Ossetia is no exception. Though Ossetians were the majority, they shared space with a sizable ethnic Georgian minority as well as a scattering of Armenians and Caucasian Jews. Ossetians to the north of the border vied for space with Ingush, Kumyks, and Chechens.

Aleksandr Dugin wasn't concerned about that quintessentially Caucasian knot of a problem. What mattered to him was that most Ossetians had ethnolinguistic roots in Iran—a society he was coming to valorize as a fount of authentic spirituality—and they were politically and culturally oriented toward Moscow. The force opposing them, meanwhile, wasn't just another local tribe. Georgian president Mikheil Saakashvili had come to power in 2003 on a pro-Western platform. He was cozy with George W. Bush, and earlier in 2008 he had taken formal steps to apply for membership in the NATO military alliance with the West. If that initiative was successful, it could bring the United States military to yet another of Russia's borders.

The separatists would soon open fire toward the south. Not on the capital Tbilisi, but on small Georgian villages within South Ossetian territory. A campaign of ethnic cleansing? Part of an effort to craft a more Ossetian Ossetia? No doubt, though it was more than that. The hope was that these actions would provoke the Georgian central government into military retaliation. Thereafter Russia—the Ossetians' longtime ally against Georgian nationalism—would have the pretext to cross the mountains in an apparent defense mission and blast Georgian forces out of the area, either annexing South Ossetia or allowing it to declare independence.

That's why Dugin was here. The conflict in the mountains wasn't one between a state and a restive minority group, but rather between Russia and the West, between rooted Eurasia and the gallivanting Atlantic. Between Tradition and modernity.

AS DUGIN RECOUNTED in an interview with author Charles Clover, his story began in earnest in 1980 in Moscow when he joined an underground intellectual and social society known as the Yuzhinsky Circle. The name referred to the barrack apartments in central Moscow where the original group, a gang of oddballs, began meeting during the 1960s. At first, the all-male Yuzhinsky Circle was a repository of things rejected by polite society and the mainstream intelligentsia. Their interests were fascism, Nazism, nationalism, occultism, and mysticism, all mixed with extreme (by Russian standards) drunkenness justified as a tool to open minds. This collection of interests wasn't random. The group was anti-Soviet, and they sympathized with Nazism, not necessarily out of a love for Hitler or anti-Semitism, but rather because it was a colorful historic foe to their own government. Furthermore, esoteric mysticism gave them the opportunity to rebel in a place where state power couldn't reach, in the hidden world of their own psyches. As Dugin would later tell me, "the Communist party owned all of us—owned the mind, the spirit, the emotion, the body. Everything was under control, except one thing. The innermost part." Ironically, however, and despite their rogue natures, many Yuzhinsky participants had family connections to the upper ranks of Soviet society, making dissidence less risky than it otherwise might have been.

As the years went by, the circle grew even more gnarled. By the 1980s it was coed, and its rituals included not only alchemy, drugs, and séances in addition to multiday drinking binges but also sexual experimentation. The Nazi antics continued: the group's nominal leader at the time even called himself the führer and encouraged attendees to dress in Third Reich uniforms and shout "Sieg Heil!" It was also becoming more integrated with radical and spiritual movements outside of Russia. One of the group's leaders, a man named Vladimir Stepanov, had become a world-renowned instructor in the school, or "Work," of George Gurdjieff, whose teachings, as mentioned earlier, emphasized enhancing human consciousness (which, again, was a pursuit and a prize beyond the reach of state authorities). Stepanov was also a follower of an obscure French mystic Dugin had never heard of named René Guénon.

Aleksandr Dugin absorbed these influences with bracing fervor. He was only eighteen years old when he began attending gatherings, and he had a profound impact on the others. Wild and daring, he was charismatic and intelligent, conversant in the works of a range of authors and fluent in multiple languages despite little formal education. A skilled poet and guitar player, he was devoted to the group and its leaders. He embraced the Nazi dramaturgy with rare enthusiasm and brashness, but his manner of speaking and carrying himself also signaled to the others that he came from a family of privilege. That was especially apparent in 1983 when the Russian state police—the KGB—apprehended him for anti-government activities. Surprisingly, he was released.

Someone with power was protecting him. That, however, wasn't enough to save Dugin from the fate of others in the Yuzhinsky Circle during the waning days of the Soviet Union. Negative attention from the KGB pushed them out of polite society and into low-level jobs. Some spread out across Russia and the globe. Some committed suicide. Dugin resigned himself to an inglorious existence by day, even working as a street sweeper. By night, however, he continued his secret socializing and study. An epiphany came when he and others in the circle discovered books by Julius Evola in the V. I. Lenin State Library. How those books had found their way into the open stacks was a mystery—it was likely a mistake by a library staffer. Evola represented the apotheosis of everything the group had idolized: mysticism, occultism, and fascism. Dugin reportedly learned Italian just to translate some of Evola's texts.

Dugin had found his ideological and spiritual home: he was a Traditionalist. And he was convinced, further, that the writings of Guénon and Evola could be used to help Russia at this critical juncture in its history.

By 1990, as the Soviet Union was coming undone, its elite was anxious to imagine alternatives to their current political system, and Dugin fancied himself apt to participate. He not only read and translated material but began to write and publish. One of his notable initiatives was a press and a journal called *Arktogeya*; the name meant "northern land" and referenced the myth of an Arctic origin of the Aryans. Outlets like this one functioned as arenas for playing with ideas, and Dugin committed much of his efforts toward imagining a fusion between Traditionalism and Russian Christian nationalism. He wrote essays promoting Evola's belief that political states ought to be steered by a spiritual elite, and that, similarly, it was time to reinvigorate the Russian Orthodox Church and to treat it as the heir to the Greek Byzantine legacy that fused the kingdom of heaven with a kingdom on earth, where priests were political leaders and vice versa. It was the germ of an idea that Dugin would develop and elaborate on for years to come: the concept that Russia the state had a metaphysical mandate to assert itself.

THE WEAPONRY on the South Ossetian mountainside was in fine order. Dugin fraternized with the soldiers as he walked from post to post, and plenty were kind enough to let him inspect. He lifted a golden mortar up and studied its inscriptions. He rested a rocket-propelled grenade launcher on his shoulder and peered through its optical sight. Turning south, Kalashnikov in hand, he rounded an impressive tank, stopping briefly at one of its ends to pose for a photo—he wasn't afraid to be seen down here. It was a Soviet tank, a T-72, the same kind used by Moscow's forces to confront a Chechen separatist uprising over a decade earlier. However, if you looked up at the side of the tank's turret, you'd see not the hammer and sickle, but the white, red, and yellow bars of the Ossetian flag.

The Ossetian separatists were already participating in a low-level exchange of fire with the Georgian army. Nothing major, just skirmishes that kept the conflict afloat, though the actions during the month of July grew more and more intense. Ossetians had recently attempted to ambush the local pro-Georgian politician while he was traveling. They failed to hit their target, but they killed a few police officers in his convoy. Meanwhile, the Georgian military had established a position on the Sarabuki heights outside South Ossetia's largest city, Tskhinvali, overlooking the Liakhvi River basin and the S10 highway connecting to the capital, Tbilisi. This allowed them to regulate traffic going north and south and, if necessary, to more easily lay siege to the city below. Ossetians understood the strategic importance of this base and had made multiple attempts to take it, though they were thwarted each time and lost a handful of soldiers to snipers from above. The Georgians had the figurative and literal upper hand. But Ossetian leaders trusted that fortunes would soon swing in their favor, so long as the Russian government would come to their aid.

Aleksandr Dugin thought he could help make that a reality. His influence at the time was informal and often mischaracterized, but he was about to make it manifest. It grew out of the collapse of the Soviet Union in 1991, a moment that appeared to many as the final victory for Western liberal democracy. The United States and its political models no longer had a distinct and worthy adversary, and many Russian intellectuals and politicians saw integration into the global capitalistic system as an obvious next step. But the more contact Dugin had with the modern West, the more he began to sympathize with and long for his former hate object: the Soviet state. If he had once celebrated fascism as a counter to communism, now he was poised to champion both fascism and communism against his (and their) real foe: the United States. In 1993, he formalized that agenda with the creation of a new organization, the National Bolshevik Party. The name was a tribute to Nazism and communism, the German and Russian movements from the World War II era that once served as counterweights to American expansion. The same was true of the new party's symbol—a red flag with a white circle, like the Nazi flag, but with a black hammer and sickle instead of a swastika at the center.

Dugin enjoyed the innovation and energy of the political margins, but his clumsy political party was hardly a smashing success. Meanwhile, he remained hungry for influence, and his pathway to it came from a most unexpected source. Old contacts in the Yuzhinsky Circle had led him, surprisingly, into the orbit of those inside or speaking to the military leadership. The Red Army had its share of occultists, too, and they gave Dugin a channel to communicate with their more intellectually adventurous comrades.

This prompted Dugin to vary his style, and also led to new publishing opportunities. In 1997 he released a book called *Foundations of Geopolitics*. In it, he outlined a plan for Russia to regain its prominence in international relations while lessening the influence of the United States and its Western European allies. It was a conflict, as he put it, between a liberal "Atlantic" and an opposing "Eurasia," between societies whose coastal geographical position made them cosmopolitan and landlocked societies oriented toward preservation and cohesion.

Russia is destined to predominate in Eurasian territory, Dugin asserted, territory aligning more or less with the boundaries of the former Soviet Union. But Russia's was not an imperialism akin to that of the United States. The spread of Americanism was homogenizing the world, bulldozing over local diversity with its demands for global capitalism and universal human rights. He claimed that Russia, on the other hand, had always been a federation—a force insistent upon political dominion within a bounded territory, but disinclined toward interfering in the cultures and lifeways of others. The future of cultural and spiritual diversity hinged on the ability for someone to counteract the U.S. march toward global domination, and *Foundations of Geopolitics* recommended methods for achieving this. One suggestion Dugin made in the original publication, and which I would return to often amid the investigations of Russian influence in the 2016 U.S. presidential elections, urges Russians to "introduce geopolitical disorder into internal American activity, encouraging all kinds of separatism and ethnic, social and racial conflicts, actively supporting all dissident movements—extremist, racist, and sectarian groups, thus destabilizing the internal political processes in the U.S." Dugin added that "[i]t would also make sense simultaneously to support isolationist tendencies in American politics."

Traditionalism and mysticism were driving Dugin's thinking, but he restrained his instinct to enunciate that in this book, writing it instead as a dry strategic guide to geopolitics for an audience of governmental military officials. Those were the exact circles where it found its audience. Because *Foundations of Geopolitics* impressed a hard-line minister of defense under Boris Yeltsin, Igor Rodionov, it became standard assigned reading into the twenty-first century at the General Staff Academy—the main institution for training leaders in Russia's military as they worked to reformulate policy after the fall of the Soviet Union. Its success also gained Dugin a hearing with top-ranking politicians in the Kremlin. During the final years of the Yeltsin administration, he became the adviser on geopolitical affairs to Gennady Seleznev, a high-ranking member of the Russian legislature and Communist Party opposed to Yeltsin.

Shortly after Putin's ascension to the Russian presidency in 2000, Dugin began to enhance his network of channels into the Kremlin. He drafted policy proposals that were circulated throughout ministries of domestic politics (primarily via political operative Gleb Pavlovsky); his own protégés like Pavel Zarifullin and Valery Korovin gained government positions; and he was given not only a special Kremlin-assigned liaison for communication but also opportunities to meet Putin directly and privately—all while his books and rapidly expanding media outreach were ensuring that his words would reach Russia's military and political elite.

By 2001, the newspaper *Versiya* began describing Dugin as a geopolitical expert contributing to policy under President Putin. Journalists may not have understood how complicated— meandering, informal, and mediated—the pathways of his influence were, but the characterization was true nonetheless, despite the fact that Dugin held no official position in Putin's inner circle. Indeed, he didn't want to pursue influence through standard routes. Rather than simply joining Putin's ruling Unity party, he thought he could gain more exposure by founding an eccentric pro-government party devoted to advancing his geopolitical and spiritual vision. And so in 2002, after a remarkably easy bureaucratic process, he founded the Eurasian Party. While National Bolshevism had a crudely familiar emblem, the Eurasianists represented themselves with a mysterious icon: a symbol with eight arrows pointing out from a central core. Was it meant to represent a desired expansion of Russia? Maybe. The fact that it also appeared superimposed on a map of Russia on the cover of *Foundations of Geopolitics* makes that an intuitive interpretation. However, the symbol itself was known in occultist circles from the 1960s on, particularly those involved in so-called black magic. It is the symbol for chaos.

By the time of the founding of the Eurasian Party, the Kremlin had already been releasing foreign policy guidelines using Dugin's peculiar terms and concepts, like a call for a "multipolar world order" opposite American unipolarity in geopolitics. Over time, journalists noticed that Putin seemed to be echoing—sometimes in a matter of hours—expressions Dugin was using in media broadcasts, whether describing Russia as "Eurasian," naming "fifth column" conspiracies, referring to Georgian actions in Ossetia as "genocide," or reviving descriptions of Eastern Ukraine as "Novorossiya," or New Russia. A symbiotic relationship between Dugin and the Russian government was emerging, in which Dugin's commentary was influencing the government and in turn the government was increasing his media exposure. Indeed, Dugin was soon to become a featured personality on state television.

Meanwhile, starting during the early years of the twenty-first century, Dugin began a series of diplomatic missions, sometimes at high levels. He participated in closed negotiations surrounding the end of the Second Chechen War between the Kremlin and local Chechen leaders, leading to the emergence of Chechnya as a largely self-governing republic in Russia run through clans and Islamic courts. The Chechen side actually requested his presence. But in subsequent years, his own media sites documented a stream of other official meetings, with figures including with Kazakh president Nursultan Nazarbayev, with the ambassadors of Iran and Syria, and eventually with European far-right parties.

It wasn't immediately clear whom he was serving in each exchange. Sometimes he was invited by the foreign nationals. Sometimes it was the result of friends with money: he acquired the financial and logistical support of Russian oligarch Konstantin Malofeev, who himself was functioning as an unofficial Kremlin fixer, dealing out aid and financing projects with ostensibly private money that was nonetheless funneled his way by the Russian government. One covert move got out, though. According to U.S. intelligence, in 2004, Putin himself sent Dugin to Turkey in anticipation of his own official state visit, all in the hopes of convincing Turkey to move away from its Western NATO allies and toward closer ties with Russia. It took a WikiLeaks release of a classified U.S. embassy report to confirm this years later.

Dugin's official status throughout all this remained that of a philosopher. His appearance, fittingly, had come to resemble that of Grigori Rasputin, thanks to Dugin's long beard in the style of Russian Orthodox priests. And his chief diplomatic intervention with Turkey, in the eyes of U.S. intelligence, for example, came when he rewrote the introduction to one of his books to describe a vision for a Eurasia more open to the Turkic world.

As Dugin the individual began moving through halls of power across the anti-liberal world, the Eurasian Party floundered in Russian elections. It was a nonstarter, a de facto social club like the other political parties Dugin had dabbled in during the late 1980s and early 1990s. But while the party struggled, its foreign initiative, the International Eurasian Movement, fared better. This wasn't a political party, but a network of individuals—some politicians but mostly zealous youths—throughout Europe, Asia, and the Middle East who were sympathetic to strengthening Russian influence and hostile to the United States and the European Union. Part lobbying initiative, part intellectual circle, part protest force, and part paramilitary, Eurasianists began emerging in key places of political conflict. In 2007, for example, a group of Eurasianist Youth Union members climbed Mount Hoverla in Ukraine and vandalized a national unity monument erected by the government in Kiev. They raised the Eurasianist flag in its place and declared the mountain renamed "Stalin's Peak." Russia needed to reassert its presence in this place, and some Eurasianists were willing to take up arms to assist. Like their leader in Moscow, the more insightful among them knew that Ukraine's time would come, but that they were not first in line.

THROUGHOUT JULY and into August 2008, Russians began pouring through a nearly two-and-a-half-mile Roki Tunnel under the Caucasus mountains and into South Ossetia. Russia had an established and much-criticized peacekeeping mission in the area, but these weren't peacekeepers. They were bringing armored vehicles and soldiers, too. Indeed, as the month wore on, the separatist army's ranks grew increasingly international, with personnel from the Russian army as well as volunteer fighters from neighboring regions to the north.

Heavy shelling in South Ossetia began on August 1, 2008. Separatist forces targeted Zemo Nikozi, Kvemo Nikozi, Avnevi, Nuli, Ergneti, Eredvi, and Zemo Prisi—all ethnic Georgian villages inside of Ossetian territory. Their combined population of roughly 14,000 slowly began to flee into Georgia proper. Meanwhile, the separatists also attacked Georgian security forces with roadside bombs and conventional fire. The central government in Tbilisi thought that its past standard of limited sniper fire was an insufficient response to the latest escalations. So on August 7, it launched a full-scale military assault on the South Ossetian city of Tskhinvali, surrounding and pounding it throughout the day and night, and pushing into the city center during early morning. Tskhinvali had been taken by the Georgians, so it seemed.

Aleksandr Dugin was back in Russia by then, though he followed events in the Caucasus closely. He knew that not only the separatists but Russia itself was going to respond. South Ossetia would not be in Georgian hands for long. But he also saw a critical opportunity and was eager to see that the leadership in Moscow pursued it.

On radio and through his online channels, he began to speak out—not only for the ostensible liberation of South Ossetia but for more. "Wage war against Georgia right up to the capture of Tbilisi"—that was his simple message. What was at stake was Russia's ability to establish boundaries for the infectious spread of American hegemony, to show that the fate of the world was not to be subsumed into a single unipolar global liberal order, but instead that it would be multipolar, where different actors with varying visions had to coexist and respect one another's claim to their own present, past, and future. Achieve that by drawing this line in the sand, and Russia—demoralized by the outcome of the cold war—will have reentered history. "It is not a choice for every responsible Russian," Dugin concluded. "Tanks to Tbilisi!"

That last line, "Tanks to Tbilisi," became a mantra and spread throughout Russian media almost instantly. It appeared on bumper stickers and was the central chant during a demonstration Dugin organized with his Eurasianists in front of Russia's Ministry of Defense on August 10. Technically speaking, he was criticizing the government. But his public platform was expanding with ease and his public demonstrations proceeded undisturbed—state authorities seemed to like what he was doing.

To the south, a storm of Russian military power crashed over the mountains by order of the Kremlin. By land and by air they drove the Georgians out of their position in Tskhinvali. The Georgians made a number of attempts to retake the Ossetian city. Their anti-aircraft systems were sophisticated, managing to down some Russian planes. But their ground initiatives provoked a Russian counterattack that was, in the words of one Georgian general, "like hell." Georgian military casualties skyrocketed as the reality of the power imbalance became apparent. The Georgians began to retreat, pursued by the Russians every step of the way. That front moved southward and passed over nearly empty ethnic Georgian towns, subject now to lawless Ossetian militias who followed in the wake of the Russians.

The Georgians were in direct confrontation with one of the most powerful militaries in the world. They were hoping for a miracle when, on August 11, U.S. president George W. Bush spoke from Beijing. "Russia has invaded a sovereign neighboring state and threatens a democratic government elected by its people. Such an action is unacceptable in the twenty-first century." *Unacceptable* was the word he used. And this statement is basically all he said. The United States wasn't intervening. Little Georgia was facing massive power alone.

Morale among the troops cratered. Russia had now pushed them out of the entirety of South Ossetian territory. But things could get worse. Retreating forces began to hear chatter from comrades and generals. The Georgian city of Gori was being bombarded by the Russians, they said, and troop movements suggested a ground assault was imminent. This was arresting news: Gori isn't part of South Ossetia. It's beyond the boundaries, just fifty miles from the capital, Tbilisi. Russia was coming for Georgia.

# SOLAR EUROPE

MY FACE WAS IN MY HANDS AS I SAT IN THE BACK seat of a taxi on Ferenc Avenue, heading toward a bridge over the Danube River that connects the cities of Buda and Pest in Hungary. I was scheduled to be on the other side of the bridge right now for a meeting with a former leader of a political party called Jobbik. We were stuck in traffic. Minutes ticked by, and I watched as public transit trains, which I foolishly thought would take longer, rushed past us, one after another. I had been in the eastern Hungarian city of Debrecen the night before, and would be leaving for Washington, D.C., later today. It was my one shot to meet this politician, and my interest in his background ran deep. Not only was he the only major politician to have ever identified himself as a Traditionalist, he was also one of many leaders in Europe's far right to have been courted and influenced by either Steve Bannon or Aleksandr Dugin.

I continued to ponder those two figures—Bannon and Dugin—and the possibility of a connection, or at least a state of mutual admiration, between them. And it occurred to me as I thought further that their similarities extended beyond a shared interest in Traditionalism, even beyond the fact that they were considered gurus to anti-liberal world leaders. Both had been working for years to invigorate nationalism in Europe. A cynic might even say that they had been working to colonize the continent with their own ideals: Europe was like a board game, with Dugin playing from the East and Bannon from the West, though seldom were they each other's opponent. Each exercised soft power, attempting to influence others through culture and intellectualism. Their common aims were the reduction of immigration and the destruction of the European Union. And though each figure was at times associated with the national government in his respective home country—especially so in Bannon's case—they pursued their causes in Europe as individuals.

And yet as I reviewed their history of activism, taking into consideration their public media appearances, exposés from former collaborators, and data from my own fieldwork, I also saw differences in what they were doing. Bannon allegedly promoted nationalism to strengthen the sovereignty of individual nation-states and their native citizenry, thereby ensuring the nations' continued vitality and the perpetuation of a culturally intact "Judeo-Christian West." Dugin believed that a Europe fractured into smaller units would also disperse and weaken the power emanating from the United States, and perhaps allow Russia to regain a cultural and political presence in those territories of the continent where history sanctioned it to do so—principally the Slavic states.

Each man targeted a different contingent of Europe's far right, with Bannon's incursion from the West focusing on more moderate parties and causes, and Dugin extending his reach further into far more radical wings: to political actors who not only resented multiculturalism and feminism but who also rejected

democracy as a whole and who might be persuaded to realign
their countries away from a liberal West and toward a Traditional East. Parties like Jobbik, whose name translates roughly
as the Movement for a Righter Hungary.

A far-right party mobilized to promote ethnic Hungarians,
Jobbik didn't hesitate to say who their enemies were. The threat
on the streets came allegedly from the Roma. The threat from
above, through nongovernmental organizations and financial
and political meddling, came from Jews. Jobbik would fight the
fight in either venue: with the pseudo military guard they organized, or with their robust delegation of governmental representatives. But the most unusual thing about Jobbik was that it
once had a Traditionalist leader: Gábor Vona—the man I was
late to see.

I JUMPED OUT of the taxi, grabbed my bags, ran into the
shopping mall, and darted up the escalators toward the café
where we were supposed to meet. Thankfully, he hadn't left,
despite my tardiness. In fact, Gábor Vona seemed to be making
a point of being especially gracious, treating me to an espresso
and helping me with my bags. Why? I wondered if it didn't
have something to do with my last name. Vona made a baffling reversal in his ideology a few years ago, renouncing anti-
Semitism and anti-Roma sentiment, issuing apologies to those
communities in Hungary who felt harmed by Jobbik. He resigned his position in 2018, having set his party on a course
for partnership at the municipal level with Hungary's socialists.
Perhaps being nice to me, as an apparent Jew, belonged to his
reinvention effort.

I wanted to ask him about a key period of time around 2014.

It was then that his Traditionalism deepened and he came in contact with Aleksandr Dugin. In 2012, after Vona had been party leader for four years, he hired a Traditionalist adviser for himself—a *spiritual* adviser, they both agreed, but you can't use a label like that in Hungarian politics, so his official title was "adviser to the party president." The adviser, Tibor Baranyi, was a stout man in his forties with a salt-and-pepper goatee, dusky eyes, and a raspy voice like that of Don Vito Corleone in *The Godfather*. Baranyi was a hard-core Traditionalist—perhaps the most serious in the world, as some of my contacts would put it.

The appeal of Dugin's ideas didn't just stem from the fact that Vona and Baranyi also saw themselves as followers of Julius Evola. Dugin's writings about Eurasianism resonated with a perennial ideological movement in Hungarian nationalism known as Turanism. It is the belief, historically dubious though not entirely devoid of truth, that ethnic Hungarians originated as nomads in Central Asia and migrated into the Carpathian Basin of Central Europe in the distant past. Aleksandr Dugin's theories about West and East added incentive for Jobbik to embrace this history: within wings of the party's upper ranks, an ideology began to solidify, contrasting Europe on one side—with capitalism, feminism, multiculturalism, secularism, and chaos spearheaded by Jews—with Asia on the other—a home of Tradition, patriarchy, ethnic purity, order, and the most vigorous spirituality alive in the world today, Islam. Traditionalism and Turanism had united in Jobbik's leadership. The child was an eccentric right-wing orientalism—a nostalgia for a more Eastern time and place that was the hidden birthright of contemporary Hungarians.

In 2013, Dugin brought Vona to Russia in order to speak with students at Moscow State University. There Vona commiserated with the professor and his students about the follies of the European Union, the spiritual vapidity of the West, and the potential for Hungary to someday join in a Eurasian union, one that would be true to its essence, and where Traditional values would flourish against the materialistic rot of the West. Dugin would later bring members of the Greek party Golden Dawn—the only other party in Europe to rival Jobbik in terms of its radicalism—to Russia for the same purpose: to push a platform of unity between Greece and Russia based on historic ties.

Meanwhile, following his visit to Russia, Vona traveled to Turkey, where he delivered a series of sensational speeches at universities that caught the attention of national and international media. At one stop, he approached the microphone with a Palestinian scarf draped over his shoulders and let out a rallying cry: "I did not come to Turkey to build diplomatic and economic relations, but to meet my Turkish brothers and sisters!" The international Muslim press in attendance couldn't believe it, and the so-called right-wing extremist from Europe would shock them further with his calls for unions between Christianity and Islam, Hungary and Turkey—founded in "shared blood," and by his outright reverence for Islam's distinct role in the world. He said it with bravado: "Islam is the last hope of humanity in the darkness of globalism and liberalism!" Most far-right parties in Europe can be described as Islamophobic. Jobbik seemed Islamophilic.

It hardly seemed like good politics. Nonetheless, thanks perhaps to the wellspring of support for far-right nationalism in Hungary, Jobbik surged during the election on April 6, 2014, gaining 20 percent of the vote and becoming the second largest party out of nine major contenders. Far-right parties were scoring tallies in the 20 percent range throughout Europe, but none as extreme as Jobbik. The percentages were large enough to at least agitate Prime Minister Viktor Orbán, whose party Fidesz—the clear leader with 44 percent of the vote—was merely nationalist and populist.

That he had a threat coming *from his right* says something about politics in Hungary at the time. There, the key ideological divide was between the far right and the extreme right. Dugin was behind Jobbik and Gábor Vona. As for Hungary's prime minister? He would eventually find a different Traditionalist collaborator from the West: Steve Bannon.

BANNON HAD BECOME HEAD of Breitbart News in 2012, and by 2014, both he and the news site were in the process of expanding. While Dugin's efforts trafficked in lecturing and interpersonal networking, Bannon sought to promote European nationalism through sophisticated media campaigning, and he found both a method and a cause to apply it to. With the backing of American billionaires Robert and Rebekah Mercer, he reached out to a data mining and behavioral science conglomerate based in the UK named Strategic Communication Laboratories (SCL) and, with an infusion of $20 million, created a new U.S.-linked subsidiary called Cambridge Analytica. There were various political interests riding the moneyed coattails of the Mercers: Christopher Wylie, former director of intelligence at Cambridge Analytica, would later recall that the initial meetings for planning the development of the company were attended by the Mercers, SCL executives, Steve Bannon, and representatives from UKIP—a British nationalist party working to break the UK off from the European Union. Steve was eager to see all these forces work together.

The company launched in summer 2014, not long after Hungary's elections, with Steve Bannon as vice president. They developed techniques to harvest a startling amount of data about hundreds of thousands of private persons, and their initial target subjects were Americans. They used Facebook and census data to learn about individual voters' financial status, political tendencies, and cultural tastes. With that information, they then began to classify voter profiles and test methods of motivating and demotivating people from participating in elections—at times by targeting individuals with certain advertisements; at other times by developing push-poll opinion surveys. Bannon, Christopher Wylie wrote, was particularly interested in finding ways to coax white self-identified Democrats into affirming anti-black views with the surveys, exposing what he believed was a latent hypocrisy in America's left and providing methods for manipulating voters' activities through references to race. While working at the firm that first year, Wylie noted unusual visitors at his UK office, representatives from Russia's LUKOIL company—a likely front for their national intelligence—appearing to inquire about the company's data on Americans.

The type of activism being supported by Cambridge Analytica was an enhanced and innovative form of something referred to in far-right circles as metapolitics. The strategy involves campaigning not through politics, but through culture—through the arts, entertainment, intellectualism, religion, and education. Those are the places where our values are formed, not in a voting booth. If you succeed in altering a society's culture, then you will have created a political opportunity for yourself. Fail to do this, and you'll have no chance.

Metapolitics held special appeal to far-right actors striving for power in the post–World War II, post-fascist liberal West: those who saw themselves as fighting against not a given political party or a militia, but against *consensus*—the sentiment of the age according to Traditionalists, the commonsense understanding held by most that far-right politics need not even be considered in public debate. To address such an impasse, metapolitical campaigns have typically taken one of two forms: either activists seek to inject their message seamlessly into existing cultural channels, or they aim to create alternative channels of their own to compete with those of the mainstream. It's the difference between editing Wikipedia articles as opposed to creating an alternative online encyclopedia; infiltrating a youth subculture or starting a new one of your own; altering public education curricula as opposed to founding a private school devoted fully to your cause. The first approach attempts to sow political sympathy among the general populace and emphasizes outreach. The second aims to form a parallel society within a society, one large enough and radical enough to confront others in a fight for power. And you didn't need to be read in the works of Traditionalist-inspired right-wing intellectuals to arrive at this strategy. Andrew Breitbart put the idea in his own words: "Politics is downstream from culture."

Bannon was pursuing both forms of metapolitics. Cambridge Analytica tested ways of infiltrating general media spheres (Facebook and Twitter rather than an underground blog portal), making it so that an individual's forays into the mainstream would be laced with dissident messages. In the same breadth, however, the goal was to pull targeted individuals out of the mainstream and deeper and deeper into a tailored sphere of messaging (like Breitbart) that would delegitimize standard sources of information and radicalize support for a chosen political cause.

Metapolitical weapons seldom produce quantifiable results. But Bannon would soon get the chance to test his in an official vote tally. In October 2015, Cambridge Analytica was approached by representatives for an organization called Leave .EU, one of the two main forces campaigning for the United Kingdom to leave the European Union, or Brexit. Its primary spokesperson—indeed, the primary spokesperson for the Brexit cause—was a UKIP politician and close friend of Bannon's named Nigel Farage. They were interested in both fundraising and data analytics for a referendum vote scheduled to be held the next summer, on June 23, 2016. Bannon and his backers signed on, and their involvement deepened with time. Even the other major pro-Brexit organization in the campaign, Vote Leave, would partner and channel money illegally to a parallel subsidiary of Cambridge Analytica that in turn would hit a select group of voters in the UK with ads that were viewed 169 million times during the final days of the Brexit campaign. All this took place shortly after Bannon had expanded Breitbart to Europe, with a new UK office that pumped out anti-EU commentary. He was crafting propaganda along with research and a tech tool to get it in front of the right people.

Nigel Farage would later describe Bannon's efforts as key to the victory.

2015 WOULD ALSO be a watershed year for the Traditionalists operating in Hungary. As Gábor Vona explained to me over our espresso, 2015 was the year when things started falling apart for him and for Jobbik. During the fall of 2014, Dugin had planned to speak at a gathering in Budapest organized by white nationalist Richard Spencer and cosponsored by Arktos Publishing, which was in the process of relocating to Budapest from India. However, the Hungarian government considered Dugin too radical on account of his warmongering and alleged fascism (Richard Spencer, it seems, was a comparative unknown to them), and told him he would be arrested on sight if he entered Hungary. Jobbik members planning to speak at the event took this as a cue to withdraw.

The party had plenty else to keep it busy, notably its own campaign of metapolitics. Its efforts were less technologically sophisticated than what Steve Bannon was doing in London, but were nonetheless appealing to far-right nationalists throughout Europe. Vona's Traditionalist adviser Tibor Baranyi spearheaded an effort to create a party-affiliated school called King Attila Academy. It had been running since 2012, and by 2015 nearly ninety students had gone through its program, which focused on religion, politics, and Traditionalism. A critical mass of zealots—a new generation of Traditionalists—was being trained in Hungary.

The creation of schools of this kind was becoming a fad among Europe's nationalists, with programs across the continent adopting a similar three-part curriculum addressing practical politics, ideology, and personality or lifestyle training. It was low-tech metapolitics at its most intense; a means of targeting a smaller number of individuals for in-depth indoctrination. Italy's Northern League party (later simply the League) had done it, to be followed by nationalists in France. Dugin was creating a self-contained program inside a major university in Moscow, and eventually Steve Bannon would attempt to found a school of his own, too.

In Hungary, Jobbik's Gábor Vona also participated as a guest lecturer for his party's academy. He enjoyed the exposure, but his focus would shift with time. After the 2014 elections, and after it became clear that Gábor Vona posed a serious threat to the future rule of Prime Minister Viktor Orbán, political forces across the spectrum and their media wings mobilized against him. And media of various kinds also began to identify Vona's strange spiritual guru, using Baranyi to portray Vona as either extreme or just plain weird and unserious.

The media messages were sensational: Vona's Rasputin Tibor Baranyi idolizes Julius Evola, wishes Hungary were still controlled by the Hapsburg monarchy, is a Holocaust denier, thinks men are spiritually superior to women and better suited to politics. Article after article, in Hungarian and in English for an international audience, was meant to expose Baranyi as a sexist and a racist in the eyes of the left, and a false nationalist to the right. And before long, the academy, too, came into the crosshairs of the media. Videos of young men practicing archery and doing push-ups in formation fueled claims that Jobbik was using the school not to train politicians and religious leaders, but instead to build an army.

These were not the kinds of headlines Vona wanted, especially when he began to see his political opportunities slip away. At the beginning of 2015, Orbán had low approval numbers. But by fall he had received a political gift from the south: the migration crisis. Waves of asylum-seekers from Africa, the Middle East, and Asia were pouring into Europe. Their destination was often Germany, Austria, or Sweden, but their paths northward went through Greece to Serbia and to Hungary.

While other European Union leaders issued statements of welcome to the migrants, Viktor Orbán took the opposite tack. He built a fence along the border to Serbia and patrolled it with military and helicopters. He would later close and fortify the border with Croatia, and bus those migrants already in Hungary to Austria. In releases to the media, he said unequivocally that the migrants had no place in Hungary. Nor was he shy about condemning his European counterparts for, as he put it, encouraging the migrants while not having properly prepared for the hardships. He even mocked Austria's chancellor personally during press conferences, and with time he started emphasizing Gábor Vona's words about Islam and connections to Turkey.

The result? A massive rebound in the polls for Hungary's president. Some opinion polls were showing a near 10-point upward swing in his approval ratings. Jobbik was helpless to reverse this trend. The anti-immigrant rhetoric, the castigation of European leaders, the construction of the border wall—they wouldn't have done anything differently. Nativistic anxieties stoked by the migration crisis had produced political dividends, but Orbán was snatching them all for himself and co-opting the most popular elements of Jobbik's platform in the process.

And it wouldn't take long until Orbán started adopting even more of Jobbik's worldview, including traces of its Traditionalism. By fall of 2018 the president, who in 2013 made a point of touting his nation's European bona fides by expounding on the Hungarian language's links to Finnish, began declaring Hungarians—the people and their language—as Turkic in larger and larger forums. And not just that: in a speech given to the Cooperation Council of Turkic Speaking States, Orbán declared an end to the days when "capital and knowledge flow from West to East in search of cheap labor." Hungarians were now proud to be of the East, not only because it was their true identity, he claimed, but also because the East was the new vanguard in anti-liberal global politics. "The only states which can be strong are those which are proud of their national identities and are able to preserve them. Today's Western teaching does not recognize this truth." A few months later Hungary would become the first country in the European Union to buy armored vehicles from Turkey.

Vona was panicked to stanch the bleeding when it began in 2015. Pieces of their policy and ideology were thriving, but in the hands of others. Searching for differences between Jobbik and Orbán—when both were beginning to share the same Turanist nationalism—seemed to be the best technique to regain control of the situation. He even offered a Traditionalist-sounding interpretation of the migrant crisis, suggesting that Germany's and Sweden's secularism made them culturally and spiritually weak and vulnerable: "masses from Asia and Africa would start head-ing toward the weak, paralyzed, spiritually sick Europe." It was unlikely that putting things in such terms—telling nationalis-tic Hungarians they could stop immigration by enlivening their own spirituality—would bring voters back to Jobbik.

No, as Vona would tell me in Budapest, he was souring on his adviser at this time, with the school that had become a lightning rod for bad publicity, and on Baranyi's notion that such obscure and vague teachings as Traditionalism could be brought into the realm of practical politics. I tried to discuss this history with Baranyi, too: I had visited him in his hometown of Debrecen for a long interview the night before my meeting with Vona. I would later transcribe the conversation, draft a few sample chapters based on it, and send it off to him for review. Something I wrote, I never found out what, upset him. Before long, my contacts in the area were reporting that he was enraged at me and was con-vinced that I was some kind of secret agent bent on harming him and those like him. He wouldn't be the last to voice such suspi-cions, and he later demanded that I not use any material from our interview, a request I honored.

My account of what happened in Hungary during 2015 and 2016 was largely tied to Vona. "I tried to explain it to him," Vona recalled. He attempted to tell Baranyi that the increased invest-ment in Traditionalism would have been counterproductive to his core aims as a politician, which were to gain popularity and actual power. A "Traditionalist party"? That would attract maybe ten or twelve people. The philosophy once sounded good to Vona, but now he saw that it was just too alienating for ordinary people. Baranyi didn't seem to care, for even a small group led by an in-spired and charismatic leader would attract more followers, and even a minuscule amount of growth would be a giant leap for the cause of Traditionalism. That was more important than Jobbik or even political advance in general. Baranyi was playing the long game. The practical-minded Vona wasn't. Baranyi's school effectively closed by the end of 2015, and he would resign from the party the following year.

They were thinking in different terms, it seemed. Politics was politics for Vona. For Baranyi, Jobbik itself seemed like a metapolitical instrument, a vessel like any other to spread a message. He couldn't see Traditionalism subordinated to politics—not when politics was bound to be corrupt in the darkness of the Kali Yuga.

But while Jobbik hemorrhaged support as the prime minister co-opted their politics, the 2015 refugee crisis and the anti-immigrant sentiment it incited continued to offer rewards for nationalist causes throughout Europe, especially to those who were prepared and organized enough to capitalize on it. People like Steve Bannon and his partners in the UK.

ON JUNE 24, 2016, early in the morning following the Brexit vote, Aleksandr Dugin made an appearance on Tsargrad TV in Moscow. "The European Union's cycle has passed its noon. Sunset begins," he declared. Dugin had helped create this channel in collaboration with his own billionaire backer. Tsargrad TV was based on Fox News in the United States, and strived to provide a voice for conservative Orthodox Christian Russians. It would serve as his platform that day, and he was eager to voice his interpretation of what had transpired in the United Kingdom the night before.

"Brexit is the collapse of the West and a victory for humanity, which is opposed to the West and seeks to go its own way."

It was a close contest, but the United Kingdom had just voted to leave the European Union. According to Dugin, it was the beginning of the slow death for a system of global power centered in the United States, but which relied upon the servitude of the European Union and its fanatically pro-American linchpin, the UK. The foundations were now undermined, and the fortress was teetering.

The screen was split, with Dugin on the left side speaking from the Tsargrad studio and Brexit icon Nigel Farage being interviewed by reporters on the right. Dozens of trimmed and chummy young men were vying to give Farage a hug, a pat on the back, or a chest bump. Should they be celebrating? As Englishmen, yes, Dugin thought. They had freed themselves from their overlords, and now they were poised to, as he put it, "follow their own destiny" as a distinct, bounded people.

"People intuitively understand that today England was freed from the diktat of the European Union, Brussels, and tomorrow the other European countries will follow its way. And we are not far off from the day when the people begin to follow their own destiny."

The disintegration of the world and the birth of multipolarity. Britain had started something; now it was time to wait for the next stage.

Brexit hadn't been Dugin's project. Indeed, with only wavering and indirect support from the Kremlin, he was more limited in the types of initiatives he could pursue. Dugin's outreach to eccentric parties like Jobbik and Golden Dawn notwithstanding, most of his efforts centered on building a groundswell of sympathy in the murkier regions of the far-right netherworlds—among ideologues and journalists rather than party politicians—which then established a foundation for high-level Russian state initiatives to develop.

This played out in Italy like a choreographed dance. Dugin had cultivated a presence in Italy since the 1990s, especially through Julius Evola followers. Throughout the early twenty-first century, far-right networks and media channels throughout the country identified Dugin as an ideological inspiration, and the result was a spreading of his ideas—and thereby greater sympathy for Eurasianism and for Russia—among the growing anti-liberal sector of the Italian population. Political scientist Anton Shekhovtsov highlights this history when describing the receptiveness on the part of Italy's most prominent far-right party, the League, to Putin's overtures. Beginning in 2013, Putin allowed Dugin's high-level sponsors to court the Italian nationalist politicians through dinners and conferences. Dugin himself also participated by headlining events for the newly established Italian-Russian friendship think tanks. These efforts would eventually culminate in direct contact between the League's leader Matteo Salvini and Vladimir Putin in Milan on October 17, 2014, where the two would commiserate about their shared belief that Western sanctions against Russia were unfair. Further, through affiliated think tanks, the League began cooperating in Russian business ventures, and in that way found a roundabout means of gaining financial support from Putin's government.

In Italy, as in France and Austria, Dugin's was an intractable kind of influence, the kind easily overblown or minimized by commentators. He served as a networker and visiting dignitary, but in all cases his involvement was premised on his philosophizing. His books and lectures provided ideological content that European activists absorbed and which later served to make the continent's far-right more pro-Russian than it otherwise might have been. Bannon, in contrast, pursued his vision of dis-integrating Europe through innovations of form rather than content. He laid siege to the European Union by creating new media outlets and by developing new methods of surveillance and advertising. Combined, their efforts helped make European nationalism more politically formidable and successful, and also more ideologically radical.

Both men began retreating to their home positions after

Brexit. Dugin began shifting his attentions more toward the East, beyond Russia, to Iran, and especially to China. Bannon turned his focus toward U.S. politics. On August 17, 2016, the presidential candidate Donald Trump, at the behest of the Mercers, named Bannon campaign CEO. Dugin would continue to invest in higher education and publishing as a means of gaining influence. And for Bannon? The preliminary work he had done in Europe would support his agenda in the Trump campaign. He used data and insights gained by Cambridge Analytica in fights for and beyond the White House.

# 6

# THE METAPHYSICS OF THE PEASANTRY

AS I TRAVELED BACK TO MANHATTAN FOR MY NEXT scheduled interview with Steve Bannon, my thoughts were consumed by the juxtaposition between him and Aleksandr Dugin, two Traditionalists working from West and East to promote nationalism. Their parallel actions revealed a common agenda bigger than the geopolitical aims of their home nation-states. Bannon was American and Dugin was Russian, yes, but both were fighting to resurrect what they saw as the pre-modern world. I knew that Steve was at least aware of and, I suspected, to some extent fond of Dugin. Did their contact extend further?

I wanted to probe the topic with Steve, but we had agreed that today's interview would focus on a different subject—about a day he loves to reflect on, a moment when his vision for the future took a gigantic leap forward: Tuesday, November 8, 2016, election day in America.

It started early, he explained—at twelve-thirty in the morning, in fact. That's when 4,200 people had packed into DeVos Place Convention Center in Grand Rapids, Michigan, for a last-minute rally in support of their man, Donald Trump. The crowd was raucous, warmed up by a performance from the foul-mouthed country-rock singer Ted Nugent and, theoretically, by Trump's sleepy vice-presidential candidate, Mike Pence. Trump didn't take long after bursting onto the stage to get to his main campaign messages: "They're ripping the auto companies apart, they're taking your jobs, they're closing your plants, moving them to Mexico . . ."

Bring back jobs from abroad—that was one of the three pillars of his pitch, the other two being the reduction of legal and illegal immigration and the cessation of foreign wars. Combined, these themes formed the message that Steve, then Trump's campaign manager, believed could overcome almost any hurdle, including sensational demonstrations of sexism and racism. But the success of that plan hinged on the campaign's ability to get their message to the right place and the right people.

Michigan was an unusual place for a Republican to choose for a final campaign rally. The state had both a sizable African American population and was also a national center for union laborers. Those contingencies were historically aligned with the left. A Republican presidential candidate hadn't won here since the 1980s.

But the people coming to rallies like this one—the rural, less educated, primarily white working class; the "hobbits" and the "deplorables," as Steve affectionately called them, referencing one of Hillary Clinton's characterizations of Trump's far-right supporters—were Trump's key to victory. Many of them had been Democrats, too. As campaign manager, Steve had what he called a maniacal focus on identifying this demographic, which had voted for Obama twice. Steve thought the demographic could be persuaded to switch parties, and even a small shift could make all the difference. The counties where they predominated were spread throughout the northern United States in a sagging crescent shape, from northern New England across upstate New

York and rounding the Great Lakes region through Pennsylvania, Ohio, and Michigan before curving up through Wisconsin and to the Iron Belt of northern Minnesota. This was postindustrial America, a place of unemployment and growing social problems, a place where factories and young soldiers had been shipped out and fentanyl shipped in. Through projects like Cambridge Analytica, he had learned who they were and what messages would motivate them to vote.

Steve explained that back then he had been fighting with the campaign about it all. Pull out of Nevada, he thought. Pull out of Colorado and Virginia, too. March instead to the upper Midwest—to the heart of the old left.

But the people in those states weren't just a data point for Steve, not just the strategic means to another end. Instead, he saw them as an almost magical, spiritual, and metaphysical force, as keepers of an eternal essence of Americanism. That's why, as a filmmaker, he had promoted other icons of white rural America, like Sarah Palin and the bearded television-reality-show duck hunter Phil Robertson. Take up their cause, he thought, and you will have more than a tool for winning a particular election. You will have gathered an army of spiritual soldiers for a war against modernity.

AT FIRST GLANCE, it doesn't make any sense for a Traditionalist to promote populism. Traditionalism is hierarchical and elitist and celebrates past precedent. Populism even as Bannon conceives it adopts the opposite agenda. It is an anti-establishment, anti-elite, and revolutionary political cause championing the masses. As Columbia University political scientist Nadia Urbinati recently put it, a populism that succeeds may threaten democratic institutions based on its uncompromising promotion of a majority made up of economically, culturally, or racially "normal people" against their domestic enemies, but populism is still (paradoxically) born out of a democratic mind-set. I initially thought that the improbability of combining Traditionalism and populism bolstered accusations of commentators who alleged that in Steve, there was no "there" there—no ideology, in fact, but just the empty ramblings of a blowhard.

However, throughout our conversations, and across many a meandering sentence and tangent, despite his sloppy use of sources, his erratic analyses, and confusing presentation, Steve had been showing me that he had developed his own distinct version of Traditionalism where some of these conflicts were mitigated. A scholar colleague I occasionally consult with had even described what I relayed as a "post-Traditionalism" that was intelligible, consistent, and sophisticated in its own way. Steve is hardly remarkable among Traditionalists for wanting to modify the thinking of Guénon and Evola, for few associating themselves with the school today adopt wholesale the thinking of its founding figures. Bannon's modifications of the Traditionalist standard often derived from his attempts to avoid the school's most politically damning dogmas—notably its theorized subordination of women, nonwhites, and the poor—and also execute a daring fusion with populism and American nationalism. His arguments contain internal contradictions and lapses, though that is unremarkable: the same is true of all belief systems, especially those that we hold in our heads without trying to organize them on paper.

I couldn't help but think that Steve's and my conversations were providing him a canvas for such systematization, but I've worked his thoughts into a more intelligible presentation as well. I've come to think that the best way to make sense of what we talked about is to understand it as a process in three steps. First, it is a criticism of rigid caste boundaries and the individuals who typify them today. Second, it is an assertion that Traditionalism's hierarchy nonetheless expresses an ancient, sacred ordering of spirituality over materialism. And third, it proclaims that during modernity, one particular class of people has a rare ability to attain his highest ideals.

Understand these things, and you will begin to understand why his passion was not only to win an election but to do so with the very type of people who showed up at DeVos Place Convention Center in Michigan, on that early November morning.

THE ESSENTIAL CONCEPTS of Traditionalism, Bannon told me, were "the rejection of modernity, the rejection of the Enlightenment, the rejection of materialism," along with the understanding that "culture, true culture, is based upon immanence and transcendence."

It all sounded rather vague, as these conversations often did when we moved into philosophical topics. And when I asked him to clarify, the first thing he mentioned was what in Traditionalism he considered inessential: caste hierarchy, being placed into a role that you can never escape. He was particularly concerned about those deemed ineligible for spiritual advancement.

His aversion toward caste hierarchy wasn't just a matter of its fatalism and the limiting role it would place on a person's life, however. It was also that he doubted modern society's ability to populate Traditional castes with authentic representatives. If castes ever did reflect differences in people's character—one's archetypal disposition toward history, the world, and the divine—they don't anymore.

This was part of a wider criticism of modernity he had articulated to me on multiple occasions, maintaining that the values, institutions, and endorsements we live by today are hollow and meaningless. This was especially clear to him in regards to the offices of the priest, the warrior, and the merchant. Look around: ordained priests are not especially spiritual and pious, career military leaders may not embody ideals of honor and patriotism, and merchants may not gain their status by the production of goods and wealth. Steve extends this way of thinking about people to also criticize the occupants of modernity's core institutions, who claim expertise and functions they do not possess. The media doesn't report, scientists don't do science, universities don't teach anymore and are a "fucking waste of time," and political think tanks don't understand policy. Inauthenticity and the meaninglessness of titles, posts, and institutions—that's the common thread. Ours is a world of simulations. So why think that society could create and maintain a meaningful caste system?

Steve was reiterating familiar concepts from Traditionalism. Guénon describes one of the signatures of the Kali Yuga as the complete upending of value systems. He described this feature of modernity as "inversion," and becoming privy to it encourages one to distrust modern officialdom. Everything you think is good is bad. Every change you consider progress is actually regression. Every apparent instance of justice is actually oppression. Every extension of credentials ought to disqualify the recipient.

Traditionalism thus prepares a mystical pathway toward anti-establishment sentiment—at least unless it comes to power. And the thinking shapes attitudes toward concepts as well as people. Prevailing belief systems that emerged during the Enlightenment and modernization will, according to the theory of inversion, present the opposite of the truth (Evola famously derided the theory of evolution, arguing that we could never properly evolve to become better, only devolve, implying that nonhuman primates portray our short-term human future rather than our past). And it calls for a reconceptualizing of social change as well. Consider all of the emancipatory movements of the modern West: democratization, secularization, feminism, multiculturalism. If you think that time is decline, if you think that a product of decline is society's confusion of virtue and vice, how could you not oppose those movements—all of them?

Indeed, because of Steve's modifications to the philosophy, you can easily miss how many of Traditionalism's basic concepts remain in his thinking. As I pointed out to him, returning to the topic of hierarchy: "Even though you don't want a class system, you do seem to want spiritual values and spiritual journeys—even if there's not a set of ambassadors who are designated to have that spiritual role—you do seem to want that to be the primary driving force in society." He nodded in agreement, and labeled his system "a hierarchy of values."

Our conversation made explicit what was implicit in much of his commentary—namely, that he observes an ordering of ideals proceeding from the body, to money, to earthly creeds, to spirituality. It is a hierarchy of values, further, subject to the same historical and political pressures that the original Traditionalists saw shaping a hierarchy of human castes. The gradual degradation of spirituality and immaterial principles results from modernization and the spread of chaos and nihilism. His ideal society is not one where certain human types lord over others, but where considerations for spirituality and cultural essence guide social and political life—even geopolitics.

Crucially, access to those highest values are not the prerogative of one type of people in his telling, but instead are available to all. Instead of having fixed stages, the hierarchy is like an open pathway for individuals and societies. What Steve advocated, therefore, is something that I would like to call "spiritual mobility"—like the liberal insistence on the right to improve one's material situation or economic mobility. He summarized, "My point is, every person ought to be a priest."

As I pondered Steve's variation, I visualized two triangles. You could represent the original Traditionalist approach with a standard pyramid hierarchy, one with four stacked horizontal layers with sprawling materialist castes on the bottom rigidly separated from small elite spiritual castes on top. In Steve's version, the horizontal lines separating castes are turned upright, fanning out from the apex of the triangle like rays of light emanating from the sun. Each ray represents a distinct cultural or religious channel, a different Traditional pathway, toward spiritual truth. The only impermeable boundaries are now side to side, not top to bottom; horizontal rather than vertical stratification, and individuals at the bottom can follow their path from material depravity to transcendent virtue.

The approach validates Steve's autobiography. When he describes his own past, it is a story of laborious, stepwise advance professionally and spiritually: a narrative of change and progress leading to contact with the eternal. A worldview that demands people stay in the spiritual position they are born into—that worldview would deem Steve Bannon a mishap at best, an abomination at worst. It would also conflict with his American nationalism and its commitment to the self-made man, here transferred from economics to spirituality.

During our conversations he was eager to champion the ability for someone to ascend the hierarchy and embody its highest values authentically. It is also the root of his passion for the movement surrounding Donald Trump.

IN THE WEE HOURS of election day in Grand Rapids, Trump was approaching the climax of his stump speech, with lines reflecting Bannon's vision. "Today the American working class strikes back!" Cheers were boisterous: it was an atmosphere of wild enthusiasm that many journalists covering the campaign knew was absent at Clinton's events. "We will Make America Great Again!" Trump concluded. "God bless you everyone. Go to bed right now. Get up and vote. Thank you, everybody, thank you, Michigan. We'll be back." Trump walked off the stage to the sounds of the Rolling Stones' "You Can't Always Get What You Want."

But the truth is that Steve thought many of the people in that audience *could* get something they want—indeed, that they had access to things others could only simulate.

Traditionalism's social hierarchy captured something important, he explained to me, an ordering of values moving from the material to the spiritual. Thinkers like Evola and Guénon were also correct in noting that the turning of the ages entailed an assault on spirituality and a prioritization of materialism over all else. The task for the enlightened is therefore to embark on a journey themselves, to ascend the hierarchy of values to achieve spiritual advance. And that journey is open to anyone who wants to take it.

The tricky thing is, Steve thinks that certain types of people are better suited than others to reach these ideal values and live them out authentically. It's just that they are the opposite types of people from what Evola and Guénon would have expected. He doesn't call them "slaves," but the masses of a society, placed at the bottom of hierarchies based on economic wealth and institutional merits—those who may not be consumed with fornication and gluttony, but whose lifeways still circulate around their bodies because they are laborers: the working class or the peasantry. They're the ones positioned to do the metaphysical work that Evola reserved for his Aryan priests. In my notes from interviews, I started referring to this theme in Steve's thinking as the "metaphysics of the peasantry."

In language that sounds more like that of the nineteenth-century romantic nationalist Johann Gottfried von Herder than a Traditionalist, Steve describes the working class or peasantry as being the caste that gives a society its defining characteristics. This is a departure from Evola, who argued that the materialist masses were themselves raw material to be shaped by the priestly and warrior culture makers at the top of the hierarchy. Instead, Bannon asserts that the working class is the fount of authenticity in inauthentic modern society, serving not only as ambassadors for the spirit of a nation forged ages ago but also as the source for genuine incarnations of the four castes in the Traditionalist hierarchy. To take them in ascending order, the "slaves" and their culture establish the conditions for economic growth and successful mercantilism. That understanding is reflected in an exchange we had about his home society:

"I ask people, I say, 'Why is the United States so wealthy?' 'Oh, you've got the most robust capital markets, everybody wants to put their money here, they want to invest.' I go, 'Why is that?' 'Well, you know, because it's so liquid and guys can come and make money and put money in,' and I say, 'But why is it liquid?' And they go, 'Well, because people have put so much money in it.' I go, 'No, there's a reason they put so much money in it.' And they go, 'Why, because they get better returns?' and I go, 'What is that based on?' And it finally gets down—if you play Twenty Questions—to the safety and security of the American capital markets. And the safety and security of the American capital markets is based upon a social structure that is all the grundoons! It's the firemen, the cops, the teachers, it's a stable social society. Right?"

Those same people are the ones who embody the next caste in an authentic way. Steve claims that in modern society, American society included, warriors almost always come from the working class. Almost never do they come from the elites, the aristocrats: "The aristos don't fight! They strictly don't fight." And what is true of the second-highest caste is also true of the first: purveyors of some of the most powerful spiritual truths and wisdoms come from the lowest ranks of official modern society, what Gurdjieff identified as actual serfs and peasants. "They have a real understanding of life," and don't need professional philosophers and smart guys and a church bureaucracy.

Ours may be a world of simulations and imitations. But shine a light on the working class, and you will find them there, hidden in plain view—real merchants, warriors, and priests; beacons of premodern authenticity. Their ability to embody authenticity is for Steve a token of their temporality. They are out of time, insulated from the corrupting influences of modernity; vessels for eternal ideals and carriers of a spirit that unites a society internally and separates it from others elsewhere.

And so it is that Steve finds his calling in politics, at least in his conversations with me: to protect and promote the spiritual well-being of the American working class. But how do you do that?

Our conversations, which until then had proven surprisingly coherent to me, were about to take a number of surprising turns. To begin with, though Bannon may claim to value the spiritual over the material, his plan to save the working class focuses on economics. Spiritual exploration and development can germinate only when material needs are met.

Going into the 2016 election, he saw in the United States a system to keep working- and middle-class people in a state of tension and insecurity. Crushing debt, rising costs of living, and stagnant wages prevents young people—say, millennials—from forming families. "You're just a . . . you're just this proletariat, can't possibly work towards any self-actualization." The working class is funneled—asleep, he says—into an inescapable and aimless cycle of life, onto what Buddhists call the Wheel of Saṃsāra.

Practical economic reforms can help the working class break

free from that cycle. He has proposed, and mentioned during our interviews, the increase of estate taxes as a means of breaking the rich's death grip on the working class. He mentioned the reduction of immigration, which as he saw it introduced into the U.S. economy unfair competition for working-class jobs. But he also thought culture and identity were involved. "The elites, I think, they like the identity politics because it separates out people and puts them at each other's throats. Thinking that is what separates them when it's really, if you had class solidarity, right? I mean, economically, we'd be able to move the ball forward."

Allowing the working class to mobilize on the basis of its shared economic interests was the prerequisite for improving its economic conditions and positioning it to pursue spiritual transcendence. Identity politics is a diversion from that initial movement toward unifying the working class, he reasoned. That he himself has been accused of stoking identity politics—defending white identity expressions like the statues of Confederate generals, for example—wasn't the most unexpected aspect of what he was saying. Did Steve Bannon just celebrate class solidarity? Is he combining Traditionalism and Marxism?

Weird. But his words were timely, because something wasn't making sense about everything he had been saying to me, at least not when I compared the theory being described with the Trump electoral campaign. Class solidarity had not been the apparent drive and focus of the effort. Not every working-class demographic felt as though Trump was addressing them—especially not urban minorities.

I KNEW THAT Steve would distance himself from Evola's ideas on race, and if I pressed, gender, too. It was one of the first things he said to me when I asked about his interest in Traditionalism, and a message he had been consistent about when discussing forms of nationalism and Traditionalism since at least 2014 when he made his Vatican address. With me, he even marshaled Traditionalism itself as an explanation. "Traditionalism is a total rejection of [racism], in that it is a brotherhood of the spirit. It has nothing to do with your DNA, or your actual, physical body." There are plenty of Traditionalists who agree with this interpretation, though also some who do not.

I wanted to turn to the issue of race again, an issue that had bedeviled the Trump campaign and Bannon's involvement in it, and an issue lurking in our conversations about social relations. "When you refer to the United States and its working class, the peasant class," I asked him, "how much does their whiteness matter to you? The fact that it's a white working class or a Scots Irish working class . . ."

"You know, I don't think so. I think the working class today is African American and Hispanic. Also, nobody wants to talk about that, but, you know, there's no more hetero-leaning society than [the] African American working class. It's tied to the Christian church."

Fair enough, but there was also something in my conversations with Steve that I couldn't overlook. He occasionally specified the race of the working class, always as white without my prompts, and he did so in particular contexts:

"I mean, it was literally the destruction of that kind of rural, you know, white working class. That kind of Scottish Irish, that was the kind of backbone of society . . .

"Until the pathologies of the underclass get into the white working class, society will be okay. As soon as the pathologies get in there, you're going to see a dramatic deterioration."

I was accustomed to hearing politicians talk about destructive tendencies taking root in minority groups in the United States, sometimes describing the problems as indicative of a flaw in a specific group's dominant culture, sometimes adding that the isolated community needed to "come together" to solve *its* problems. But I can't recall having ever heard someone discuss the struggles of, say, urban black society as poising to undo *America's* preexisting national essence.

Come election day in 2016, the people who supported Trump had a distinct profile. They weren't especially vulnerable to competition from immigrant workers, nor did they suffer appreciably from unemployment. Instead, they were working class, less educated than the norm, and as one study put it, more likely to be found "living in racially isolated communities." And there were a lot of them: one, in Michigan, I know. Aleksandr Dugin knows him, too.

# STRANGLE THE TIGER

LATE IN THE EVENING ON NOVEMBER 8, 2016, A FEW hours' drive away from the spot of Trump's final rally in Grand Rapids, a young man named John B. Morgan walked into the bar of the Gandy Dancer restaurant perched on the banks of the Huron River in Ann Arbor, Michigan. John had been the founding editor in chief of a Traditionalist publishing house called Arktos. Now he worked for another publisher, Counter-Currents, which was more plainly white nationalist than Traditionalist. It wasn't a perfect fit for John, but nothing was.

John lived in Budapest, and India before that. But Ann Arbor still felt like home, and he was in the midst of a pilgrimage. This election was something special. Trump had no chance of winning, he thought. And John couldn't really call himself a fan per se. But the fact was that someone who was less than completely hostile to his ideals of white identity politics was in contention for the U.S. presidency. John wanted to vote in person to commemorate that unbelievable state of affairs. This was a once-in-a-lifetime event.

He was meeting an old friend at the bar to watch the results that night. They were drinking beer, paying little attention to the TV screens showing CNN's coverage of the vote. The hour arrived at and passed seven. They noticed when the states of Indiana and Kentucky were called for Trump. That was expected, but still, it was nice, John thought, to confirm that Trump had won something. Back to what their conversation: old jobs, old places, old people, old . . . shit!

Wolf Blitzer was saying on CNN that Trump was competitive. Of course he's winning the southern states, and he's leading in Florida. Hillary is struggling to wrap up Virginia. But the real battle is taking place around the Great Lakes, in America's industrial region—the Rust Belt. He's got a chance there. Here.

Another round of beers. Blitzer was back on TV before long, interrupting their conversation. Trump is a favorite, even likely at this point. Was John drunk?

His friend had to work the next day, so they parted ways and John hustled back to the apartment where he was staying. He poured himself a Dark Horse beer and turned CNN back on. Trump was going to win. States including Michigan, Pennsylvania, and Wisconsin—his part of the country—were pivotal. He was thrilled, proud—full of solidarity with the working people of Michigan whom he'd lived among for so many years. He was jumpy, almost. For about thirty seconds.

Then a different sentiment washed over John. He took another deep draw of Dark Horse. "Now we actually have to do something."

We? The alt-right, or whatever people are calling them. Those on the edges—the extremes rejected by mainstream conservatives—who dare to make politics an explicit fight for the fates of white people. If they had a role in electing Donald Trump, then they could also have a role in helping him govern. But they had a considerable resource on the inside. John thought to himself, *There is this Bannon guy, I've been reading about him.*

*He's one of us! Maybe he'll be sitting there in the White House, telling Trump Traditionalist ideas.*

On that night in front of the television, John felt something he had never felt following U.S. politics: optimism. It was almost frightening, he later told me, and profoundly un-Traditionalist.

GENERATIONS OF TRADITIONALISTS came to regard activism—and its implied belief in one's ability to shape society—as a temptation, and most claimed to have learned a lesson from it, to never fool themselves into thinking that they could change anything about the world. Julius Evola had guided them on this path.

Early in his life, Evola thought that societies could counteract the Traditional time cycle. Through reckless ambition and industry, they could push themselves backward through time to access a greater righteousness. It was on these grounds, in part, that he supported fascism. Having come to regard the Italy of his day as a society teetering on the edge between bourgeois plutocracy and communism—as heading from the age of the merchant to that of the slave—he saw fascism as a surprising and sudden movement in the opposite direction, a move backward toward a military state. Aesthetics as much as politics led him to this conclusion, for he saw in fascism a new value for "warrior ideals." Consider the ways that Hitler and Mussolini appeared in public: they were marvelously decorated soldiers.

Fascism counted as a promising start—a revitalization of the society of the warrior. Warriors are better than merchants and slaves, yes, but they aren't quite ideal. Furthermore, fascism was too populist, too materialist (especially in its strictly biological racism), and too aligned with the Christian church to suit Evola. If only fascism could be imbued with spiritual content, if only the warriors of his day could be somehow enchanted and mystified, they could complete the unwinding of time and push society backward from the age of the merchant to the age of the warrior and then to that of the priest—back into a golden age.

Evola's moment of optimism died in the flames of World War II. The victory in Europe of Russia and the United States—of communism and liberal democracy, of two sides of what Traditionalists see as the slave ethic—was a crushing and total defeat of his vision, too. He came to think in retrospect that what he had witnessed in nascent fascism wasn't a fundamental shift in the currents of time. Rather, Mussolini and Hitler represented what René Guénon described as a "readjustment," a fleeting reaction against the advance of ages that briefly delays but does not reverse direction, a nostalgic tribute to an era that, in the near future at least, was lost.

Fatalism gripped the postwar Evola. The writings he produced from this point forward turned toward grappling with the challenges facing anti-liberals living in the liberal age. The success of the Allies ushered in an era in which individuals like himself were targeted, formally and informally, by a public to whom their views were unequivocal anathema. Open resistance to the dark age, he thought, was suicidal. If the Traditionally minded person was to experience virtue, it could take place only privately, in the hidden space of his own home or psyche. "The desert encroaches from all sides; woe to him whose desert is within" was one of Evola's favorite quotes by Nietzsche. And for society at large to reach a golden age, it had to move forward, rather than backward, in the time cycle, approaching and weathering the collapse of the Kali Yuga to reach a rebirth.

Evola famously used an East Asian parable to describe his solution for the Western anti-liberal. It is a parable that opens with a man confronting a tiger in the wild. Unable to outrun the tiger and lacking any means to attack it head-on, he instead leaps on the beast's back to ride it. This ride may last a lifetime and may require the rider to watch in silence as the tiger dismembers others in its path, but at least he will avoid its bites. And when age takes its toll and the tiger begins to weary, then the rider may move to strangle it and thereby find freedom.

Evola declared that modernity, like the tiger, cannot be fought directly. Cries against its order will at best sound like white noise to those around. More likely, vocal opponents of modern liberalism will be devoured by state-sponsored repressive measures or devastating social censure. The survival strategy for such opponents is similar to that of the individual confronting the tiger: withdraw and wait. Don't start a political party or an armed revolution; maybe don't even tell your friends what you really think. Don't be honest with the outside world. Heck, pretend to hold the opposite values if that's what it takes. It doesn't amount to surrender or cowardice in Evola's mind. A disruptive anti-democratic radicalism is hiding in this apathy, in refusing to treat politics as a reflection of your vision or as an avenue toward change. Self-preservative acts are carried out with the knowledge that liberal modernity, like a living organism, has a limited lifespan and will eventually succumb to time.

The pessimism of the time cycle thus conceals hope. Those living in the liberal West can take special consolation from the fact that the decadence and social chaos of their society signals they are at the front end of the wave: Westerners entered darkness first, and they, too, will be the first to transcend it into gold. This could even instill in Traditionalists a right-wing melancholia—a drive to relish misery and sadness as signs that relief is near. And trusting that the social forms of today are predestined to collapse and usher in a return to the world of Tradition, activists must shift to the clandestine cultivation and preservation of resources that, in Evola's words, "could eventually become the premise for a future, formative action" when the moment is right and the tiger begins to weaken.

Not violence, not grassroots organizing, not propaganda, but time was the weapon of the Traditionalist, according to that way of thinking. Silence and withdrawal—the refusal to speak words or take actions that could incriminate you—gives you access to time; the less you put yourself in danger, the more time you get.

This is the reason for John Morgan's feelings of turmoil amid Trump's victory. It is also why it didn't make much sense for Aleksandr Dugin or Steve Bannon to be calling themselves Traditionalists. Dugin pushed policies, staged protests and propaganda campaigns, called for invasions, and traveled the world communicating with and lobbying governments throughout Eurasia for mysterious reasons. Bannon was a hurricane of action and activism himself. He had scores of failed initiatives behind him, but he had also spearheaded remarkably effective efforts to reshape political culture and society in the United States and Western Europe. These were hardly the behaviors of people who thought activism was meaningless.

AS STEVE AND I were concluding our conversation in Manhattan about the night of Trump's election, I asked him to think not about Trump, but about what that moment meant for Traditionalism. There were no comparable examples of someone with such a depth of interest in Evola and Guénon gaining that much formal power, I explained, preparing the way for myself to try dropping a name. I continued, "I mean you could talk about, say, Dugin—"

Steve reacted instantly. "I told you I've spent a long time with Dugin?"

No, he hadn't. I simply wanted to confirm that he knew of the person I was referring to. That he had met with Dugin was a shock to me. It happened just weeks earlier, he explained, in November 2018, following the midterm congressional elections in the United States. Steve's willingness to mention this so casually took me by surprise. Now I was the one struggling to form a sentence. He knew he was giving me sensitive information. "If they . . ."—the American media, that is—"if they knew I had a meeting with Dugin, literally it would be front page of the *Washington Post*. It's 'Bannon's a traitor,' and they'd go nuts." *He's right about that*, I thought. Especially if our media understood who Dugin is.

Where had they met? In Rome, Steve said, they spent an entire day together—alone at Steve's luxury hotel in Rome. *Of course*, I thought to myself, grasping onto the one aspect of what he was telling me that felt predictable. Let me explain: Bannon accompanied Trump into the White House as an adviser following the shock presidential election of 2016, but after he left the administration in summer 2017, his geopolitical activism shifted to two regions, namely, Europe (again) and China. Both of those campaigns crossed paths in Rome—the same Western European city where he was most likely to find Dugin, too.

From 2017 and into 2018—while in political purgatory in the United States amid a public feud with Trump—Steve turned his attention toward Europe and attempted to collaborate with people like National Rally leader Marine Le Pen in France, Geert Wilders of the Dutch Party for Freedom, and Viktor Orbán in Hungary. His efforts were formalized on July 20, 2018. Then he assumed co-leadership of a Belgium-based organization called the Movement designed to assist European nationalist parties with tech savvy and policy design, to produce and share polling data, and to target advertising campaigns. At the same time, he began planning the creation of a new school in Europe—a "gladiator school" as he took to calling it—for training future nationalist leaders in politics, ideology (including Traditionalism), and basic life skills. Even in the age of super-charged data mining, schools remained a key metapolitical outlet for far-right nationalist Europe, and Steve wanted to participate.

Most of those activities were highly publicized in international media, as was Steve's wont. But in August of 2018, a few months after my first contact with him, he took on an additional project that hardly anyone knew about. Guo Wengui, an exiled Chinese billionaire hostile to the ruling Communist Party of China (CPC), began paying Bannon for "strategic advisory work regarding media investments, marketing and advertising, joint ventures, and cryptocurrencies." Steve had been a vociferous critic of China for years. For him, the international spread of Chinese money and infrastructure represented a pernicious globalism at war with his vision for a world of sovereign nation-states. The country's monitoring and repression of spirituality, further, made it a threat to his Traditionalism. He was poised to work against China, but the contract with Mr. Guo provided added incentive: Steve's salary was $1 million annually.

Steve's various agendas came to a head in Rome. He was hoping to place his gladiator school in the eight-hundred-year-old Trisulti monastery just outside of the city. He wanted to solidify a presence there in part because of a side project to attack the Vatican and its liberal Pope Francis (who called the Trump administration "un-Christian"), in part because he was convinced the Chinese were going to throw major money at Italy as part of their One Belt One Road Initiative to forge railways and sea routes for global trade. The Chinese wanted a major hub in Venice—"where Marco Polo started," Steve noted in a conversation with me—and he was concerned that the Asian nation had a receptive audience with Italy's government. He was especially concerned that the nationalist leader of the League party and one of his closest allies in Europe, then deputy prime minister Matteo Salvini, was not attuned to the threat. Steve saw an opportunity to intervene.

But he was targeting the same Matteo Salvini whose party had long coordinated with Russian interests and was blatantly attempting to secure Russian funding in late 2018; the same Matteo Salvini who had been meeting with Vladimir Putin since 2014 and expressing support for Russia's side in the Ukraine conflict; the same Salvini who had met with Aleksandr Dugin in 2016.

Rome, in other words, was friendly territory for both Bannon and Dugin. But I wondered whether their visions for Italy—and the world—aligned.

At first, Steve gave me only the basics of his and Dugin's conversation. It was mainly about the relationships between Russia and the United States, he said, about the need for Moscow to join America in facing new challenges. What challenges? "Islam?" I asked. No. "The globalists?" Not them, either. Instead, he explained, Russia and the United States needed to unite as members of the Judeo-Christian West to fight against China, and its partners Turkey and Iran.

That Russia and the United States disagreed fundamentally on issues like democracy and human rights seemed but a minor issue for Steve. He wasn't envisioning an alliance based on whatever political values happened to be in vogue today; ancient and primal commonalities mattered more. I thought of an old quote attributed to Otto von Bismarck, that the most important geopolitical factor in East-West relations during the latter half of the twentieth century may be "that, after all, the Russians are white."

Still, why Steve would think his message would resonate with Dugin's virulent anti-Americanism, fanatical love of Iran, and increasingly conspicuous ties to China was beyond me. And indeed, he mentioned that moments in their conversation had been contentious, but he insisted the effort was essential, and added that it was a pleasure in addition to a duty. "You know, I'm, I'm such a fan of his writing . . ." Steve said about Dugin, mentioning the Russian's book *The Fourth Political Theory* in particular.

We both heard a knock at the door. "That's my guy." Father George Rutler, that is. A potential collaborator on Steve's campaign against the Vatican? I wondered. But my turn was over. I thanked Steve for his time and departed.

I had only scratched the surface of this revelation: two political ideologues of considerable influence, both disciples of a minuscule and radical philosophical and spiritual school, meeting in an attempt to coordinate geopolitics. Two Traditionalists who, if ever they believed in riding the tiger, now thought it was time to act.

I was right to have suspected something about them, though their connections were deepening before my eyes, it seemed. I would have liked to explore this further with Steve, and there would be time for that. For now, he had given me another lead by saying he had read Dugin. The Russian's writings hadn't been circulating in mainstream channels. Virtually all of them in English had come from an underground source, one that I now knew Steve had accessed, one that tied Steve and his Traditionalism to a particular, radical milieu.

IDEAS DON'T SPRING out of thin air. They come to life and gain influence in specific social environments—in a certain time, at a certain place, and among certain people. One strand of right-wing thinking in American politics today can be found among the country club and chamber of commerce types, those nurtured in college Republican and Ivy League business schools and wooed after graduation to free-market think tanks. They may or may not overlap with the members of political Christian evangelical groups, who circulate around D.C. organizations like the C Street Fellowship or the Faith and Freedom Coalition. Such groups are flush with legions of immaculately groomed, starched, and ironed white men whose hands rise and fall to bestow God's graces and lower taxes. And then there are the rogues, the antiestablishment Tea Party activists who stormed the U.S. capital in 2010, the street activists who march and protest, hold cookouts and meetups at the grassroots level, though conspicuously on mass display with the help of Fox News.

Steve Bannon weaves in and out of each of those circles—a partial participant in all, a perfect fit in none. This is because of the piece of his thinking that isn't known and wouldn't likely be shared by others involved. There is no Traditionalist milieu in Washington politics, no faction of lobbyists, advisers, or politicians with an annual Christmas party and favorite haunts, working to advance the dreams of Réne Guénon in American governance. The circles that lived Traditionalism's precepts and attempted to spread its messages are as removed geographically, socially, and spiritually from Washington as you can imagine. I can't picture any American Republican—the country clubber, the evangelical crusader, the Tea Party firebrand—feeling the slightest bit at home in these settings or even stumbling across them by accident.

I knew about those milieus, had visited some, and had interviewed and written about the key participants for years—often with the idea that I was conducting salvage research on an isolated scene of far-right activism destined to be forgotten. Never did I think that their stories would someday contain a link to formal political power. But when Steve Bannon told me he had been reading the works of Julius Evola *and* Aleksandr Dugin, then I knew that I had failed to comprehend the potential of the circles I had once followed, of the publisher that was more than just that. What they had produced would reach and influence at least one major world leader.

Home again in Colorado the day after my interview with Steve, I found the number, punched in the international code for Hungary, dialed, and heard a soft voice answer. "Hello? It's Ben Teitelbaum. Could we chat for a moment? I've been thinking about Integral Tradition Publishing and Arktos, about the early history and the stuff you guys published." The things Steve had said to me during our last interview were helping me place him in an ideological context with a paper trail. Now it was time to go to the source.

That is why I decided to call him, the wayward Michiganian John Morgan; as much to learn the details of certain intellectual projects as to remind myself of an atmosphere unlike any I would think to connect with the White House or salons of power in Rome. "Can you tell me about the early days leading up to Arktos, John? Can you tell me what was it like? During those mornings?"

# 8

## THE RACE OF THE SPIRIT

*August 2009. Mumbai, India.*

BEADS OF SWEAT ROLLED DOWN JOHN MORGAN'S BROW as he lifted his head from the small, soaked pillow. Even now, at four in the morning, Mumbai's heat was punishing, and John had yet to adjust. Short, with curly brown hair and a soft, cherubic face, the thirty-six-year-old from Ann Arbor, Michigan, had been living in India for three months. His mannerisms, his voice, and his conduct all resonated humility and compassion. Perhaps that is why the leaders of this Hare Krishna ashram in the northeastern edge of the city granted him the impious luxury of a pillow. The other dozen or so devotees in the room slept with nothing but a chatai mat and the hard floor beneath them.

John rolled up his mat, placed it under his pillow, and walked to an adjacent room with a drain in the floor, where he poured ladle after ladle of water from a bucket over his body. Still in darkness, he wrapped a white dhoti cloth around his legs and waist and slid a flowing white collarless kurta over his upper body. *Now for the finishing touch,* he thought as he dipped his right ring finger into a bowl of yellow paste, pressed it softly to the middle of his nose, and increased the pressure as he drew his finger up across his forehead to the base of his hairline. It was the U-shaped tilaka mark typical of Hindu Vaishnavites.

John turned and joined the procession of immaculately prepared but groggy-looking young men walking toward the temple. One figure stood out. John briefly locked eyes with his business partner Mark, the only other Westerner living in the ashram. John stopped briefly, his eyes shining, and smiled at Mark. Here they were, spiritual refugees from the West finding a home in a faraway land, showing that they were more than armchair Traditionalists, committing themselves to an authentic Aryan religion. By living in India and seeing through a project that for years had been their dream, they might bring this truth to the others.

Some people would call them white nationalists, and were you to have asked them if they embraced the label, they would have replied with contorted faces, tilting heads, and a chorus of *well*s and *um*s. It is true, they had all experienced what they called an ethnic and racial awakening, thanks in part to the broadcasts of American white nationalist icon William Pierce. That early influence made them who they are. But their paths eventually crossed in a conviction that white nationalism alone, and its gratuitous focus on the body at the expense of the soul, was lacking—not because it was immoral, but because it was incomplete.

Change began when they discovered the writings of Julius Evola. John's partners first heard the renegade Italian referenced by one of their favorite black metal icons, Varg Virkenes. Upon accessing one of Evola's only texts available in English, the seminal *Revolt Against the Modern World,* they began reading and rereading sections aloud. The book's influence on them was transformative. Contrary to the messages they were hearing from organized white nationalism, Evola helped them see that the woes of the world were not the result of nonwhites and Jews per se. Modernity, rather, was the underlying cause, immigration and multiculturalism its by-products. And a meaningful escape could be found only in modernity's opposite: Tradition, with its rejection of progress and equality and its embrace of a hierarchy that placed Aryan men on top.

These young men fancied themselves a part of that chosen caste, though they shared it as much with those at the ashram in Mumbai as with the blond men of Scandinavia. As far as they were concerned, the Aryans were scattered across two continents, their territory marked by the historical extent of the Indo-European languages, which stretch from Sanskrit in the Indian subcontinent, northwest through Persia, and to the Hellenic, Slavic, Latin, and Germanic languages in Europe. This territory is the historic home, roughly, of a body of religious practices with similar features—polytheistic faiths, some labeled "pagan," which professed cyclic time and different destinies for different types of people. All were vanquished by the spread of monotheism from the Middle East—all, in their minds, except for one.

Hinduism was the sole Aryan spirituality to have maintained itself as an unbroken practice. And for these young men, the pathway toward it would be standard for Westerners: the Hare Krishna movement and its branch of Hinduism, Gaudiya Vaishnavism. In this movement, they found people who appeared the polar opposite of the modern Westerner, people who were disciplined and orderly thanks to their commitment to what Evola taught them were real Aryan values. These people were everything they had hoped to find but didn't in the chaotic and decadent white nationalist scene.

John Morgan's path to the ashram began a few years ago in Michigan, back when he grew interested in alternative spiritualities after following what he describes as his discovery of a deeper extra-material reality thanks in part to experimentation with hallucinogenic drugs. (He wasn't ashamed to talk about this, for his idols Julius Evola and Ernst Jünger, an anti-modernist

German philosopher and World War II soldier, used hallucinogens to the same ends.) Traditionalist philosophy managed to unite this burgeoning interest in hallucinogens with his reactionary politics. Entranced by Traditionalist texts and disillusioned by the spiritual vapidity of his home life and culture, he began looking for a Traditional religion to practice. Nearby Detroit offered a rare access to Sufi Islam, and he began hanging out with local Naqshbandi Sufis and even managed to meet the famous Shaykh Hisham Kabbani, the founder of the local order. And John would have gone that route, too, had it not been for a query he received online.

In 2006, two Europeans had started a publishing house, one that would feature English translations of Guénon and Evola. The market was wide open, save for a small New Age press in Vermont, they had no competitors, certainly not for the radical right-wing readership they hoped to target. They called it Integral Tradition Publishing. John, whom they had come in contact with via an electronic mailing list, seemed an ideal candidate to be their editor. He was a native English speaker, smart, scholarly in his own way, and passionate about Traditionalism. He started working for them part-time in 2006. But in 2008, they approached him with a more exciting suggestion: why not move to India, join them in a Hare Krishna ashram, and start initiation into the religion that Guénon wrote about most. Meanwhile, they emphasized, your cost of living will be unfathomably cheap and that, combined with new print-on-demand technologies, will allow us to succeed where all other business initiatives on the far right fail. All that was going on back home was the financial crisis, and the silly politics of Bush and Obama.

So John went. Some mornings the routine felt oppressive and academic to the Westerners. But today the spirit was with them. John turned to watch one of his partners. He sang the words of the mantra steadily, defying the heat and the exhaustion; his back arched as he looked up and spread his arms to the sky. Aryan body and soul were one.

Notes of incense, chimes of kartal finger cymbals, and the rhythm of the mridangam drum filled the air as the devotees entered the temple. Candles cast the only light, and the heat grew nearly unbearable as bodies crowded together in front of the altar. The deities were awake, everyone knew, though a veil still covered their faces.

The conch horn sounded. In the Bhagavad Gita, horns fashioned from large seashells were used as a summons to battle, blown by none other than Lord Krishna himself. Today their deep cry signals the start of the morning service, the mangala arati. John turned toward the altar as the veil dropped, revealing a scene decorated vibrantly with all the colors of the rainbow. Gaura-Nitai, the twin deities of the ashram, stood in the center. The devotees respond by also raising their hands high and commencing the service with the mantra that Gaura brought to Earth. "Hare Kṛiṣhṇa, Hare Kṛiṣhṇa . . ."

Though the Westerners had moved beyond the American white supremacist movements, their thinking about race was complicated. For them, race was more than just skin color. Evola declared that it was also a particular way of relating to the supernatural, of wondering about existence, and of understanding the metaphysical dimensions of time and the universe. This "race of the spirit," he explained, was the only thing one could inherit from ancestors, the only aspect of race that could live on while bodies die: bodies are time, spirit is eternal. That our spirits match the race of our body is hardly guaranteed, however, and mismatches would occur as Tradition is lost in an age of darkness. To adopt the spirit of others—or worse yet, to abandon spiritual yearning altogether—was to lack race in the truest sense, to deprive oneself of the tools to be deeply and authentically linked to past generations of your own kind and differentiated from others.

Racelessness may sound like a modernist ideal alongside secularism, but for Evola it was an evil that encroached on all sides. Indeed, when as a young man he first encountered Nazism during the 1930s, he considered its fanatical racism little more than a promising start. The Nazis' focus on biological race and the body showed that they were unwittingly consumed by modern ways of thinking and knowing—foremost of all, science. For a period of time Evola took it upon himself to improve the German campaign, to breathe mysticism into their sense of race, hoping to create a thoroughly Aryan population that strived for purity of both body and spirit. His bizarre theories weren't popular in either of Europe's fascist regimes. Guido Landra, a racial theorist under Mussolini, claimed Evola's concept of race would "be of exclusive benefit to the Jew" because it allowed for various peoples to claim an Aryan spirit. Heinrich Himmler's SS staff likewise labeled Evola a "pseudoscientist" with the potential to cause "ideological entanglements" in Hitler's Germany, and recommended he be marginalized.

But years later, John and his partners found Evola's thinking illuminating. The drunken fools in the white nationalist movement were mutants, perhaps possessing an Aryan body, but with corrupted spirits. As with the Nazis of old, their political obsession with skin color revealed that they had assimilated modern values: they were materialists, unable to see past physical matter, accomplices to decadence and equivalent to the lowest castes of humanity. John felt more kinship with his fellow devotees in the ashram. They shared the same Aryanism, one born of a core that long ago was the wellspring of both of their bloodlines. And the racism that prevailed in India was for them far more palatable, far more Traditional. Hinduism, often implicitly or informally, associates skin color, social standing, and spiritual opportunity. The lower castes, committed to physical labor, were often darker-skinned, while the upper castes, notably the Brahmins, who historically were religious authorities, tended to have lighter skin. This way of thinking gave the wayward Westerners a chance to combine their values and elevate themselves in the process. Pale skin may have been a boring and unattractive feature back home. Here it could be a sign of holiness.

This morning, indeed, was devoted to celebrating the holy. The ritual as a whole has an arc. The opening texts and songs are delivered powerfully but with a slow pace, to create a somber and contemplative ambience, much like that of a Christian mass. As the service proceeds, however, the atmosphere shifts: tempos accelerate and the devotees' movements grow more rapturous. One of John's partners always found this part alienating and foreign—*this is how you connect with the divine?* he wondered. It resonated with John, however. He sang the final song while the mridangam drum beat faster and faster and voices sang louder and louder. Laughter rang out from the assembly as the mood reached a fevered pitch. Devotees raised their hands and began jumping and spinning in ecstatic dance. John was floating.

THERE HAD BEEN CHATTER about John in the ashram, because it would soon be time for him to make a decision, to choose his path. Devotees at his stage either went the way of the householder (grihastha), which would entail an arranged marriage and a family, or followed a rabbinical path committed to ritual and study of scripture. John was earnest in considering the rabbinical path. Most of the sacrifices would be steep but doable, save one. Becoming a monk would mean he couldn't work, would never have an ordinary job of any kind. He would have to give up Integral Tradition Publishing.

Work, however, was going well. ITP had been slow to live up to its title as a book publisher. Its retail operations consisted in large part of products they didn't produce, especially a large catalogue of CDs of a murky underground music genre called neo-folk, popular among Traditionalists. But now, having moved to India, they were pushing some exciting releases. They had published *Metaphysics of War* in 2007 and would soon finalize *The Path of Cinnabar*, both by Evola. The first was a compilation of essays and articles Evola had written during the early stages of his career, the second a sort of autobiography. John had worked tirelessly on both, penning forewords and adding footnotes throughout. *Metaphysics of War* was an especially exciting initiative. Its chapters included some of the only texts Evola produced on his arcane theory of race to be published in English. It was sure to catch on with the more sophisticated minds in the European and American radical right.

Business opportunities were expanding as well. John's partners would soon initiate exchanges with a Swede named Daniel Friberg. Friberg had come straight out of Sweden's white power skinhead scene. He was tough as shit, with battle experience facing off against anti-fascist street gangs. Like them, Friberg was disgruntled with the state of white nationalism and was drawn by the prospect of building a more intellectual movement. He had a publishing and translation outfit of his own called the Nordic League, specializing in Swedish-language productions— books, magazines, blogs, online encyclopedias, and music—and he was looking to break out. Maybe ITP would want to join forces? Friberg was slightly less devoted to Traditionalism. Were ITP to merge with his initiatives, they would likely need to drop their previous requirement that all staff members practice a Traditional religion. But they were still aligned on the big issues.

By the end of the following year, the merger was a reality and a new company, Arktos, was born. It wouldn't take long until their business model—based on print-on-demand publishing and operating out of low-cost economies like India—allowed production to soar. They were soon the largest publisher of new English-language Traditionalism and far-right intellectualism in the world. And this meant that they had resources, not only to pump out new translations of Evola's writings but also to invest in contemporary Traditionalist authors. One author in particular was poised to expand their reach. He was Russian, and Arktos was set to release the first English translation of one of his major works in 2012 and would work to promote him through conferences and speaking events. His name was Aleksandr Dugin, and he would become Arktos's greatest commercial and intellectual success.

9

# THE MAN AGAINST TIME

BANNON IS SAID TO HAVE CALLED HIMSELF A LENINIST once at a party: "Lenin wanted to destroy the state, and that's my goal, too. I want to bring everything crashing down, and destroy all of today's establishment." That statement was according to someone else in attendance, though Steve claims to have no memory of saying it.

Regardless, it's the sort of thing I could easily imagine him saying. It fits with the rest of his thinking, at least as he presented it to me now, several months after our first conversation, as we sat alone late at night in yet another hotel room in El Paso, Texas.

He seemed to make a point of looking me in the eye when asserting that Lenin was not his hero, that the way Russian communists disassembled their society is hardly anything to emulate. But it's true, he said, that there is a role for destruction in politics in general and in our time in particular. Destruction "is just part of the cycle."

Steve believes in them: time cycles. He believes that human societies rotate through a series of ages leading from collapse to regeneration to collapse again, and on and on. Some people know this about him. Near the beginning of his stay in the White House, journalists learned that he celebrated a book originally published in 1997 called *The Fourth Turning*—a popular work claiming that modern history cycles through four approximately twenty-year eras, the last of which is an of era of crisis and deconstruction ahead of an era of rebirth. But Steve calls that book the "simplistic" version of Guénon and Evola, of the deeper stuff you'll find published only by presses like Arktos: real Traditionalist texts whose accounts of a four-age cycle leading to a dark age—the Kali Yuga—are flush with ecumenical religious justifications and spiritual analyses. Granted, Steve is not the type who pays too much attention to the details in Traditionalism's teachings on time. To him, they represent an inspired attempt to explain something unknowable, to be taken as a guideline.

It is not a particularly Christian guideline, he'll admit. He relayed to me a strand of Christian theology claiming that the world used to be bound in cyclicality, but that the arrival of Jesus had broken the pattern and initiated progress—linear history pointing toward the ultimate and final salvation. "I still got to be sold on that one," he said to me, grinning, again showing an eagerness to break with the dogmas of his professed faith. "Not so sure I buy into it. I still think you see cycles."

More than that, he thinks that we are at the terminal stage of a cycle right now. What tells him this? He mentioned observations both concrete and vague. "I think you see it a little bit every day. Things are just . . . feel like they're getting rougher, right?" He also talked about the increasing unpredictability of social and political life, about the ways certain people seemed to be funneled into positions of political influence, not because of their individual yearnings and activities but by unseen forces churning around them. He mentioned Donald Trump and Alexandria Ocasio-Cortez as examples: it was an inversion of the previous status quo that allowed for their rise. But he also saw a broader movement toward conflict. He had seen traces of it before. As he explained: "There are certain times in history that no matter what good men say or do, inexorably you're drawn to something that turns out to be a conflict. You see this before World War II; you see this before the Civil War. You know, people forget how many peace conferences they had, how many deals people were trying to cut, and how many things—it didn't matter. Inexorably, you were drawn to something that had to be done. And that's where we're going, that's what we're doing today."

Violence could be on the horizon globally, he thought. If a single power or a coalition of powers attempts to gain control of the Eurasian landmass, thwarting an old tenet of American foreign policy, that will bring about a conflict, he assures me. Domestically, though, within the United States, it wouldn't have to be that way. Our internal conflict wouldn't need to be dealt with militarily or through violence, but it would require destruction, particularly destruction of our public institutions, many of which, Steve believes, are in need of revitalization or, he suggests, being "blown up." He mentions Joseph Schumpeter's notion of "creative destruction" and Henri Bergson's idea of élan vital, in addition to the Traditionalists. "It's this thing that you have to go through, that you do have to destroy to rebuild."

It sounds like an agenda of chaos. Steve wants to see mass disassembly of our largest governmental agencies, and all this alongside his other agendas of breaking up the European Union and stopping the free international flow of people, goods, and money. But an arch-Traditionalist in the mold of Julius Evola wouldn't necessarily see it as chaos. Remember, what is dark about the dark age was the eradication of hierarchy—hierarchy, which is a form of order. Dispense with hierarchy and you find yourself in chaos, born of the inability for any of us to distinguish ourselves vertically or horizontally. Put that in more general terms, and you're talking about the replacement of a segmented society with an undifferentiated mass: chaos and confusion enter our lives as we scale up, placing ourselves in contexts too large to reflect anything genuine about us or our yearnings. The shift from tribe to chiefdom to nation therefore constitutes a movement from order to chaos, not to mention a shift from national to supranational entities. Differentiation is what's lost in these cases. It may take a chaotic act to destroy the mass entity, but if its collapse produces a smaller body of variegated entities, you will have moved from chaos back to order again.

A pane of glass is insanity; harmony lives in its shattered pattern on the ground. In modern politics, that means pursuing breakdown—the disassembly of sprawling "administrative states," as Bannon so often puts it. One way to do that is to start from the top, by placing people in positions of power who are hostile to the institutions they serve; who will work to skunk the institution's mandate and functioning. *It all makes sense*, I thought as I listened to Steve, recalling a series of actions he took a few years ago.

IN THE WEEKS following his victory over Hillary Clinton, Donald Trump began choosing individuals to serve with him in his government. He wasn't making these decisions on his own. Steve was transitioning from his old role of managing a candidate to that of chief adviser to the president, and his primary function at this point was to assist Trump in staffing his new government.

On November 23, 2016, Trump nominated Betsy DeVos for secretary of education. Earlier that year, DeVos had called for scrapping the public school system in Detroit and replacing it with a voucher system where students take a share of public money and apply it to the cost of a private school of their choice. She was an advocate of religious education (let's presume Christian, not Islamic) and of the belief that breaking down public education would allow for a diversification of the culture and spirituality transmitted to American students. In 2001 she and her husband, Dick DeVos, speaking to a private gathering, specified that they aimed to infuse education with Christian messages and to upend what they saw as the hierarchy of institutions in society. As Dick put it, "the church—which ought to be in our view far more central to the life of the community—has been displaced by the public school as the center for activity, the center for what goes on in the community." And for the DeVoses, uninverting this imbalance didn't entail eliminating public schools altogether, for these institutions presented opportunities for activists like themselves, as Betsy explained. They provided a channel "to confront the culture in which we all live today." Public schools were a battlefield beckoning the conservative cultural warrior—a space for metapolitics. They implored Christians to infiltrate these channels into the cultural mainstream, "not to stay in [their] own little safe territory." Circa 75 percent of the schools Betsy DeVos would oversee in the Department of Education are public.

On December 7, 2016, Trump announced that he would nominate Scott Pruitt to head the Environmental Protection Agency. The nomination was watched closely: during the early stages of the presidential campaign, Trump said of the EPA, "We are going to get rid of it in almost every form." Pruitt had served as Oklahoma's attorney general, and during his stay in office he sued the Environmental Protection Agency thirteen times. His instinct was to partner with the private industries that were the primary target of environmental regulation. In fact, their collaboration was so close that industry spokespersons sent him talking points to use when arguing in public about policy. Perhaps these actions led him to label himself as "a leading advocate against the EPA's activist agenda." He was an ideal person to head the agency itself, in other words, if your goal was to see the EPA deconstructed.

On December 13, 2016, Trump announced he would nominate former Exxon Mobil oil executive Rex Tillerson, a political unknown, to be the new secretary of state. His foreign policy views seemed conventional—surprisingly so given Trump's expressed desires to transform the geopolitical role of the United States. Bannon pushed for his nomination nonetheless, and the appeal became clear during Tillerson's confirmation hearings, where he clarified an agenda: "it is just in my nature to look for inefficiencies and to streamline, and that will start, if confirmed, it will start right there in the State Department." He added, "I think we are naturally going to capture some efficiencies and cost savings." Indeed, at the outset of his tenure, Tillerson told staff that he planned to cut the department's budget by a third, to eliminate thousands of jobs, and to cut billions in foreign aid. By late spring, Tillerson had imposed a near total hiring freeze. By October, he was offering more than two thousand employees of the State Department a $25,000 bonus in exchange for their retiring within a year. The White House, for its part, had not been nominating people to staff top positions under Tillerson. Likewise, the usual lag in filling American diplomatic and ambassadorial posts after a change of administration had now stretched to alarming lengths. Nearly a year after Trump's election, forty-eight ambassadorships were vacant. The U.S. diplomatic mission to the world was contracting.

On December 16, 2016, Trump nominated Mick Mulvaney to lead the Office of Management and Budget. It is the biggest agency within the White House, but the move positioned Mulvaney to enter into another role, namely, to head the Consumer Financial Protection Bureau. The bureau was created in 2011 as a means to allow private persons to better check the actions of large corporations. Mick Mulvaney, a former representative to

Congress, had been a fierce critic of the CFPB, allegedly on account of its built-in immunity from political oversight. In a 2014 interview he said of the bureau, "It's a wonderful example of how a bureaucracy will function if it has no accountability to anybody. It turns up being a joke, and that's what the CFPB really has been, in a sick, sad kind of way," adding that it was "extraordinarily frightening" and needed reform. What kinds of reforms? the interviewer asked. "Some of us would like to get rid of it." It took a protracted legal battle and a public pressure campaign, but in November 2017 Mulvaney assumed leadership of the bureau. He would begin his work by firing swaths of staff, hiring next to none, freezing all cases before the bureau pending adjudication, and submitting a planned $0 budget. This institution, too, had an enemy at its top.

They were on kamikaze missions, those filling leadership positions—each conspicuously striving to undermine the fiefdom over which they presided, each making a contribution to the broader deconstruction of the administrative state. However, their plans would be frustrated by a glitch in the system. They may have been destabilizing and undermining their respective agencies, but they were subject to the same from above. Trump, too, undermined the functioning of the institution he presided over as president. Personnel turnover in the White House would be pronounced, and people like Tillerson and many other staff members served relatively brief terms before coming into conflict with Trump and exiting, often to be replaced by figures with similarly ephemeral tenures. Wreaking havoc among his immediate subordinates, those whom he relied upon to advance his agenda, was surely not a conscious aim. Steve certainly hasn't given me any suggestions to the contrary. Instead, it seems the internal strife was a consequence of Trump's nature, some sort of unfortunate collateral damage wrought by the introduction of a force with rare destructive capacity.

That force had to be there, Steve thought, especially if Trump was to rise to meet his own destiny.

THE PROSPECT OF there being not just a plan but an elaborate theological agenda behind the apparent chaos of the early Trump administration turned my attention toward the defining phrase of the president's campaign: "Make America Great Again." The slogan, which Trump patented in 2012, was a succinct expression of the will toward national rebirth, what British historian and political theorist Roger Griffin calls *palingenesis*. It refers to a moment of unspecified greatness lost in the past and thereby proclaims ours as a time of decline. It is easily misconstrued as an expression of nostalgia, of longing for a more virtuous past. One thing the four-word phrase does profess to know, however, is that American greatness does not belong to the past, but is instead a creature that can be made to live in the here and now. Its life is not linear—it doesn't have a beginning or an end. The slogan is therefore not a call to move backward and regain the past, nor is it a promise of something novel in the future. It attempts to regain an eternity.

Here is a paradox of the time cycle concept: it recognizes no real past, present, or future. This is part of what Bannon enjoys about it, part of what makes the notion of cyclic time both a descriptive tool for understanding how the world is and a prescriptive tool for creating the world that ought to be. "Politicians talk about grandchildren, and yes, we have to think about that," he said to me. "But as importantly, we have to think back to what we owe to those who came before us." Those attuned to cyclic time do not attempt to progress toward a previously unrealized state of virtue, condemning the present and the past in the process. They rest rather in communion with their timeless kin, coalescing around the moon, sun, and stars rather than the latest layer of stone or pavement. Eternity—the supposed insight that would lead a political leader to channel the will of grandchildren and ancestors at once—is something that we can have or not have. The cycle also entails a motion from the central core, away to its edge, and back again—centripetal and centrifugal. It entails movement of departure to the illusion of time and progress, and movement of return back toward the core of eternal truth, on and on. But this all plays out according to a set schedule, an order during which different ages unfold. Or does it?

More than once I've pondered the Julius Evola of the 1930s when mulling about Steve. During the 1930s, Evola began to suspect that the time cycle was something society could control, something *he* could control. He had been expecting to see a shift from the bronze age of the merchant to the dark age of the slave. Instead, a warrior appeared in Benito Mussolini, signaling a potential change in the cosmic currents and the potential to experience utmost virtue without having to plow through death and destruction first. Like the young Evola, Steve might also claim to have witnessed a reversal of time. For he, too, rose to influence during a revolution headed by an ostensible archetype of one of the Traditionalist castes. Only for him, the figure wasn't a warrior, but a merchant—an icon not of the Kshatriya but of the Vaishyas. However, for Steve, Trump's appearance did not signal a reversal in temporal currents the way Mussolini's did for Evola. The direction of time remained intact. As he told me, "to Make America Great Again, you've got to . . . you've got to disrupt, before you rebuild."

In Bannon's eyes, Donald Trump is "the Disrupter." I've heard him say "destroyer" as well. That's Steve's understanding, at least. Steve recalls having a quick conversation with Trump about it all in the White House in April 2017, following some media coverage of his reading of *The Fourth Turning*. The president wasn't amused. He saw his role as that of a builder rather than a destroyer, and was turned off by all the weird talk of doom and destruction and collapse.

Steve didn't push it. It was just a quick exchange. And besides, there was no need to make Trump see the world the way he did. The president can think whatever he wants to think. "Remember," Steve said to me about Trump, "he is a man of action. The power of men of action is that a lot of men of action are not . . . you know, you don't have to read books and think about time cycles. You just do it."

ON JANUARY 20, 2017, the same day that Donald Trump was sworn in as president of the United States, he signed an executive order. Executive orders and presidential memoranda are declarations issued by the president, typically concerning the functioning of the U.S. government, that carry the force of law. And on this day, President Trump chose to issue an order, 13765, titled "Minimizing the Economic Burden of the Patient Protection and Affordable Care Act Pending Repeal." Its purpose was to prompt federal agencies to stop enforcing key aspects of President Obama's healthcare reform legislation, and it appeared the opening move in Trump's plan to repeal the program altogether.

That was Friday. The following Monday, on January 23, President Trump issued a number of presidential memoranda. One removed the United States from a twelve-nation trade agreement across the Pacific region. The other prohibited any federal moneys—through foreign aid or other means—to go to organizations that provide abortion services to women.

On Tuesday, President Trump signed executive order 13766, "Expediting Environmental Reviews and Approvals for High Priority Infrastructure Projects." He also issued a flurry of memoranda promoting the construction of a series of oil pipelines—including one that crossed key waterways and which Native Americans claimed threatened the environmental integrity of their sacred sites—as well as a memorandum aimed at easing regulations for manufacturing.

The president took the next day to proclaim the entire week, by means of a presidential proclamation, National School Choice Week in recognition of nonpublic and charter schools. He also issued executive order 13767, "Border Security and Immigration Enforcement Improvements," calling for the immediate construction of a physical wall along the U.S. southern border with Mexico and the acceleration of processing and deportation of illegal immigrants. This was accompanied by a second executive order, 13768, "Enhancing Public Safety in the Interior of the United States," seeking to block federal funding for U.S. cities that deliberately limited the capability of the government to enforce immigration law (so-called sanctuary cities) and giving officials permission to initiate deportation proceedings against those only suspected of posing a safety risk.

On Thursday, he rested.

On Friday, he issued a memorandum entitled "Rebuilding the U.S. Armed Forces," directing a review of the nation's nuclear and missile-defense capabilities and the drafting of a plan to boost preparedness. That same day, he issued another executive order, 13769, "Protecting the Nation from Foreign Terrorist Entry into the United States." The order reduced the number of refugees to be admitted and blocked the entry of Syrian refugees indefinitely. It also suspended visas for citizens of Libya, Somalia, Sudan, Syria, Yemen, Iraq, and Iran. In references to comments Trump made during the electoral campaign, the press dubbed this order the "Muslim ban."

The president was on pace to sign more orders in his first hundred days than any other U.S. president since World War II.

Not only was Steve Bannon the source of the content of some of these declarations—including the "Muslim ban"—he was also invested in the broader strategy of issuing declarations in such short succession. One might have reasoned that having won an election with a minority share of the vote and amid resounding public outcry and fear over the direction of the new administration, the president should have eased into major political battles so as not to embolden the opposition. Bannon instead told me and others that he advocated this technique to disorient the president's foes, principal among them, in his mind, the media. Hit what they care about most: health care, the environment, abortion, immigration. Hit them so fast they can't focus. This would cripple the opposition, allowing the president to advance his cause unabated.

THERE WAS ORDER, direction, and purpose to Trump's destruction. That's how Steve saw it, at least. And speaking with him about the first days in the White House made me suspicious about something else he had said to me during one of our first informal conversations, a peculiar phrase that could have been mere coincidence or a deliberate characterization derived from Traditionalism's darkest corners. In a flurry of verbiage, he referred to Trump as "a man in time."

The use of that term in right-wing Traditionalist circles comes from a woman named Savitri Devi. Born Maximine Portaz in Lyon in 1905, she took the name Savitri Devi (Goddess of the Sun Ray) after having converted to Hinduism as part of a quest to discover a living Aryan tradition. She was a devout National Socialist during the war, to the point of spying on British forces in India for the Axis powers. But her real work began after 1945 when she attempted to forge a new religion out of the wreckage of the Third Reich. She compared herself to Saint Paul, who built a new faith based on a figure whose life on earth ended in political defeat. The teaching she produced, however, came to be called Esoteric Hitlerism. Devi seldom put it this way, but as much as she was a follower of Hitler, her thinking also reflected the influence of Guénon and Evola.

Devi believed in the Traditionalist notion of cyclic time, but she emphasized something different when thinking about it. As time proceeds and social order disintegrates, she claimed, violence and destruction increase. This makes violence a blessing in disguise. Just as nature's wildfires herald regrowth, destructive human aggression is necessary to clear the way for social and spiritual renewal. Time *is* violence. Both entail pain and suffering, but likewise the promise of salvation.

Certain influential individuals play an outsize role in this process. Devi claimed they came in three forms: men in time, men above time, and men against time. Everything that Devi saw as defining the passage of time—that it entailed decay by way of selfishness, chaos, and violence—is embodied in the men in time. She claimed that these figures need not be aware of their role in a cosmic time cycle. Void of reflection and curiosity, they fall into the darkening spirit of their age, pursuing bodily pleasure and material wealth with such ruthlessness that they become distinguished forces of harm. And we should thank them for that. Devi described herself being "overwhelmed by a feeling of sacred awe at the thought of the grand-scale exterminators without ideologies." They are flashes of fire serving never to create on their own, only to destroy: they are lightning.

If the men in time are fully engrossed in violence, another category of figures—men above time—escape such bondage. They do this by means of enlightenment, by gaining insight into the truth of time, by knowing the feebleness of human campaigns for progress, and by understanding that salvation exists in eternity rather than the "future." You could find them among the aesthetes who reject the world, the mad mystics in the wilderness, or they could be in a role altogether unrecognizable to those around them. During the golden age, these same figures would be regarded with utmost reverence as spiritual authorities. But in later ages, society ignores them as irrelevant or invisible. That doesn't mean they are without impact. They may function as saviors for those around them—redeeming not groups or societies but individual souls who follow their example. Their wisdom is never spread by proselytizing or force. Rather, like the sun, which is their symbol, it radiates from their being, and in no particular direction.

But the climax of Devi's thinking comes when describing a third figure, born out of those with insight into the mysteries of the universe and the truth of time, but endowed with the nature of the warrior caste. They know that the currents of time point toward destruction, but they also see glory on the other side. Far from the tiger riders of Evola's postwar withdrawal, they are charged with fanatical ambition and inspired by the highest ideals rather than selfishness, taking it upon themselves to carry the world into and through darkness. This makes them both lightning and sun, men "against" time.

True men against time are not humans per se, but rather avatars. As Devi wrote, "The last Man 'against Time' is, in fact, no other than He Whose name, in Sanskrit Tradition, is Kalki,—the last Incarnation of the divine Sustainer of the universe and, at the same time, the Destroyer of the whole world; the Savior Who will put an end to this present 'yuga' in a formidable display of unparalleled violence, in order that a new creation may flourish in the innocence and splendor of a new 'Age of Truth.'" She wrote of Adolf Hitler as a man against time, thanks to his vigorous commitment to violence and devotion to what she saw as Aryan ideals. But Hitler lost, of course. And for Devi, this meant that the true man against time had yet to come.

BACK IN STEVE'S HOTEL ROOM in El Paso, I asked him whether he had heard of her, Savitri Devi. He said he knew the name. I explained that she was the person with whom I associated the expression *man in time*—that she had used it to describe figures whose behaviors advanced time, which is to say perpetuated violence and destruction. They didn't have any understanding of their own importance or their role in history—they didn't need to *know*, they needed to *act*. What I was describing matched his characterization of Trump ("you don't have to read books and think about time cycles. You just do it"), though I didn't say that. "She had a whole theory to go with this," I continued, "a theory of men in time, above time, and against time."

"Okay, but here—give me one sec . . ." He wanted to respond but was distracted by his phone. He texted someone back, then continued: "She had a thing that was a what now?"

"She believed that there were three types of avatars in history, men who were in—"

"Three types of avatars, what's that?"

His earlier use of the phrase *man in time* notwithstanding, he wasn't sounding especially familiar with Devi's ideas, but I continued, "So as the time cycle is moving forward you will get historic figures who either just destroy, and that pushes the time cycle forward." I then began to explain the men above time. "Or they pull themselves out of it, time, because they are enlightened and they experience transcendence and they are no longer subject to time essentially, and to degradation. They don't need to—"

"Well, who in history has done that?" Steve seemed excited by the ideas. He was eager for me to go on, I could tell. "I mean, Jesus Christ, or Buddha?"

"She mentions the sun-worshiping kings of Egypt."

"Oh, so she goes way back, yeah."

He was digging it. "Way back," I echoed, "yeah. Genghis Khan is a man in time. He didn't have higher ideals, but he served the progress of time because he destroyed things and brought us closer to the rebirth after Kali Yuga. And then there's the man who's against time, who—"

"What's the man against time?" he eagerly interrupts.

"The man against time is someone who has the higher ideal *and* is willing to destroy at the same time."

He leaned back, folded his hands behind his head, and looked up at the ceiling. "And why—if he has the higher ideal . . ." He paused to think, and then continued: "Because he understands that he has to destroy to rejuvenate?"

"Yes."

Steve shrugged, turned to look out the window, and said nothing.

# 10

## ESOTERIC GATHERINGS

I SPENT DECEMBER 2018 AT HOME IN BOULDER PLAYING catch-up with events that had taken place on the global political stage during the past months. This was the time of midterm congressional elections in the United States, and the Democrats had taken the House of Representatives but failed to wrest control of the Senate from Republicans. The outcome could have been worse, Steve thought, though he anticipated that the Democrats would now use their power to try to impeach Trump. There were various defense mechanisms in place, but it was a setback, no doubt. Ups and downs—Steve had his eyes on the long game, on spoils greater than any single congressional election, larger than Trump, larger even than the fate of the United States.

I had learned that Traditionalism motivated him to connect with one other major global figure—Aleksandr Dugin—and that his access to Dugin's thinking, if nothing else, had come via Traditionalism's far-right underground channels, through the publishing output of Arktos. I was on the hunt for details about this, though Steve had said he wouldn't be available for an interview for a few weeks. That's when something unexpected happened. There was chatter among Traditionalists online about yet another figure in the upper reaches of powerful governments, someone unfamiliar to me, someone connected with the political upheaval taking place in Brazil.

A renegade politician, Jair Bolsonaro, dubbed the "Trump of the Tropics," had just won the presidency in Brazil. Bolsonaro's victory marked yet another startling success for the global far-right populist wave. He rattled international observers through his overtures toward state violence, political violence, and the consolidation of executive power, as well as his contempt for the media and political establishment, socialism, Islam, LGBTQ people, and other minorities. And whereas populists elsewhere combined cultural conservatism with celebrations of social safety-net welfare policies, Bolsonaro's hostility toward socialists in his country inspired him to demand free-market reforms. His platform and demeanor were unthinkable even in the raucous world of Brazilian politics, and the opposition to his candidacy was fierce (he survived a knife attack a month ahead of the first round of voting), but he prevailed nonetheless, bolstered by a deep reservoir of resentment against the political establishment and progressive political movements. He also had a prominent ideologue stirring these sentiments through social media.

I looked up his acceptance speech, posted online just weeks before, on October 29. Bolsonaro made it an informal affair, streaming the address from his home via Facebook Live in an affront to Brazil's standard media channels. He seemed not to be speaking from a teleprompter or from notes. Instead, he had laid four books on a table in front of himself and would use them as mnemonic devices to help him organize the seemingly ad-libbed speech. A theatrical move, I thought, portraying him as a leader of conviction following the steady compass of words committed to paper, like when Napoleon staged a portrait in the presence of scrolls.

He put his hands on the Bible and the Brazilian constitution—two of the four books—when reiterating his campaign messages of honesty and anti-corruption. "You will know the truth, and the truth will set you free," lines from John 8:32, were his introduction to calling for a new era in which Brazilians enact a revolution of realism and transparency.

"What I most want is, by following God's commandments along with the constitution of Brazil . . ." Bolsonaro shifted his hands again, set down the constitution, and lifted book number three, an abridged version of Winston Churchill's *Memoirs of the Second World War*, waving it at the camera as he spoke. ". . . being inspired by great world leaders . . ." He immediately set the Churchill tome down as he continued: ". . . and with good technical and professional counseling free from the usual political calculations, build a government." His eyes continued wandering as he spoke. He was looking for the fourth book, lying on the table but apparently out of his view, written by Olavo de Carvalho, the man who would be his counselor: *O Mínimo que Você Precisa Saber para Não Ser um Idiota* (The Minimum You Need to Know Not to Be an Idiot). I paused the video.

Olavo, as he is simply known. He's the one my contacts were talking about. And I was growing more and more certain that Steve had referred to him in an offhand comment as I was entering his hotel earlier, as a great "theorist" of the Bolsonaro regime whom he was coming in contact with through his existing links to the president's sons. (He had met with Eduardo Bolsonaro, the new Brazilian president's most politically prominent heir, in New York City during the summer of 2018.) Shortly thereafter, Brazilian media reported that Bannon would be advising the Bolsonaro election campaign.

Meanwhile, Olavo was causing alarm. Liberal international commentators were lamenting that the vote would empower not only an unqualified person hostile to the environment, minorities, and education to be president but also the mad pseudo philosopher at his side. Olavo lived in rural Virginia, which is a bizarre piece of this story in and of itself. But he and Bolsonaro had been close for years. In 2014, they began streaming online chats together, where they gossiped about politics and culture. Olavo was eccentric in ways the future president and his family of soccer fanatics weren't, but the two connected in their contempt for the media and universities. However, it was Olavo's scorching critiques of contemporary Brazilian politics paired with his call for a new pious Christian honesty that most won Bolsonaro's admiration. Olavo, for his part, liked Bolsonaro's unrefined nature, his willingness to speak in crass terms, and his penchant to sprinkle his speech with references to God and Christ. He understands that society needs a spiritual basis, Olavo thought, and that the real people of this country are Christians.

At first glance, Olavo seemed no different from the fire-and-brimstone Christian nationalists I was used to seeing in the Anglo-American world, but looks can be deceiving. I would soon learn that Olavo, like Bannon and Dugin, was some kind of Traditionalist, and that his credentials in the school far surpassed that of his counterparts in the United States and Russia. Steve has a long history of reading Traditionalism and interacting with a few of its key interpreters. Aleksandr Dugin had also intersected with its latter-day celebrants, including those on the radical right. Olavo, in contrast, had *lived* Tradition, in the ways and even in the institutional line of its original founders. Among the three, Olavo's journey to power and influence seemed the most unbelievable, especially when you consider how it began.

Olavo de Carvalho was born in 1947 outside of São Paulo, and for a stint during his college years was a communist. That was standard behavior for rebellious youth during the reign of the U.S.-backed Brazilian dictatorship. But Olavo's penchant for dissidence was not limited to politics. During the mid-1970s, he delved into alchemy and astronomy, and started hanging out in occultist circles in São Paulo. Soon he began writing for the French-based occultist magazine *Planète*. It hardly counted as standard journalism: he interviewed extraterrestrials, dead people, and so on. At the same time, he started teaching, offering astrology lessons in bookstores, and later lecturing in astrology at the Pontifical Catholic University of São Paulo. Esotericism was his overarching passion.

It was all great fun. But in 1977, Olavo's girlfriend brought him a book that would change his direction: *The Sword of Gnosis*, an anthology of essays by Traditionalist writers, including René Guénon. It was edited by American Jacob Needleman—the same Needleman who years later would mentor Steve Bannon. The text inspired Olavo to read all of Guénon's books. After having mastered Traditionalism's primary sources, Olavo decided that he was done with study. He had to find a way to start practicing.

And that was how Olavo found himself at an unusual ceremony on the outskirts of Bloomington, Indiana, in 1986, mesmerized by an ensemble of voices, bodies, and drums. I knew about the place—anyone who studied the history of Traditionalism did. Through online documents and eventually by speaking with Olavo himself, I could imagine the environment and just how bizarre it was. And to think that someone's journey could lead from here to the upper echelons of Brazilian and American power.

THE STICK-END PLUNGES into outstretched hide, sending reverberations through the drum barrel and out into the thick Indiana air. Each lift of the stick is an escape; each strike, a homecoming. There is no motion other than that: going from and back to the core—centripetal and centrifugal. No other motion save, that is, for the movement of the dancers. The pounding of the drum drives them round and round in a circle. White sashes and beaded tassels trail behind their bodies as they move. Only women danced in the outer circle, and these were their only clothes, meant to expose them and the life force they carried. Their circular path symbolized the extent of the universe, its bounds and its current. They were in a state of being, never becoming, forever and ever. And they all encircled the creative force, the axis rising high and standing still, whose nature cannot be female—the tree and the man next to it wearing a horned headdress.

Olavo de Carvalho stood to the side and watched as the dance unfolded. He was short and slightly plump, with dark hair combed to the side and thick round glasses, and he wore a buttoned-up pinstripe shirt. His appearance made him appear normal, maybe even boring—an accountant, a salesman, something like that.

The community, tucked away in a leafy forest about twenty miles north of Bloomington, Indiana, had a hundred or so permanent members, almost all white Westerners, and called itself a tariqa—a school or order of Sufism. There can't have been many groups like this one in this area, in rural Midwestern America. Male initiates referred to one another with the title of respect Sidi (Lord). The organization and its offshoots were structured with the Sufi position titles of muqaddam, shaykh, and khalifa. Participants—sometimes secretly from the outside world— considered themselves Muslims. But these practices were relics of a few years ago, when the community followed the laws of Islam more stringently. Since the tariqa had arrived in Bloomington in 1980, its rituals had gradually broken from its roots—observing, though officially never fusing into synthesis, other Traditional faiths in addition to Sufism. Olavo was considering starting a branch back home. For that, he would need the approval of the leader of the tariqa here, the shaykh, whose books he had poured over in Brazil; the horned man in the center of the dancer's circle, on the compound in the woods.

Frithjof Schuon looked like no one else. His aquiline flat nose seemed to pull his entire face down, forcing an expanse for itself between his mouth and his deep-set eyes. His beard made his face look longer yet. It stretched down inches below his jawline and was squared at the edges. A wild vertical halo of hair emanated from behind his head, and he dressed eccentrically.

On this day, he stood in the center of the circle next to the tree with the cyclone of skin whirling around him. He wore a cloak of flowing animal hide, an ornate bead breastplate in whites and reds, and a warbonnet headdress with buffalo horns at the temples and trails of feathers leading across his forehead and down over his shoulders and back to the ground. He was clothed in the ceremonial style not of a Sufi, but of the Oglala Sioux Indians, who during the 1960s adopted him and gave him the name Wicaphi Wiyakpa (Bright Star) to accompany his Sufi name, Shaykh Isa Nur al-Din. The dance was based on the Sun Dance of the Sioux, though it also resembled the circular dhikr dances of the Sufis and those of the Hindu Vaishnava bhakti, too. His donning of Sioux dress paid respect to their Traditional pathway, though he held no particular allegiance to it, nor to the Islamic-inspired garb he was most often seen wearing. Like the faiths they represented, the garments were only wrappings, different shells of a common core manifest and delivered, not in another set of garments, but in the naked body of Schuon himself.

Olavo de Carvalho had come to the kind of place that parents warned their children about. Religious cults had haunted the United States in particular since the 1960s thanks to a string of sensational flashpoints: Jim Jones. David Koresh. Bhagwan Rajneesh. No single religion held a monopoly in such cases. The constant instead was the presence of charismatic leaders who claimed to be unique conduits of divinity, making themselves indispensable to the spiritual and social needs of their disciples. Conventional wisdom taught that involvement in breakaway religious sects like this lead to brainwashing, extortion, and abuse. Conventional wisdom, however, was the last thing Olavo was interested in.

Frithjof Schuon waved a feathered staff in his right hand as the dance proceeded. His followers were all watching him as they were supposed to, though they kept tabs on one another as well. You wouldn't believe the infighting in this place. The tariqa observed varying levels of initiation, entailing differing degrees of access to Schuon himself, and everyone seemed to be maneuvering to climb a step higher.

A lot was at stake in that play for positioning. The most initiated men could hope to speak directly to the shaykh, to see the most holy and revealing paintings he made of himself, and perhaps to be named his successor when the time comes. For women in the tariqa, those highest in the hierarchy might lead dances, sing during ceremonies, facilitate communication for others, and maybe come in contact with the core in ways no man could.

Born in Switzerland to French and German parents, Schuon came to see himself as the heir apparent to René Guénon. He had been a somewhat rambunctious follower of Traditionalism's patriarch from the early 1930s on, begrudgingly following Guénon's direct advice to convert to Islam and pursue the path of Sufism, though his original interest was in Hinduism. Sufism, however, proved to be a good home for Schuon. After having been initiated into a Sufi order in Algeria and after having declared himself a leader—shaykh—based on a vision rather than on the call of an elder, he started a tariqa in Basel and began initiating others. By the time Schuon and his first wife moved their tariqa to Indiana in 1980, they could claim followers throughout the Americas and Europe, and even a few Muslims by birth in the Middle East.

By that point, Schuon also functioned as the unofficial figurehead for individuals throughout the globe looking to deepen their understanding of Traditionalism. René Guénon died paranoid and embroiled in conflicts with his former followers in 1951, and Julius Evola spent his last years holed up in his Rome apartment with a tiny group of exceptionally radical and dangerous followers—simple terrorists, some of them—and scorned by many Traditionalists. Schuon would lead the spiritual effort forward, but not without major modifications of his own.

His changes weren't necessarily those of moderation: he celebrated Indo-European caste hierarchy (believing that castes should be based on "natural" rather than "institutional" qualities and affiliations). And like Julius Evola, he, too, had a race theory to go with his Traditionalism, one that saw extensive mixing of "white," "black," and "yellow" races as a product of modernity's formlessness and chaos. "White" was a race, in his mind, native to the wider Indo-European world (encompassing India and the Middle East as well as Europe).

But he also was more open to what was called universalism than Traditionalists of the past. Guénon's way of thinking was that, with the ancient ur-religion having been lost, seekers needed to settle for just one exoteric religious way today in hopes of uncovering traces of what once was. To choose this path was to admit a defeat: what in the past was a unified whole had through time been divided piecemeal among a number of faiths, any of which would demand devotion to obtain its modest yield. Schuon, however, would suffer no such concession. Though he embraced Sufism, he gradually warmed to and participated in other religions at the same time—notably Native American spirituality and Orthodox Christianity—suggesting that he was above the need to limit himself to one path, but might instead encompass them all at once. The underlying logic seemed a rejection of Traditionalism's time cycle and its fatalism: Schuon could bring about the reconstruction of the ur-religion in the here and now.

THE DANCE CONCLUDED. People dispersed every which way—some to head home, some to change their clothes for additional events. Olavo struggled to reach Schuon. Since his arrival in Bloomington, Olavo had not been able to speak with the shaykh directly. Schuon was surrounded by his inner circle, and they regulated where he went and who could come close to him. This was part of the hierarchy that Olavo had yet to climb, that was surely the official explanation. But to him, it seemed more like a bureaucracy. It was off-putting. Didn't the shaykh know how far he had traveled to be here, and didn't he know of the rarefied recommendation that accompanied him?

Olavo's path to Bloomington began with disillusionment. Back in São Paulo in 1982, he discovered a local tariqa, thanks to a tip from one of his students. It was part of an international Sufi order headed by Omar Ali-Shah with his brother Idries— both British Muslims of Indian, Scottish, and Afghan origin. Upon arriving at his first prayer session, Olavo was surprised to find essentially all his students in attendance. They had been recruited, without his knowledge, based on their affiliation with him. But he was encouraged to stay, and so he did. He even introduced additional students: one young woman—Roxane, a Catholic former communist with flowing red hair who had taken his classes—came to the tariqa in 1983 specifically to spend more time with him.

Still, Olavo participated in gatherings and rituals with some hesitation. The deeper he got into the community, the more he came to see its leader, Omar Ali-Shah, as a con man who used the tariqa for money and influence. His brother Idries would even claim to be the heir to the spiritual project of George Gurdjieff, mainly as a ploy to gain money. This was not the experience of transcendence that Olavo imagined. And he might have left the scene altogether, had it not been for a tip from a friend to write directly to a prominent Traditionalist Sufi for advice.

The prominent Sufi's name was Martin Lings. He led a tariqa in the London area while also working as an Islamic scholar for the British Museum. Not only was Lings renowned for his writing and his personal warmth, but his circle of contacts came to include composer John Tavener, who wrote pieces dedicated to both Schuon and Guénon, and Charles, Prince of Wales—the future king of Great Britain. Further, he would be traveling "nearby" Olavo—perhaps the two could meet? "Dear Senhor Olavo," Lings wrote on June 2, 1985, "I received your letter and hope that you will be able to come to Lima."

The two met face-to-face on a cool August morning in Lima, Peru, that same year. A gentle, sweet, honest guy, Olavo thought, and immediately felt at ease in Lings's presence. They talked about the Ali-Shah brothers. Lings knew all about them. And he had a solution. "You have an experience of fake Sufis," he said to Olavo. "In order to restore your spiritual situation, you need to go see real Sufis."

Olavo needed to find a new tariqa network to belong to, one that was linked with the Traditionalist linage of René Guénon, one with an authentic spiritual master at its head—no more con artists. Lings wasn't promoting himself; he was referring to a tariqa in the United States. Its shaykh was Lings's shaykh, too, and he said of him: "I knew when I was in his presence that I was in the presence of a true saint and the spiritual master that I was seeking. And when I say true saint, I don't mean just a saintly man. I mean a saint of first magnitude, such as one could not expect to meet in the twentieth century."

Lings suggested that Olavo complete the process of converting to Islam before going to meet the great Shaykh Isa Nur al-Din. Something happened afterward, because when Lings wrote again, on September 8 of that year, with additional instructions to Olavo for arranging a visit to Bloomington, Indiana, it opened, "Dear Sidi Muhammad . . ."

NOW, IN BLOOMINGTON, Olavo was feeling duped again. The all-too-familiar game of petty personal politics appeared to rule this order, too. Perhaps he could even leave and go home early.

Then a surprise. A communication from the shaykh: He, Olavo, was to be appointed as a muqaddam. Already. Just after he had arrived. That meant that he would be allowed to run his own tariqa. Olavo de Carvalho: Sidi Muhammad, muqaddam of the Maryamiyya tariqa of Brazil.

He was excited, yes, though it was a little strange, he had to admit. This whole thing, this place, its rules and ways, and the shaykh, too. Then again, he had taught himself not to question much, to instead be patient, knowing that the most important truths—hidden truths—require time and devotion to reveal themselves. That's the way of esotericism.

Esoteric. The term in its narrow definition describes knowledge that has been rejected, most often knowledge rejected *in favor* of reason and science, and which therefore is not apparent to most in modern Westernized society. In religious contexts, it could also describe ineffable personal spiritual sensation in contrast with the outward "*exoteric*" trappings that may accompany it—the rituals, names, places, and histories surrounding inner experience. For the seeker of esoteric insight or spirituality, sources tend to be marginalized or hidden. Rejected knowledge may be conferred though accessible vessels like a church or books in a public library. But it can also be tucked away in the codes and rituals of a clandestine organization. In some cases, the source of the esoteric is a single person who shares it in the ways and under the conditions that individual chooses.

Traditionalism counts as one of the clearest examples of religious esotericism. It opposes itself to Western modernity and science. In its doctrinaire form, it repudiates the hope of going mainstream and changing society as a whole, and it strives toward an undefined and unexplained body of knowledge (the core religion, whatever that is). Further, while Traditionalists write, they urge followers to align themselves with a relevant practice, sending them off into the world of clandestine initiatory spiritual circles where the unarticulated and unspecified would be made clear to a chosen few. It was a matter of time until Traditionalism manifested itself as it did in Indiana.

OLAVO HAD BEEN appointed as a muqaddam. What was the process? Don't even ask—they won't tell just anyone. But immediately after his initiation—after entering one circle—he found another group forming that he was excluded from.

A select number of members gathered at another part of the compound to attend what was called a "Primordial Gathering." This circle was made up mostly of women. No one who had read Schuon extensively should have been surprised that so many of his rituals treated men and women differently. The sexes were in his mind manifestations of different cosmic forces that shaped the cosmos. He saw modernist feminism as an attempt to strip women of that force and its characteristics: beauty, passivity, purity, goodness, love, and logic. As he wrote, "Feminism, far from

being able to confer on woman 'rights' that are non-existent because contrary to the nature of things, can only remove from her
her specific dignity; it is the abolition of the eternal-feminine, of
the glory that woman derives from her celestial prototype."

That he spent far more time writing about women than men
may have had to do with a series of visions he had throughout
his life, those most prominent involving semi-sexual encounters
with divine female figures: the Virgin Mary in one instance, and
Pte-San-Win of Sioux mythology in the other. One result of
these visions was Schuon's insistence on including prayer to Mary
in his routine of Sufi practices and eventually to name his tariqa
order Maryamiyya—an Arabic, adjectival form of her name. But
before that, the encounter gave Schuon, in his words, a "need to
be naked like her baby." Nudity became an expression of divinity
for Schuon, "a return to the essence, the origin, the archetype,
thus to the celestial state." His own nudity, further, may also
have been intended to draw an association between himself and
Jesus, just as his position at the center of the circle gyrating to
the strikes of the drumstick linked him to the Sun, to Krishna,
to God, to eternity.

Some troubling things were taking place in Bloomington.
At least one community member would report of rituals for the
inner circle of initiates that shed pretenses to the exoteric and
focused instead on bringing participants into contact with the
esoteric truth—that is to say, rituals bringing female initiates
into contact with Schuon's naked body. He was seventy-nine at
the time, but rumors were spreading about the age of the other
participants involved.

OLAVO RETURNED TO BRAZIL and began arranging his—or
Schuon's—tariqa. It was sure to be a success; his own students

would follow him, he knew. Roxane, the former communist student, was a sure bet.

Still, there were so many technical details to work out, and as disciplined and studious as he was, he didn't yet know a lot about Sufism and the running of a tariqa. Worse yet, the workings of a tariqa were not written down, but were instead determined by the shaykh, and Schuon wasn't always responsive. Luckily, Martin Lings from London was happy to correspond with Olavo on these matters as an approved authority on the shaykh's rules.

I found a copy of a letter Martin Lings sent to Olavo. It had no date written by the author on it, but it must have come shortly after Olavo's return from Indiana. The only date on the paper was from years later—a stamp from the Justice Court of São Paulo on January 27, 2014.

"Dear Sidi Muhammad," Lings wrote. "Thank you for your recent letter. Here are the answers to your questions." Lings then went on to answer Olavo's questions with businesslike efficiency.

Olavo had asked about how much members of the tariqa needed to contribute financially (zakat) to be in good standing. Each should contribute 2.5 percent of one's yearly income, Lings replied, though there are many exceptions. Olavo asked about the chanting of the shahada, the Muslim profession of faith—who should lead it, how many times it should be repeated, and how tariqa members should arrange themselves during the process. You lead it, Lings replied, and you can chant it up to a thousand times. Sexes should be segregated throughout, with women standing behind men, as was done in Bloomington. Oh, and about them—women—a final question: Olavo wondered how they were to be initiated into the tariqa. Lings's reply to this final question was curt and direct: "The woman is initiated by man during the sexual act—assuming no interference by birth-control devices. There is no initiation apart from this contact."

Financial contributions, the chanting of the shahada—that

was all fairly standard Sufi practice. But this last part? That was Frithjof Schuon, the Maryamiyya order, with all its sectarian intrigue in tow. It had spread to the tropics via Olavo de Carvalho, who would later find himself advising the president of Brazil and collaborating with powerful Traditionalists around the globe.

# LET US TRANSCEND MODERNITY

DURING OUR INTERVIEWS IN THE WINTER OF 2018, I had been surprised by Steve Bannon's willingness to speak with me about his incendiary intellectual influences. But I was dumbfounded when he casually told me that he had been meeting with Aleksandr Dugin. This was, after all, during a time of intense inquiry into Russian influence on the Trump campaign and the 2016 election. What I didn't mention to Steve was that years ago I, too, had met Dugin. He and I crossed paths in a milieu where Traditionalism and far-right nationalist politics were beginning to meet and intermingle.

I remember the occasion vividly. Daniel Friberg, the CEO of Arktos, introduced Dugin and me in the foyer of a lecture hall in Stockholm on July 28, 2012. Tall and goateed, Daniel did the honors in his exceptionally deep voice. "Professor Dugin, Ben is a Ph.D. student from Brown University, right? He is writing a dissertation on our movement here in Sweden. He speaks very good Swedish."

*Surprising words,* I thought. This was also my first encounter with Daniel. At this point he was exploring the prospect of moving Arktos to Hungary from India, but here he was just visiting his native Sweden. The professor, on the other hand, was a mystery to me. I knew that he had been visiting John Morgan in India earlier that year. For a second, I thought about trying out my mediocre Russian on him, but after our brief exchange, Dugin turned immediately toward Daniel—he wasn't interested in me. "I have some upcoming books that I would like to talk to you about. Maybe you would want to continue publishing . . ."

I blended back into the crowd entering the hall at the Army Museum in Stockholm. The roughly ninety-person assembly was funneling in to hear the opening speeches of a conference called Identitarian Ideas, identitarianism being the moniker for a then small but innovative and energized faction of anti-immigrant nationalists in Europe, more likely to be familiar with Traditionalism than other groups. I was indeed a doctoral student doing research for a degree in ethnomusicology—the study of music and culture—and for over a year had been following, interviewing, even living among activists in Scandinavia's nationalist scene, everyone from the populist far-right Sweden Democrats party to the militant National Socialist Nordic Resistance Movement.

This scene used to be as much about music as politics, and that is what first drew me to it as an ethnomusicologist. Since the 1980s, white power skinhead music had been a main outlet for condemnation of immigration, multiculturalism, and nonwhite minority groups throughout Europe. This was especially true in progressive Sweden, a country that had kept nationalism and anti-immigrant sentiment out of its government until recently, and therefore a society that had confined those sentiments to the underground, a place where youth protest music thrives. It also didn't hurt that people in the scene seemed far more willing to speak to me, a music scholar, than to other researchers or journalists. I wasn't interested in anything "serious," after all.

There would be hardly any music today, though. I had been

following Scandinavian nationalism just as it was gaining ground in the mainstream due to the electoral success of anti-immigrant political parties and the increasing reach of far-right media. Nationalist music, I theorized, was fading throughout this process. These people saw themselves on the verge of exchanging symbolic power for real power, and that changed the way they socialized, organized, and presented themselves.

The goal of the identitarian movement in Sweden was to kindle a new intellectualism within the far right. The audience today was hardly composed of converts. I looked around the room as people were taking their seats and recognized almost all the local leading figures of white nationalism and National Socialism in attendance. Granted, these men—there were only a half-dozen women—were dressed for the occasion. Many had close-cropped haircuts testifying to their former tastes for skinhead fashion, but here they were in suits and ties.

Attire that screamed Nazi or hooligan would have been out of place. The headline announcing the event in friendly local far-right media outlets read, "Unmodern thinkers gathering in Stockholm," and that language reflected the wishes of the organizers. The publishing house Arktos and Daniel Friberg were the main sponsors of the event. Since its founding in 2009, Arktos had increased its production more than tenfold. They continued to sell paraphernalia: bumper stickers fashioned for street activists, clothing, miscellaneous items like a *Blood-Soil-Faith* patch, and a healthy assortment of neo-folk CDs. But their book selection had grown significantly, mostly in works by Traditionalists or by their contemporary fans. And they were breaking into new territory with their latest release, *The Fourth Political Theory*—the first English translation of a book by Aleksandr Dugin, who also was the keynote speaker this evening.

Dugin's network of platforms and channels to power had been shifting in recent years, but it also seemed to be growing.

Amid his fiery rabble-rousing during the war in the Caucasus in 2008, he gained a professorship in international relations on the Faculty of Sociology at Moscow State University. There he immediately founded the Center for Conservative Studies, launching it with a conference hosting French New Right icon Alain de Benoist. Dugin developed a curriculum for his center with courses treating topics like ethnosociology, geopolitical processes, and religious studies—all taught with a healthy dose of Guénon. This was his brand of metapolitics.

While that may have been a product of intervention by the Kremlin on Dugin's behalf, the government endorsement of him became explicit during 2012 when his exposure on mainstream state media exploded. Putin was at the time in the midst of giving himself a definitive ideological brand as an anti-Western, anti-liberal conservative after having leaned in the opposite direction at the beginning of his rule. It seemed part of that rebranding effort involved inserting Dugin into the public conversation to stir sympathy and attack naysayers. (As Charles Clover would note, Dugin's visibility in Russia always seemed to increase when the Kremlin's relationships with the West worsened, and vice versa.) Dugin and Putin had no official relationship, in spite of the hyperbolic claims of Western commentators. Still, his high-level meetings with Turkish officials continued, and he was becoming a favorite guest on Iranian state media, pushing partnership with Russia and rejection of the United States. And just recently, in March of 2012, he began serving as an adviser to Sergey Naryshkin, at that point the speaker of the Duma and future head of the Foreign Intelligence Service.

Having access to political leaders in any capacity separated Dugin not only from the other contemporary authors published by Arktos but also from everyone else in the room in Stockholm. Being part of the radical right in Western Europe had been tantamount to political impotence and irrelevance. But Dugin's influence had grown thanks in part to his ability to contain and conceal his occultism, mysticism, and Traditionalism. The texts that he injected into the Russian education system and most of his consultations with policy makers focused on geopolitics— geopolitics with a fanatical vision for revamping the global order, but presented in thoroughly pragmatic terms. The book he had just published through Arktos, however, and the speech he was about to give in Stockholm put mysticism back into his agenda. And its message to those gathered at Identitarian Ideas would be an amalgamation of familiar rallying cries and discomforting challenges. He was attempting to embrace but also influence what he correctly identified as a rising political force in Western politics. I had never heard anything like it: even in this context, even though his style cut a sharp contrast with the militant neo-Nazis in attendance, he stood out as the radical one.

"ALL THAT IS anti-liberal is good."

It was one of the blunt declarative statements that chopped up his speech. And thank God for them. Aleksandr Dugin's English vocabulary was impressive, but his heavy accent and stilted pronunciation made the hour-long event sound like a meandering, mumbled, drunken tirade. It surely didn't help that a sizable portion of the audience before him was, indeed, inebriated. Booze had been flowing from a cash bar all day. Identitarian Ideas had been styled as an academic conference, but old habits die hard, and by the time Dugin took the podium at eight P.M., many in the audience had been downing wine and beer for hours. This wouldn't have been a problem if you were planning to pump your fist to white power music, but an academic lecture, and this one in particular, would require unusual mental focus to get through.

Dugin's frequent references to liberalism could confuse.

Americans like me often think of liberalism as one side of our political spectrum, as synonymous with leftism and the Democratic Party. Europeans use the term to describe the ostensible opposite—a free-trade, small-government political right. But for Dugin, as for most professional historians and political scientists, liberalism was something more: namely, the common ground between the mainstream left and right throughout the West— the values that a survivalist guarding his property in Montana, an immigrant rights protester in Paris, an investment banker in Frankfurt, and a feminist activist in Brooklyn all share. It is the core concept of liberty, of the urgent need to be liberated from something. Liberated from government. Liberated from one's class. Liberated from the circumstances of one's birth, be they economic, political, or social. The destination of this exercise is individualism, to claim the status or products resulting from one's particular essence and industries.

Individualism is key to the liberal form of government known as democracy, whose validity rests on the notion that elections register the free thoughts and action of each citizen. Dugin's contempt, however, centered on how it defines human beings. He explained that in liberal societies, "There is nothing above the individual. Individual is axis. No collective identity can be recognized in liberalism. Peter is Peter, nothing else. He is not Christian, not Muslim, not European, not black, not white. And this is important: liberalism taken to its logical end cannot recognize gender. Because to be a woman or to be a man, that means that we have a collective identity."

This way of thinking about people, defining them as ideally disconnected (liberated) from religion, family, nation, even their own bodies is historically exotic and insidious, he claimed. And as even a proponent of liberalism like Francis Fukuyama understood, it would leave us yearning for community.

That problem, Dugin argued, birthed the two main challenges to liberalism in the twentieth century: communism
and fascism. Both ideologies aspired to promote an alternative
entity—not the individual, but two collectivities, class and race.
And each claimed the universal validity of their vision for all of
humanity, meaning they could never coexist.

Having described the differences between those three ideologies, Dugin then claimed that they all shared something. Each
made a play during the twentieth century to mobilize masses
of people around a narrative of progress. They agreed that the
past was something to be overcome, that with the help of their
reforms a greater future could come about—one that wouldn't be
experienced in the confines of a village or home, but on a global
scale. He could have added to his argument, for in his writings
he described all three as being materialist as well—liberalism
(capitalism) and communism being obsessed with money, and
fascism with bodies. To put that differently, all three were modernist, competing for the chance to modernize the world.

Liberalism won, of course. It partnered with communism to
defeat fascism in 1945, and then let communism die of old age
in 1991.

The air in the room grew thick when he addressed those who
thought they got it—those who knew who liberalism's historic
foes were and who rallied behind those foes. To identify with
communism or fascism, Dugin asserted, is to identify not just
with the losers of history but with the *modernist* losers of history.
This is not the same Dugin who during the 1990s combined the
Nazi and Soviet flags as a banner for a National Bolshevik Party.
Not that he would dismiss those sitting before him whose shirts
concealed tattoos of swastikas and German Imperial Eagles. Any
opponent of liberalism was a friend of his, and he was more than
happy to see any advance of communism or radical nationalism

throughout the globe. But to belong to the vanguard of an anti-liberal, anti-modern cause and be a part not just of destruction but of creating the post-liberal world would require more.

DUGIN'S WORDS, WHILE wide-ranging and often only barely comprehensible, still had direction. He took the political spectrum as many Westerners understood it, folded it together twice over, and placed it all at one side of the room opposite . . . what?

I remember it so plainly: as he transitioned from criticism into outlining his vision for the future, Dugin's language grew increasingly vague, but it also began to soar. "Modernity is in the hands of liberals—let it be in those hands. Let us transcend modernity. Let us go beyond, let us reject not only the results of modernity but also the sources and the roots that were the base, the intellectual and pragmatic base of modernity . . . We shouldn't fight for the values of the modern past, we should fight for the values of the premodern past, that could be and should be taken as future values . . . We shouldn't struggle for the past that has passed, but for the eternity that was reflected in Traditional society!"

For a moment, he seemed almost to be addressing a political rally. I thought I heard a note of gravel in his voice, an echo of the protester who once chanted "Tanks to Tblisi!" on the streets of Moscow. But he had more intellectual work to do.

If liberalism sought politics that would promote and protect the individual, if communism focused its energies on the working class and fascism on race and state, he wanted to see politics focus on something else, something harder to grasp: spiritual and cultural community. He envisioned a politics that honored and preserved the values that distinguish one society or tribe from another and which allowed them to make sense of the world on their own terms, to uphold their own meanings and their own way of being. He borrowed the concept from German philosopher Martin Heidegger, who calls it Dasein.

The threats against his vision were not only individualism—for these values weren't created nor could they be maintained by isolated individuals divorced from community and history—but also the imposition of one society's meanings onto another, which is to say imperialism or globalization. Dasein exists always in the plural: there can't be one for all the world, nor a universal standard by which to judge them, because all humans don't share history in any meaningful sense. Indeed, in some respects, what he was saying sounded much like a kind of cultural relativism, to use the terminology of cultural anthropologists.

Devise a system of politics whose primary goal is not wealth creation, technological advance, or military conquest, but rather the independence and freedom of each spiritual culture, and you end up with a very different political map. Dugin explained, "We will come to a place where there are not any more nation states, [. . .] but we will have civilizations. Civilizations as borders of particular Dasein. [. . .] Every Dasein is particular, is unequal, different from the others. And there is not any common scale where we could just say this one is better than that one. So we are arriving at the concept of multipolarity, the world organized on the basis of civilizations."

In order for there to be cultural and spiritual variation in the world, power needed to be dispersed as well. This was one reason why the push for a world order protecting Dasein, the push for a multipolar world where difference rather than homogeneity thrives, would proceed from challenging the United States. A nation of immigrants shedding allegiances to their historical communities and embracing allegedly universal values like democracy and equality, the United States could produce only a highly volatile, perverted Dasein, one without real historical roots, and one that only with great force could be prevented from attempting to spread itself outward and trying to blanket the world with its sense of existence. A strong Russia could blunt American expansion, and do so without imposing itself on the local cultures and spiritualities it touched.

At the time, I thought that what he had to say was unexpected, peculiar, and provocative. But was anybody in the room listening? Would anyone outside of Russia read his book?

SIX YEARS LATER, I was going to speak to Dugin again. It was 3:50 in the morning on December 27, 2018, when my alarm sounded. I hurried to turn it off and slowly got up, peering out our window toward the trees outside. Snow was whirling about, sure to add to the already massive drifts formed against the house.

I would need to dress warmly: long underwear, thermal pants, a thick sweater, a jacket, boots, gloves, and a furry cap. I tiptoed down the stairs and through a hallway, trying not to wake my daughters or my mother-in-law, who was sleeping on our living room couch. After grabbing my laptop I dashed out of the house, plowing a path through the snow and out to my car about thirty paces away. It was like an igloo inside, shielded from the wind, but my breath still froze in the air.

I flipped open my laptop and turned on the video chat. I saw myself on the screen. With all my layers of clothes, I was the one who looked Russian. But at least here I would be able to speak without waking anyone.

My contact with Steve Bannon had come about thanks primarily to luck and persistence. I had obtained a few email addresses and phone numbers, and I worked them obsessively for a year. The conversation I was about to have here, in contrast, came straight out of my network of contacts forged through years of ethnographic research among Europe's radical right. My request for an interview was accompanied by multiple introductions and references attesting to the fact that I was responsible, professional, and not working covertly for any outside interest.

I clicked on the green button, listened to the ring, and heard someone at the other end of the line answer.

"Hello? This is Ben Teitelbaum. Can you hear me, Mr. Dugin?"

"Yes, yes. I can hear you," he replied.

I recognized the voice and the accent immediately. I was speaking to him in the middle of the night 8,500 feet above the sea in the Rocky Mountains, and I had answers to those questions I had asked myself years ago. Someone outside of Russia had indeed read his books—someone big.

# 12

## THE SUMMIT

DURING MY INTERVIEW WITH DUGIN IN DECEMBER 2018, weeks after his meeting with Bannon took place in Rome, I asked him politely whether "he had ever met Steve." It was disingenuous of me, but I also didn't want to startle him and compromise my access. He had in fact leaked news of the meeting to one obscure media outlet, *Reset DOC* magazine, though nobody seemed to notice. His answer to me was puzzling. "No," he said, "but I would like to meet him." Steve had confirmed to me earlier that the two had promised to keep the meeting confidential, though it seems neither could stick to that pledge with consistency.

Once Dugin had denied that the meeting with Bannon took place, he began to speak not only about his impressions of Steve but also what he would say to him in a *hypothetical* conversation. This struck me later, for when I asked Steve to recount the conversation for me, which he did, his memory and Dugin's hypothetical conversation largely aligned. It allowed me to attempt an account of what transpired in Rome in November 2018.

I later approached Dugin with a draft of this account and

a request to speak about it. He replied with a philosophical escape. "Benjamin," he wrote, "I have no desire to speak of anything except the ideas, theories and so on. I prefer not to discuss
facts [. . .] I certainly don't want to comment [on] the text you
have sent me. In no way. [. . .] For me real and imagined, by the
way, is just the same. Because the world is our imagination."

The account is first and foremost Steve's account, and he
showed me notes he claims to have taken during their session
as well as diagrams he drew in front of Dugin as they spoke.
However, the longer quotes—rephrased slightly according to the
addressee—come from Dugin, from things he spoke to me in an
imagined dialogue, but which Steve later (when I showed him)
read as a record of the conversation that took place after their
handlers left them alone in Steve's room at the Hotel de Russie,
near the Piazza del Popolo, blocks away from Julius Evola's old
apartment in Rome.

"I knew at the time that it was a historic meeting," Steve later
told me. What both he and Dugin seemed not to know was that
each man was quietly being funded or patronized by opposing
Chinese interests.

THEY SIT DOWN on the plush couch while coffee is poured for
them and then the handlers cleared out.

Where should we begin, Mr. Bannon?

"I'm dying to hear you talk about Heidegger. You know,
Dasein is still a big part of what I believe, this concept of being."

It was a safe start. Heidegger is a mainstream philosopher
about whom Dugin has written extensively. It is an interview,
with the Russian doing what he does best—lecturing, with
heavily accented but effective English. Bannon, for his part,
breaks character and mostly keeps quiet, prodding the mono-

logue along with short queries while taking furious notes. His interest is genuine. He studied Heidegger for years, though he came to the philosopher through Dugin's books, which were his primary interest. But there is strategy here, too. *Let him talk it out,* Bannon thinks. *Then I'll turn my fire on him. We got time.*

Hours pass. At noon a knock on the door breaks their focus, and the doors swing open as hotel staff rush in. The lunch spread is made to impress. Indeed, Bannon was doing well for himself. Despite high-profile setbacks—being fired from his White House position and losing control of his media company Breitbart—he was living lavishly and sharing the wealth with those around him. He didn't tell Dugin about the million-dollar salary he collected from Guo Wengui to challenge the Communist Party of China in all ways and at all times.

"How about you?" Bannon asked Dugin. "You kind of lost your shit a few years ago, right?"

Dugin's fortunes had indeed been mixed as of late. When pro-Western forces took over Ukraine in 2014, he initiated an effort much like his past campaign in Georgia to stoke Russian military intervention. He had to act, for the uprising in Eastern Ukraine against the new pro-Western government in Kiev was based not on political ideals alone but also on language and ethnicity: the population in the east of the country identified as Russian and had a different Dasein. Breaking off from Ukraine would mark a stand for the East as opposed to the West, for identity and against state bureaucracy, for Tradition and against modernity.

Dugin's efforts involved direct fundraising for separatist militias in Eastern Ukraine, as well as a propaganda campaign to build public sympathy. While pursuing the latter during an interview with pro-separatist media, he called on listeners to "kill, kill, kill" those loyal to Kiev in Eastern Ukraine—"New Russia," as he was calling it. A massive protest ensued, targeting his em-

ployer, Moscow State University, and soon Dugin lost his professorship. In a bizarre blog post that followed, he had blamed his
firing on "Lunar Putin"—a reference to Evolian Traditionalism
missed by observers—which is to say, on Putin's allegedly weaker
liberal alter ego, as opposed to "Solar Putin," who would have
apparently saved Dugin's job. But the dismissal didn't signal that
Dugin had been completely dropped by the Kremlin, because he
still seemed to be serving as a behind-the-scenes ambassador for
Putin on the world stage.

It's fine, Dugin replies. I'm staying plenty busy.

Turkey, Serbia, China, Pakistan, Iran—Dugin is constantly
on the move. He visits these countries to speak with government officials, opine on state media, or teach. He had already
secured a new academic home for himself as a Senior Fellow at
the China Institute at Fudan University in Shanghai, where he
delivered lectures on the glories of Russia and China, the virtue of Eurasianism and multipolarity, and the depravity of the
United States. And the selection of countries he was frequenting
was no accident.

"Talking to anyone who hates us," Bannon says with a
chuckle.

Dugin shoots back an earnest glance and says nothing.
Throughout his career he has called for partnerships between
Russia and mujahideen, Iran, China—it doesn't matter. If they
fought the American evil, the evil of our time, they were a friend
of Dugin's.

AFTER LUNCH THEY FORTIFY themselves with coffee and
return to the couch.

Bannon's interview continues. More philosophy, more
Heidegger. More Dugin. Good thing that their handlers are

attending to other tasks. Most people would find this mind-numbing.

Hours pass before Bannon breaks topic. "This is such a privilege, Aleksandr. I'm really fascinated with you. I could sit here and listen to you all day long . . ." It is his way of politely saying the opposite—that they don't have all day long to talk about Heidegger, and that it is time for them to get to deeper topics. Dugin takes the cue, turning to his claim that they are seeing the emergence of a multipolar world.

Steve understands exactly what Dugin means by that: a world that isn't dominated by one force, where regional powers exert themselves only in places they are historically and culturally sanctioned to do so, where Western values are treated as simply Western and not universal—not the destiny of all. Much of it resonates with Steve's ideals.

Bannon smiles at Dugin and says nothing. There is a long silence. Bannon takes a final sip of his coffee and sets the cup back onto the saucer on the table.

You and I were born into nothingness, Mr. Bannon, says Dugin.

Bannon nods. "And yet we each found our way to it. The Tradition."

Yes, yes. Incredible. For me, communism took it away. We had lost everything, all ties with it. We created an entirely new society, communist society. The loss of absolutely everything, pure nothingness in the Traditionalist sense. Dugin speaks with caution now, parsing out each word as if translating in his head in real time: And for you America—the only state that was created in modernity. The rest of European society has institutions, rituals, the links to the past, the will to preserve. All that was destroyed in American society. It was created anew, totally anew. Evola wrote about men like us, those who don't belong to Tradition by historical ties. Communism and America. At least he had Russia, Dugin explains, buried in the ruins. So long as he was willing to dig for it. Steve had nothing, not even in the soil beneath him.

This is Bannon's cue, and he begins gently. "Yes, but, Aleksandr, I think you're missing some stuff."

Dugin seems ready for this. He inquires whether Steve has read his books.

Of course Bannon has—all that have been translated to English.

With a nod of his head, Dugin continues: America's role in globalization, this hegemony, this pressure for human rights, democracy, and so on. All the worst things in the world. It's modernism upon modernism.

"That's liberalism," Bannon replies. "Liberal modernity. It's not a people. That's a set of ideas—dangerous ones—put forward by people from around the world. When people say that America is an idea, that's what they are talking about, these so-called universal values that can't help but infect everything. But that is the thing—America isn't an idea. It is a country, it is a people, with roots, spirit, destiny. It's the working class and middle class, it's that group of people that have been perennial to us, from the fuckin' Pilgrims and the Puritans on. And what you are talking about, the liberalism and the globalism that live in America, real American people are victims of that. We're talking the backbone of American society, the people who give the country its spirit— they're not modernists. They're not the ones blowing trillions of dollars trying to impose democracy on places that don't want it. They're not the ones trying to create a world without borders. They're getting screwed in all this, by an elite that doesn't care about them and that *isn't* them."

Dugin smiles at him and peers up from underneath his overflowing eyebrows. Tell me, how was it that you came to Traditionalism?

"Gurdjieff. Reading him started my journey onward to—"

Dugin interrupts. An Armenian! Part of the Russian silver age. You found your way not as an American—such a thing is impossible. You did it as yourself. And what a radical situation. For you defend Tradition in the pure, pure of night—in the midnight of the civilization, in the midnight kingdom, the United States of America.

"Listen," Bannon responds, "America is part of the Judeo-Christian West. Modernity has advanced further with us, like with Scandinavia. But our roots still exist, and they can be revived, and they are being revived. That's what you're seeing today with the Trump movement. That is America rising up against its overlords. It's no civil war. Oh no. That's America fighting against globalism and liberalism, just like Russia fights against it, too."

Dugin starts to speak, but Bannon interrupts. "And here's the thing. That America—real America—it's not your enemy. It's your ally, and I'm not even talking about politics. Our peoples share the same soul and values. At our cores we are not communism and liberalism, we are Russia and America, both of the Judeo-Christian West. That's why we are moving together, toward nationalism, populism, and Traditionalism. There's a deeper struggle going on in the world today—we both know that—one between spiritualism and materialism. Peel back the layers on the surface that divide us and you'll see that we are the same—the essence of our nations is the same. You and the Eastern Orthodox church—you can even teach us to be better versions of ourselves. Our peoples are showing their vitality right now. They can lead this fight."

Bannon leans back in his seat with a smug smile. He won't be interrupting any more.

Dugin maintains that it's not a difference of degree. He is less interested in mobilizing within a particular spirituality—reuniting the east and west of Christianity, for example—and more enthusiastic about rallying behind spirituality of all kinds against anti-spirituality. This stance led Dugin to idolize the most robust theocracy in the world: Iran. And this would also entail raging against the beacon of liberal secularism—namely, America.

But as Dugin starts to speak again, Bannon raises one finger, dashes off to an adjoining room, and returns with a black notebook. Returning to his seat, he opens it and draws three small squares, arranged in a triangle. He points at each: "Four thousand years old, thirty-five hundred years old, three thousand years old. China, Persia, and Turkey. On the face of it, these are the countries that could be the most Traditional block. I understand why you might think that guys like us should look to them for deliverance, but this block is the center of modernism. On the one side, you have Shia and Sunni Islam, both with expansionist ambitions. And then you have China . . ." Bannon had arrived at the nation who was hosting Dugin in its most prestigious public university, and whose government Bannon was secretly contracted to work against. He continued, attempting to dispense with Dugin's notion that the Chinese were enemies of global liberalism: "The globalists are totally tied to the mercantilist totalitarian system of the Chinese. China is the economic engine that drives it all. Without China, it doesn't work; that's what's driven the system. The whole system is a step to maximize profits and their wealth creation through China."

Bannon leans back, puts his arms behind his head, and continues, knowing he has more ammunition. "What we have now is a system where slaves in China are manufacturing goods for the unemployed in the West. This is the system we've set up. And, Aleksandr, do you think the Chinese, do you think the Communist Party there is just a passive player in all this, doing the globalists' bidding?" Aleksandr doesn't bother trying to answer as Bannon bolts forward in his seat. "No, no. You look at what they are doing in Africa, you look at their new Silk Road project and their attempts to turn the world into a series of networks. You look at how they're scared to shit of populism—they talked to me about it at Mar-a-Lago, they're fucking scared! Brexit, the rise of nationalism—that's chaos to them, they can't control it. And then you look at what they are doing with robotics, trying to atomize and control society, even to the point of putting chips in people's bodies."

He takes a deep breath. "We are talking about a maniacal regime hostile to our vision of a world of independent nations, your vision of a multipolar world. A regime that wants everyone assimilated into one system. And it's one that is trying—right now—to suck the humanity and the soul out of us all with technology they can't be trusted with. I know what you think of America. But history is showing us something." Bannon was making his pitch using the terms and the values that both men shared. He presented a story of inversion—one where modernity had actually scrambled the geopolitics of a liberal West and a Traditional East: the vanguard of the Kali Yuga, of globalism, liberalism, and modernity, is in Asia.

Dugin smiles and takes a long glance out the window to the south as Bannon finishes. Corso Vittorio Emanuele runs just a few blocks away. He says nothing. More than a minute passes.

Weird. What the fuck is he thinking? Is he gassed from all the Heidegger stuff? Bannon doesn't know. But he suspects Dugin is surprised by what he has to say. He might even be digging it.

Bannon's voice deepens. "As a Traditionalist, Mr. Dugin, it is imperative that you join us against them. As a Traditionalist, Mr. Dugin."

# 13

## DINNER AT THE EMBASSY

I ARRIVED LATE, A LITTLE BEFORE FIVE IN THE EVEning, delayed during my walk from the train station by hordes of youths in MAGA hats and their clerical chaperones who had swarmed downtown Washington, D.C., for the anti-abortion March for Life in January 2018. As I turned the corner and walked up the sidewalk toward the townhouse, I saw Andy Badolato standing outside berating someone on his cell phone, sweating robustly while wearing shorts and a polo shirt in the 30-degree air. He was there to receive me. Steve knew I was coming and had asked his most notorious fixer to park me in the ground level of what he still calls "the Breitbart embassy."

Like a cruise liner, Steve Bannon's Washington townhome goes from stark to gaudy as you ascend floors. You enter the first floor into a dimly lit TV den with low ceilings and a large worn leather couch flanked by a steel table and chairs that look like they were taken from a 1990s sports bar—a space that is part run-down bachelor pad, part war room. As you move farther into the house, French doors open onto a conference room overflowing with papers and laptops, all facing a mounted monitor on the wall and a poster of D.C. that one could easily mistake for a target map.

I sank into the couch and got comfortable. I'd been through the routine plenty of times before, and had come to suspect that the waiting exercise was a deliberate strategy to humble me ahead of a meeting. Meanwhile, Andy was on and off the phone, a bottle of beer in his hand. He segued from making a business pitch to a lawyer to a conversation with someone interested in Trump's famed border wall with Mexico (was this a business pitch, too?).

After more than an hour, I was summoned. "Dinner party is starting, boss wants you upstairs."

Steve greeted me with a handshake and a hug as I entered. "Welcome, Ben." The walls of the second floor are painted with pastel scenes from Greek antiquity, while the carpeting—royal blue with white stars—says home. A dozen other guests trickled in and mingled with Steve in front of a minibar. Darren Beattie, a former speechwriter for Trump recently fired for presenting at a conference sponsored by the controversial H. L. Mencken Club years earlier, made a quiet entrance. The other attendees were Brazilians.

Then the main attraction entered, the guest in whose honor Steve had arranged the dinner. Everyone made space and broke out in cheers as he and Steve walked across the room to greet each other. One of the younger Brazilians standing next to me was fighting back tears. With smiles and laughs we made our way to the long, impressively laden table. We sat down and said grace, reciting the Lord's Prayer with our heads bowed, as is the routine for the Brazilian guest. Of course I joined them in this.

The mood wouldn't become jovial again until, after a few minutes, a middle-aged Brazilian investment banker named Gerald Brant tapped his glass and proposed a toast: "This is a dream come true," he said. "Trump is in the White House, Bolsonaro is in Brasília. And here we are in Washington: Bannon and Olavo de Carvalho, face-to-face. This is a new world, friends!"

I knew Traditionalism had motivated Bannon to connect with one other power broker—Aleksandr Dugin. But the story had grown more complex, for here was another major global Traditionalist. I had asked Steve on multiple occasions if he could help me reach Olavo, or if I could sit in on one of their meetings, and he had always been evasive—until now.

Following the October 28, 2018, elections in Brazil, the new president, Jair Bolsonaro, had offered Olavo the position of minister of education. Olavo declined, citing his desire to continue writing and agitating freely from his social media throne. The former muqqadam in Frithjof Schuon's tariqa would be serving as an adviser to the president nonetheless, everyone knew, while remaining situated at his home in rural Virginia, where he had lived without returning to Brazil for over a decade.

As is proper, however, Olavo made recommendations as to those the president might consider instead for government positions. Cultural funding and universities would be key targets of reform, so Olavo understood that the future minister of education would need robust credentials and a passion for, as he saw it, fighting against Marxist infiltration. He recommended Ricardo Vélez Rodríguez, a conservative philosopher. And while making that recommendation, Olavo offered a second: Ernesto Araújo, perhaps as foreign minister. Araújo had studied Olavo's lectures and was a skilled writer and a scholar in his own right, who maintained a blog called *Metapolítica: Contra o Globalismo* (Metapolitics: Against Globalism) and could discuss the works of Guénon and Evola fluently. More so than Olavo himself, Ernesto was a Traditionalist. In 2017 he penned an academic essay, "Trump and the West," that referenced Evola's *Metaphysics of War*.

STEVE SAT ME across from Olavo at the dinner table, with himself at the head. Darren Beattie was to my left, and in between toasts and monologues, he and I chatted about philosophy and academia. Beattie received a round of praise during the meal after Steve said that he had played a key role in writing a speech President Trump delivered in Warsaw in July 2017, which celebrated Poland and America as members of a cultural and political union of the West. "We write symphonies. We pursue innovation. We celebrate our ancient heroes, embrace our timeless traditions and customs" were some of its key lines, as well as the charge that "our own fight for the West does not begin on the battlefield—it begins with our minds, our wills, and our souls." Beattie later told me he wasn't in fact one of the lead writers on the speech, but so as not to cause embarrassment, he nodded in thanks.

We talked a lot about Bolsonaro. Some of the Brazilians seemed to have come to the dinner with the agenda in mind of selling the new administration to Steve. Olavo and a handful of the others had been to the U.S. State Department earlier in the day for what appeared to have been part of an official visit, and a puzzling one at that: neither Olavo nor anyone in his immediate entourage held official positions in the Bolsonaro government. Olavo was there to voice his condemnation of China and the urgency of resisting the spread of its influence globally: unlike Aleksandr Dugin, Olavo was a stalwart Traditionalist ally of Steve's in this regard. The officials at the State Department had seemed to agree with this assessment of China, much to the Brazilians' surprise.

Steve didn't seem as surprised as they were. Meanwhile, he wanted to know more about the composition of the Bolsonaro government. Olavo and Gerald Brant took turns describing the new administration as factionalized. Regrettably it contained elements of the old military guard, who were often the target of Olavo's screeds on corruption, but at least all parties involved seemed serious about establishing law and order in Brazil. There were the free-market capitalists, represented by Bolsonaro's minister of finance, Paulo Guedes, who was educated at the University of Chicago. He opposed socialism—that was good—but he seemed like a globalist. This made him unlike the final pillar: the patriots, the nationalists, personified by Olavo and Bolsonaro's sons—none of whom had official positions in the administration, but were instead confidants of the president with massive social media followings. Steve asked about this faction's vision, and the Brazilians around the table seemed to reply in unison, "Alignment with the Judeo-Christian West."

Olavo was in direct contact with the president, he affirmed. They spoke most recently about China and about CNN, which had established itself in Brazil for the purpose, he thought, of contesting the messaging machine of the new president. His conversation with Bolsonaro left Olavo concerned that the new president didn't see the threat CNN posed to his government. But the Chinese threat and the need for Brazil to reorient itself toward the United States—that Bolsonaro understood well, if only for economic reasons.

Steve was thrilled to hear that. Brazil had long been grouped together with Russia, India, and China in the so-called BRIC alliance of powerful, non-NATO-allied ascendant economies. Isolating China by undoing that alliance was appealing enough, but as Steve once argued to me, Brazil has hidden metaphysical gifts to offer the United States as well. Not only does the Judeo-Christian West exist in South America through Brazil, but Brazil began the process of modernization later than Western Europe and the United States. That means that its authentic

Western culture runs deeper, is less corrupted. It can serve as a reserve of culture that nations further deteriorated by modernity embrace as they strive to revitalize themselves.

Steve didn't go there this evening. Instead, he stuck to practical issues as the conversation got more serious. He shared Olavo's belief that mainstream education in the West was destroying its potential for a conservative future, and that alternative education systems were needed as a countermeasure. He had been working on a solution.

In 2009, at his then new home in rural Virginia, Olavo launched Seminário de Filosofia. It was an online school, a way for him to make use of his years of lecture notes from Brazil now that he lived abroad. A standard university position would not have appealed to him anyway. He felt leftists had infiltrated Brazil's educational system in preparation for a communist revolution. Conservative ideas could be introduced into society only through alternative channels at this point—metapolitics, that's what was needed—and the internet provided the ideal venue. Seminário de Filosofia was not designed for students to ever meet with Olavo face-to-face. Instead their tuition provided them with access to a series of video lectures, the broad topics being comparative religion, letters and arts, human and natural sciences, and communication and expression. Enrollment would eventually swell to over two thousand students, most of them young men.

Steve wanted to achieve a similar level of outreach. After all, he, too, had plans to develop a school for the implicit purpose of waging metapolitics. But Olavo was quick to distinguish himself. He had taught the masses, but he wasn't into creating templates; he focused on the individual. He said he wanted to know where each student was and to help his pupils understand what they wanted. How he could do this with so many students at once? I was curious to know. As I listened, I wanted to ask Olavo whether it was a coincidence that someone who opposed globalism also disapproved of universal educational models that didn't address the particular student.

I never got a chance to ask because the conversation took a quick turn. Olavo's school was a philosophy school, and he said his definition of philosophy was the attempt at aligning the unity of knowledge with the unity of consciousness. This meant he was interested in understanding the limits of knowledge a person had. It was a bit arcane—I didn't get it, and I don't think others at the table did, either. But I remember thinking that Olavo indicated he defined a person by what he or she knows. People are knowledge. When you change, it is because you learned something. Steve, in host mode, was acting agreeable, but I knew he disagreed with this. He thought that we possessed "being" beyond knowledge; indeed, that our economy and society is flawed because it only values people based on their intellect. When your life changes genuinely, he thinks, it is because you've had a change in being. This is why Steve loves the movie *Groundhog Day*.

Steve asked him about Guénon. "He was crazy," Olavo said. "He said a lot of crazy things. But"—and Olavo turned straight to me for the first time during the dinner and peered over his glasses while pointing his finger—"he said a lot of true things as well." What about Evola? I asked. "Evola was completely insane. He wanted to bring down the church so that he could create a new European paganism. Ha! But he is so fun to read. His book on alchemy was great. They all could write beautifully. No atheist could write as beautifully as they could."

I asked him if it was a coincidence that both he and Bannon had gained influence, and that both considered themselves affiliated in some way with Traditionalists. "No," he replied. "Because the Traditionalists put forth a criticism of science, modern science." I found it a puzzling response. They were both gurus behind major populist revolts. Was that really about criticizing science? Steve did question the reality of global warming, but he didn't present himself as an opponent of modern science. And why did Olavo seem so eager to downplay his affiliation with Traditionalism and then go on to praise its key thinkers? What had happened since his time in Schuon's tariqa?

Those were questions I would have to get to later. Steve speedily wrapped up the dinner and we bid each other farewell. I left wondering where his and Olavo's relationship was headed. Steve maintained a plethora of political partnerships—some shallow, some substantial—throughout the global radical right. But compared even with his connections with close allies like Brexiter Nigel Farage, his commonalities with figures like Aleksandr Dugin and Olavo de Carvalho ran deep and must have felt exceptional. They were political *and* spiritual kin, and they were only beginning to interact now.

ABOUT TWO MONTHS LATER, I saw images splashed across U.S. media showing Steve sitting once more at a lavish dinner in Washington, D.C.—across town this time, at the residence of the Brazilian ambassador on Massachusetts Avenue. To Steve's left sat President Bolsonaro. To Bolsonaro's left sat Olavo de Carvalho. And to Olavo's left sat Brazil's foreign minister, Ernesto Araújo. The president was making his first visit to a foreign government, and breaking with convention in the process. Typically, this first foreign visit takes place in Buenos Aires. But Bolsonaro wanted to signal to the world that Brazil's foreign policy was changing.

His decision to invite Steve to the dinner was also provocative. Steve no longer held any official position in the White House or in the government. Not only that—Trump's most recent public comments on "Sloppy Steve," as he had taken to calling him, were fiercely critical. The guest list at the embassy thus testified to Steve's continued high status in the eyes of the Brazilian government but also Bolsonaro's confidence in his relationship with Trump. He adored the U.S. president, hardly ever missed an opportunity to praise him on social media, and would greet him the next day at the White House with a Brazilian soccer jersey emblazoned with the Trump name.

The purpose of the visit was more than trading pleasantries, however. Bolsonaro and Trump hoped to discuss trade deals, the imperiled anti-American government in Venezuela, perhaps even the possibility of basing a U.S. rocket-launching station in Brazil, though all these were just elements of the bigger message: Bolsonaro was there to tell Trump he wanted a greater U.S. presence in Brazil. Implicitly, this also meant that he wanted to loosen the Chinese grip on his country and its economy. It marked the advance of an agenda from the nationalist faction of his administration, the wing driven by Olavo, the complicated Traditionalist who was striving to see Brazil shed its mercantilist geopolitics that linked it to China, and instead prioritize the spiritual roots that made it a part of the Judeo-Christian West.

It was part of the Traditionalist-inspired vision that united Olavo and Bannon, now in action.

# 14

## GLOBAL ALTERNATIVES

DURING THE SECOND HALF OF 2018, I WAS ABLE TO find the traces of a network of communication among Traditionalists with access to high ranks of power—Dugin, Bannon, and Olavo. They had a number of things in common: their broadly simultaneous arrival to power in association with an anti-liberal strong-man leader, their all being Traditionalists in some way, and the parallels in their forms of activism. None were politicians. They were advisers, influencers, and strategists. They were playing the long game, envisioning transformations larger than the term of any one leader and marshaling political and meta-political tools in pursuit of their goals. Having witnessed the meeting of Bannon and Olavo a few days prior, I had begun wondering what it all meant and what they were doing with one another. All I knew was that Steve was appealing to the other two, on the basis of shared values, to pressure their respective governments into greater alignment with the United States and into rejection of China. He was fulfilling the agreements of his day job and the agenda of his anti-CPC sponsor, Guo Wengui.

These exchanges were playing out in real time—Steve's initial contact with both Dugin and Olavo had taken place after I first began interviewing him. The other two, however, were no strangers to each other.

"Dugin and Olavo de Carvalho—don't they fuckin' hate each other?" On a brief respite from travels and interviews, sitting in my office at the university, I was chatting on the phone with a trusted contact: someone who has long been half in, half out of the circles I usually study and who is a sometime Traditionalist. "They've met?" I was surprised and a bit embarrassed.

My contact informed me that almost a decade earlier, Dugin and Olavo had clashed in a debate. He remembered that Olavo's Traditionalism seemed very unorthodox and that Dugin didn't come across especially well in the exchanges. All this didn't seem to matter, because the world of Traditionalism on the right remained fully behind Dugin's positions after the debate nonetheless. "What was it all about?" I asked. America, he replied. Olavo actually was arguing that America is a source of Tradition in the modern world, that members of its rural population are the global ambassadors of spirituality.

It was the complete opposite of what Traditionalists on the right typically think, those who usually idolized the East or Russia, thanks in part to Dugin's years of influence. But what my contact had just relayed about Olavo's ideas didn't sound that eccentric to me. It sounded like Steve.

BACK IN 2011, a year before I first met him in Stockholm, and ahead of his collaboration with Arktos in India, Aleksandr Dugin had moved from obscurity into a position of political power rarely achieved by a self-proclaimed philosopher. The number of platforms available to him were multiplying, and he was using them to further his mission of linking geopolitics and spirituality. When a group of Traditionalists from Latin America had asked if he would like to participate in a debate with one of their local philosophers, he leapt at the chance, because the topic seemed perfect for him. He was to discuss, from a Traditionalist perspective, the current state of geopolitical power dynamics in the world in general and the role of the United States in particular. Participation was easy, too: this would be an internet debate, an exchange of response papers to be posted online, and perhaps thereafter made into a book. He agreed. But who exactly was the other participant? he wondered.

Olavo de Carvalho at this point was living in Carson, Virginia. He had left Brazil for the United States in 2005—some say for tax reasons, some because of threats against him. If you asked him, he would instead point to domestic politics and the rise of the socialist Workers' Party to power in 2003.

The move to the United States appeared a sacrifice of influence. Throughout the 1990s Olavo had a string of successes as a commentator, principally by means of well-received books as well as articles in leading newspapers. He had become a public intellectual, and did so as an entertaining and articulate commentator on politics and philosophy rather than as a Traditionalist. A lover of four-letter words, he wasn't projecting the image of a stuffy and erudite celebrity professor. His columns began to feature foul attacks on feminists and sexual minorities. In a column written two years after his arrival in the United States, he ruminated on homosexuality: "I don't believe it would have been better if my father, instead of depositing his sperm in my mother's womb, had injected it into the rectal passage of his neighbor, from where the liquid in question would have gone into the toilet at the first opportunity."

In both body and mind, he was a long way from the tariqa of São Paulo. During the late 1980s he had lost confidence in Frithjof Schuon. The shaykh had not only installed a phantom leader of the tariqa ostensibly under Olavo's leadership but had also endorsed rumors that heretical practices like animal sacrifice were taking place there as well. Olavo wanted out. You can't just leave a tariqa, however, you must be thrown out. So, to make this a reality, Olavo began writing Schuon insulting letters to secure his coveted reprimand. I'm sure the letters were lively.

Frithjof Schuon died in Bloomington in 1998, and thereafter his network of Traditionalist Sufi orders—which traced their origins to René Guénon—scattered. Among those that persisted, some embraced British Traditionalist Martin Lings and others an Iranian émigré named Seyyed Hossein Nasr, who since 1984 has held a professorship at George Washington University. Olavo held no animus toward either, but he also had no plans to become one of their followers. He didn't want any more gurus of any kind in his life. He wanted to become his own guru, and serve as a guru for others.

An epiphany of sorts had set him on this path. In 1990, when he was forty-three, he was shaving in front of a mirror when he recalled thinking, "I know everything about myself—I'm not the problem anymore." His focus now was going to be on the world outside of himself. Traditionalism was part of that, but he was not going to be beholden to it or any other doctrine, save for one.

He became a Catholic while still in the tariqa—the religious syncretism of Schuon's Traditionalism allowed this—but with time he became more expressly devoted to the church. The shift sent not only a spiritual signal but also a social and political one. Catholicism was key to his intensifying opposition to communism, which throughout his life had morphed from being a vehicle of protest against Brazil's military establishment during the 1960s into becoming an accepted part of that establishment, at least in its international dealings. Toward the end of the twentieth century, Brazil's military elite had become eager to partner with current and former communist dictatorships throughout the world. Anti-communism had become the Brazilian dissident's cause.

Traditionalism had given Olavo a language through which to criticize communism as materialism. And this would not be the only vestige of his time following in the footsteps of Guénon. The community he assembled as leader of the tariqa during the second half of the 1980s had led him to a new partner. Roxane, who as mentioned earlier was a former communist who became Olavo's student, had become his wife, and unlike his previous marriages, this one held.

Roxane Andrade de Souza and their children would accompany Olavo to the United States in 2005. His visibility in Brazil, paradoxically, had increased following the move. He wrote columns for major newspapers like the *Jornal do Brasil*, but his online presence was the key change. He started a blog and began to produce online radio shows within a year. He was experimenting with social media platforms, too: Twitter, Facebook, and YouTube. Olavo's initiatives flourished—his social media output reached staggering numbers of viewers—amplifying the momentum he had generated through books and newspaper articles back in Brazil.

Both Olavo and Aleksandr Dugin had experienced a similar growth in their media presence. One thing he didn't share with the Russian Traditionalist, however, was access to policy makers. This didn't bother Olavo, though. As he would later put it to me, "I'm not interested in changing political situations. Because this is impossible. Political situations have so many factors, and so many people interfering." The future was in God's hands, he thought, with a fatalism typical of Christians, but one which in his case may also have had more eccentric roots in classic Traditionalism.

※

BACK IN MY OFFICE, I thanked my contact for chatting, hung up the phone and opened up my computer. I wanted to view the debate between Dugin and Olavo my contact mentioned in the same way it was originally aired: online.

Dugin opened the debate, writing the first post on March 7, 2011, a sunny morning that followed three days of straight snow in Moscow. He argued that the current state of geopolitics was one in which all forces opposing the United States had been vanquished or marginalized. Now America was pushing for the creation of a unipolar world government, using capitalism and calls for universal human rights and democracy to clear a path for its dominance. All this was prefaced on America's seeing its manifest destiny as being the endpoint of history, the destination of a grand progression leading from the Roman empire, through the Middle Ages, modernization, and the Enlightenment, and finally to liberalism and a society of hyper-individual citizens of the world. That this Western history is considered the history of the world is but a minor offense to Dugin. As he wrote in his stilted English, filled with gratuitous definite articles that don't exist in Russian, "The tradition and conservatism are regarded as the obstacles for the freedom and should be rejected."

Was there any hope for a revolt? Potentially. Throughout the world there were actors who collectively might have the resources to fight back. Their ranks included, most obviously, those nations who dared open opposition to Western values, the U.S., and U.S. global hegemony—Iran, Venezuela, and North Korea. But it could also include those who, for strategic reasons, appeared to accommodate Washington in some ways and reject it in others—India, Turkey, Brazil, Russia, Kazakhstan, Saudi Arabia, Pakistan, and China. Nation-states were not the only organs of resistance, however. American interests were also thwarted by extra-national forces such as Islamists or South American leftist movements despite the fact they lacked the formal structure of a modern nation-state. Dugin boldly counted his own Eurasian movement within that category.

Anti-American nations, Eurasianism, Marxist guerrilla groups, al-Qaeda—together they possessed considerable resources, but Dugin remained pessimistic. "All these groups lack the global alternative strategy that could be symmetrically comparable with the American [. . .] vision of the future," he concluded. "Everybody acts by themselves and in their own direct interests." But this debate could offer a forum for two Traditionalists to craft a broad strategy. Perhaps his opponent—this Olavo character Dugin had barely heard of—could offer an alternative message to unite anti-American actors in a fight against the materialist world order.

These were ill-fated expectations.

Olavo saw the world through a different set of lenses: not as a twofold division between a villainous West and the virtuous rest, but instead as a battle for domination among three actors, none of whom he liked. Those three actors were the Russia-China alliance, Western finance, and Islamists. It was hard to compare them with one another because their goals, their weapons, and even their leading archetypes varied. The Russia-China alliance was the only properly geopolitical force, looking at the world in terms of friend or foe nation-states, and being driven primarily by agents in the security and military sector. Western finance was run by bankers and tradesmen unbeholden to any nation-state or religious principle but instead striving to maximize efficiency and profits. The Islamist power structure, on the other hand, was essentially theocratic—invoking not military but religious authority—and their ambitions were likewise spiritual.

Olavo concluded: "For the first time in the history of the

world, the three essential modalities of power—politico-military, economic, and religious—find themselves personified in distinct supranational blocks, each of them with its own plans for world dominance and its peculiar mode of action. [. . .] It's not farfetched to say that the world today is the object of a dispute among the military, bankers, and preachers."

A Traditionalist analysis, it seemed. And as he read it, Aleksandr Dugin expected Olavo would proceed to a Traditionalist conclusion. If we saw the three upper castes of the hierarchy vying for power—the castes of the priest, the warrior, and the merchant—shouldn't we sympathize with the most virtuous one, the priest—that is to say, with spirit and theocracy? Shouldn't the former muqaddam of the Maryamiyya of Brazil, who had once answered to the name Sidi Muhammad, throw his hopes and support behind Islam and condemn the merchants of the West?

This was hardly Olavo's assessment. Instead he insisted that to condemn Western finance is not to condemn the United States, a nation possessed itself of a Tradition and a heritage predating liberalism. Real America was not the center of globalism, but its primary target. Western finance "is not an enemy of Russia, China, or the Islamic countries potentially associated to the Eurasian project, but on the contrary, it is their collaborator and accomplice in the effort to destroy the sovereignty, the politico-military power, and the economy of the United States."

Olavo's diversion from Dugin's approach ran deeper yet, and he launched into a direct assault on the Russian philosopher's chosen antidote to alleged liberal decadence: "Russia is not at all the 'fortress of spirituality and tradition,' appointed by a celestial mandate to castigate the flesh of the United States for the sins of the immoral and materialist West. Today, as in Stalin's time, Russia is a den of corruption and wickedness as never before seen, one dedicated to the spreading of its mistakes around the world." Olavo's writing became more lucid and vibrant when he arrived at this topic, as if to signal that discussing it was his main interest and objective in the debate.

Dugin was aghast. He lacked Olavo's rhetorical flare in English especially. But he knew what he was hearing from the Brazilian was not in keeping with Traditionalist orthodoxy. "The Western traditionalists (R. Guénon, for example) were on the side of the East. J. Evola was the partisan of the Western tradition but in absolute opposition to the Modernity and to the USA," he wrote as the opening sally of his response.

Dugin saw deep problems in Olavo's accounting of the power dynamics in the world as well. Could you really equate the economic and cultural globalism emanating from the United States with that coming from the others? In other words, is there really as much Russo-Chinese militarism and Islam in the world as there is crony capitalism? Of course not, and any opponent of globalism should accordingly get his priorities straight. Further, while he understood the criticisms against the Russian state, what about America's crimes? "Hiroshima and Nagasaki, the occupation of Iraq and Afghanistan, the bombing of Serbia." It seemed preposterous to separate that legacy and "Western finance" from the United States on the grounds that its native culture was a helpless victim of it all. "The real America we know well." He would later argue that any premodern pre-liberal American heritage was hardly innocent: it needed to be viewed as the soil in which globalist liberalism blossomed.

Olavo up until this point had worked himself into a bit of a knot—first claiming that there were three deeply distinct forces coveting world power, then saying casually that all three were united in their effort to destroy the real America.

Time for some clarity. The financiers of the world, he argued, were creating a system of protections for themselves—a worldwide socialist dictatorship, in fact—but one centered on consolidating state control of economies, on introducing regulations and tax schemes in which only the largest business could thrive. The result was the creation of a system in which "big government" and "big business" would both flourish, where capitalists so rich as to envision control of the market and escape from risk would find their natural allies in the most powerful state formation, in communism. Move production away from democratic nations where the ebb and flow of market forces breed uncertainty, and put it in the most predictable economies on earth. Indeed, China's ability to challenge America's global dominance "would be unthinkable without the investments of the USA and without the planned self-destruction of the American industrial park." Add to this mix the fact that, Olavo claimed, Russia and China are among the largest suppliers of weapons to terrorist organizations, who were sapping spiritual vitality out of Islam, and a unity among the major global forces starts to emerge.

Nothing was what it appeared to be: not capitalism, not communism, not the alleged conflict between modernity and Islam. They were simulations, born in what Traditionalists might call a meaningless and inverted world, all reducible to a single mass system.

What, then, did Olavo support? First and foremost, Christians from all countries, Israel, and American conservative nationalism. The social habits of rural Americans in particular appeared to capture something for him sacrosanct: in boilerplate U.S. conservative language, he saw increased cohesion, charity, and volunteerism when Washington pulled back from American society. But he didn't yearn for them to create a competing globalism out of the forces he most admired. "If there were plans for the establishment of a Christian or Jewish or redneck world dictatorship, I would be among the first to denounce them, as I denounce the Russian-Chinese militarists, the Western oligarchs, and the apostles of the Universal Caliphate."

❋

OLAVO HAD TAKEN OVER the debate as it moved into its final days and concluding exchanges. His ideas and their unpredictable course were the focus of discussion. As I read Dugin's responses, he seems exasperated and perhaps a bit annoyed. As he writes: "I thought I would find in [Olavo] a representative of Brazilian Traditionalist philosophers in the line of R. Guénon and J. Evola. But he turned out to be something different and very queer indeed." Dugin was dismissive of Olavo: that Western financiers were in a pact with Eastern socialists, who were in turn collaborating with Islamists, and that this was the core of contemporary globalism—this was nothing but "free fantasy at work." There was no need to elaborate, it seemed. Dugin simply reminded those following the debate that by linking Traditionalist virtues like order, social cohesion, and hierarchy with the East and decadence with the West, he was in keeping with established thought in the spiritual philosophy that both he and Olavo called home. But it didn't seem to faze his debate partner, whose incursions were throwing into question not whether Dugin opposed the West, but whether in opposing the West and promoting the East, the Russian was actually fighting for Tradition and against globalist materialism.

Olavo, it turned out, was saving his flourishes for the end. Dugin had been reasserting his fidelity to Traditionalism's patriarchs throughout, and Olavo sought to counter it, not with a lecture on the history of governmental regimes throughout the globe, but instead through a tidbit from sacred geography. René Guénon had in lesser-known texts written about centers of satanic influence—of "counter initiation" that could pull souls away from the Tradition. These are the Seven Towers of the

Devil, and none can be found in the West. As Olavo explained with apparent delight: "there is one in Sudan, one in Nigeria, one in Syria, one in Iraq, one in Turkestan (inside the former USSR), and—surprise!—there are two in the Urals, well within Russian territory." Olavo left out that in later years of his life, Guénon suspected that there was an additional center of evil located in California, but that would have complicated Olavo's next point—namely, that if one draws a line between these seven centers on a map, you see the outline of Ursa Major, or the Great Bear constellation.

A bear—not only a sign of Russia but also a historic symbol for the warrior caste. Was Guénon privy to ancient esoteric knowledge pointing to a hellish rise of militarism in Russia? Was Dugin himself subject to corrupting spiritual forces in his near vicinity?

Did Olavo really see something in this, or was he just playing with Dugin?

Olavo was shifty, and what he had to say was unlikely to resonate inside the tiny community of Traditionalist intellectuals, few of whom had considered a union between their spiritual and philosophical tendencies and sympathy for the United States. That probably tickled Olavo; he didn't mind being an outlier and an iconoclast. Nor did he fear accusations of irrelevance. He made as much clear back at the beginning of the debate. "In order to fulfill his plans," Olavo wrote of Dugin, "he counts on Vladimir Putin's strong arm, the armies of Russia and China and every terrorist organization of the Middle East, not to mention practically every leftist, fascist, and neo-Nazi movement which today place themselves under the banner of his 'Eurasian' project. As for myself, besides not having a plan not even for my own retirement, I count only, as far as war resources go, on my dog Big Mac and an old hunting shotgun."

Dugin was an ideologue and a power broker. Olavo was just a dude having fun—or so he wanted to appear.

As I read through those final exchanges on my laptop, I realized that Olavo's use of Traditionalism didn't seem as eccentric to me at this point as it would have had I encountered it years earlier. The notion that a hidden reserve of humanity's anti-modern spiritual force was to be found, not in Hindu ashrams or Sufi tariqas, but instead among the rural Christians of the United States—that was a concept that would reappear in the thinking of Steve Bannon, a Traditionalist whose political power would exceed that of Dugin, in a formal sense at least. I thought through the sequence of my interviews with Bannon, noting that our conversations about his views on the metaphysical powers of America's rural white working class had occurred months before Bolsonaro's election and Olavo's emergence on the public stage. Steve might have only recently met Olavo, but I suspected that he had been trafficking in the Brazilian's thinking for some time.

# 15

## ENCHANTED BORDERS

The wolf will break its bonds
And run . . .
Brothers will fight one another
And kill one another,
cousins will break peace
with one another,
the world will be a hard place to live in.
It will be an age of adultery,
An age of the axe, an age of the sword,
An age of storms, an age of wolves
——*Ragnarök, as described in the* Voluspa

LATE ON A FEBRUARY EVENING IN 2019, ON THE OUT-
skirts of Tucson, Arizona, Steve Bannon is in his element. He is
drawing a serrated knife across a piece of steak in front of him
when a waitress breaks his focus. "Compliments of another guest,
sir." She places a bottle of Coors on the table to his right. Steve
laughs. He doesn't drink, hasn't since 1998. But he still wants to

thank whoever sent it his way, so he stands up and surveys the space.

Li'l Abner's Steakhouse is an assemblage of rooms with low ceilings and wooden walls covered with handwriting, illustrated napkins, and license plates—mini monuments left by decades of customers. Most of the tables are made of wooden planks— picnic-table style—topped with rolls of paper towels: ribs are a favorite at this place, and you eat them with your hands. Packed on this Saturday evening, Li'l Abner's is noisy. The restaurant's house band has been playing there every Saturday night for thirty years, but tonight just happens to be the debut of a new guy—a solo guitar and voice act—who is playing honky-tonk with a few Johnny Cash covers thrown in.

The performer, the restaurant staff, and the guests all seem proudly unrefined. They are dressed simply, even scruffily in some cases, and so is Steve. Unshaven. Hair all over the place. Shorts and loafers with no socks, multiple long-sleeved polo shirts, and a green vest with a prominent stain on the left front chest. When Steve shakes the hand of the burly, bearded middle-aged man who sent him the beer, the two look like kin. Of course one of them was a limousine populist from Goldman Sachs who flew around the world in private jets and stayed in the most exclusive hotels you could imagine. But they are comfortable in each other's presence, you can see, as each pats the other on the back.

"I really appreciate what you do, man."

"Thanks, brother. Look, we are down here trying to learn about the stuff coming across the border, the drugs and cartels and stuff. We are going to do what we can to help you, that space down by Nogales where it's wide open. We've got a team going down there."

"God bless you, sir."

"God bless you, too, brother."

Steve is speaking to him about a part of the desert two hours south of Tucson, roughly eight miles west of Nogales, Arizona. The area contains a striking feature at a particular spot where two mountain ridges meet, framing a small basin below. The land there is dry and the environment fierce. Pronghorns, scorpions, tarantulas, mountain lions, javelinas, even jaguars roam across a patchwork of sand, grass, and cacti; eagles and vultures fly above. Bullets fly, too. Migrants young and old, U.S. Border Patrol agents, Mexican Federales, scouts, drug runners, and armed American vigilante militants do a dangerous dance round each other day and night. But they leave little trace. In fact, save for a post in the ground here and there, hardly a human-made object is to be found in the area—few buildings, signs, roads, or fences.

Yet the basin is the site of a profound feat of human imagination. For it is here where a national border enters from the east and takes an abrupt turn in a circa 130-degree angle as it heads toward California. The angle is clear on a map: it is the spot where Arizona's southern border, part of the southern border of the United States, begins its northwest/southeast slant. It is part of what gives Arizona a contour unorthodox in a part of the country where many states are drawn in straight lines, squares, and rectangles. Local lore has it that the abrupt turn was born of lust for alcohol. The story goes that when those redrawing the border after the Mexican-American War got west of Nogales, they decided they needed booze and charted the fastest path toward the saloons of Yuma, over 350 miles across the desert northwest.

STEVE HAD BEEN OUT of the White House for about a year and a half, and had watched with concern as the Republicans in the U.S. House of Representatives lost their majority the previous year to a Democratic Party bent on expanding investigations into President Trump's foreign and domestic dealings. That was certain to delay Trump's agenda, the agenda that Steve had helped conceive. Failure to deliver on campaign promises would certainly dampen enthusiasm among Trump's core supporters, throwing his reelection efforts into peril. But Steve's deeper worry was not for Trump the person, but for the fate of Trump's policy proposals, especially the promise to build a border wall. It was time, he thought, to take matters into his own hands, and he had a plan.

Much of the U.S.-Mexico border runs through privately owned land: the U.S. government may not want to build a wall, but it can't stop citizens from placing one on their own property. And so Steve had teamed up with a number of secondary veterans of the Trump campaign, "original gangstas" of the MAGA movement, as he called them, to tour the country and generate money for the project. They called themselves We Build the Wall.

Borders are essentially immaterial phenomena. That's why a border can zigzag through the Arizona wilderness without leaving a physical trace of itself: borders represent an imposition of the invisible upon the concrete. But in order for a border to be meaningful these days, in the soulless age of the Kali Yuga, it must be rendered in the parlance of the times. It must be made material.

Tucson was a natural destination for Steve to start this effort. It was home to his brother Chris and his family, including Steve's nephew and key handler, Sean—a beefier American version of Prince Harry. Tucson was also a flashpoint in the conflict surrounding border security. And so, the night before, We Build a Wall held a fundraiser/rally in a nearby suburb for a surprisingly raucous crowd of 280, all of them residents from one of Tucson's many retirement communities. The event was a success, Steve thought, generating not only money but, more important, media attention.

His visit to the barbecue joint tonight is just for fun. The entire gang of local Bannons is there gathered around one of the plank tables, along with a few visitors, including me. I sit across from Steve, and his brother Chris sits next to me to my right. Chris nurses bottles of Coors almost the entire evening, helping his brother dispose of any sent by other guests as tributes.

Sean Bannon, Chris's son, sits next to me, and across from him, to Steve's left, is Darren Beattie again. But the special spot at the table to Steve's right, in front of an empty chair, is reserved for his three cell phones. They merit their own place setting, it seems, for they are very much alive. They flash on and off the entire meal, reminding me at one moment of the multicolored Simon light board memory games of my childhood. Eventually Steve lays a napkin over them, lifting a corner and peering beneath it on occasion. A coping strategy. That made it easier for him to converse with the other guests, and with me.

"IT BECAME SO THIN," Steve says. "There was no resonance to the debate, it was—it didn't mean anything. The Republicans never addressed trade, they never addressed jobs, they never addressed mass immigration, illegal immigration as taking away people's sovereignty and taking away their jobs. They never discussed it. They had this very thin thing on tax cuts. It was, it's what I call thin, with no human substance, no lifeblood. That's what Trump provided. Trump provided a non-politically correct vernacular that hit the working class right in their . . ."

*Gut, chest, heart,* I think to myself as I nod—something visceral to tie it all back to the lack of blood in standard Republican political rhetoric he was just talking about. I couldn't help but want to finish Steve's sentences sometimes. I have heard this stuff before, and based on the postures of the other Bannons at the table, so had they.

". . . right in their thing, you know?"

Immigration and border security are Steve's cornerstone issues, the ones that he identifies as holding untapped political potential, and which he sees as encompassing a range of other concerns. That is why he often talks about borders and does it in a variety of ways. Throughout the meal, we are treated to a sampling. The narrative he offers during the beginning is the one best suited for general audiences in prime time—indeed, it is what you're most likely to hear from him in a TV interview or debate. It is simple and concrete, an account that focuses on the alleged loss of jobs and money among citizens due to an influx of migrants and moves to more abstract topics only in remarks about the loss of dignity for individuals who feel helpless to resist the transformation of their economic and social world. I knew there was greater depth in his thinking on this subject: after all, he claims that the economic stability of the working class is the prerequisite for their spiritual advance, which in turn is the prerequisite for the revitalization of America.

But when his conversation turns to China, as is inevitable, the topic of borders works its way in as well. As he sees it, borders are central to China's view of the world and their attempts to dominate it:

"What the Chinese have in mind is anti-Westphalian. This is why Olavo and I are exactly on the same page. The Westphalian system is a system of nation-states—individual, independent, robust nation-states where the citizen can get the most value and have the most ability to control his own fate. What the Chinese are doing is a network effect. They're taking the British East India Company model of predatory capitalism, spreading it out through One Belt One Road and Made in China 2025 initiatives, where they're going to be an über-EU, which is, you know, whether it's sub-Saharan Africa, Europe, the United States, Brazil, we're all just administrative units in a network, right?"

The strengthening of borders, in this case, is less a matter of domestic politics and more one of resisting a new globalist imperialism emanating from China. Sovereignty is the prize to be won in all of this, for the nation-state as well as for the individual within, who, as Steve sees it, has greater capacity to shape government in a nation close to hand rather than a supranational entity from afar.

But if championing borders can frustrate China's expansion, it can do the same thing to America. A stronger border provides a stronger sense of American particularity and boundedness, all of which could help the United States quell its own globalist tendencies. Thus the concept enters again when Steve discusses American identity politics:

"I am a huge believer that we are a country with a border and a wall, and a country that has a culture and a civilization and citizens and Americanness to it all, right? And that's a country. If that's called blood and soil, then so be it. But we're a country, we are a thing, with a people and a set of customs and traditions. We're not some idea. I hate the concept that America is an idea."

"America is an idea." It is a phrase touted by anti-Trump Republican congressman Paul Ryan, whom Bannon famously referred to as a limp-dick motherfucker. For him, it is the hallmark of a worldview that treats America as the essence of all, and therefore the exclusive claim of none. "America the idea—that gets into all the spreading, that gets us into all these wars with these people who want to walk around with this kind of airy-fairy idea of democracy and be jamming it down the throats of people in Kabul, sixteen years, at two trillion dollars, thirty-five hundred deaths, fifteen thousand wounded, and two trillion dollars—that's America the idea."

Listen to Bannon speak for a while, and you get the sense that he believes firm borders can accomplish quite a bit: invigorate the dignity of working-class citizens, prevent the expansion of foreign empires, stoke the consciousness of a nation's identity by helping it see itself as bounded and integral, and prevent it from wasting its resources in globalist enterprises. But he also thinks of borders in less conventional ways, treating their fate not as an instigator for a new order, but rather as a register of something else, something bigger.

We don't get to that stuff until the night has rolled on and he and I have returned to our standard topics of discussion, long after many of the guests at the table have turned to other conversations. The path there is meandering. A little chatter about esoteric books like Blavatsky's *Secret Doctrine*. An airing of views on Mormonism—he doesn't think Joseph Smith could have made it all up without divine intervention. Even some commentary on Sufism (if all Muslims in the Middle East were Sufis, we wouldn't have a problem at all). I began to wonder what people at the other tables would think were they to hear our conversation now.

Eventually we are back to the topic of his more esoteric ideas. It hasn't been absent in the conversation thus far. It even appeared sub rosa in his words on "illegals taking jobs" from earlier. The inability for Republicans to comment effectively on the topic; their inability to venture beyond their "thin" messaging on taxes—Traditionalism has equipped him with an interpretation for all that. Mainstream Republicans that he took on were acting as agents of modernity, demonstrating the fact that in the dark age, human existence is reduced to its basest elements—namely, goods and money. Accounting for people as being more than that, as well as accounting for nations as being more than mere economies, requires an escape from the deprived mores of our own age, an escape from time. He calls that transcendence. "Their powerful message to me, Traditionalists, is that there is a way, you have to have immanence, and that life has to have transcendence. If it doesn't have transcendence, it's going to be thin. It's going to be materialistic. And society will eventually break down. Everywhere in America now, it seems like we've lost our moral underpinnings."

TRADITIONALISTS ARGUE THAT fickle material want is destined to overrun any immaterial boundary in the dark age. This is partly because there is no means of defense. If society refuses to recognize the immaterial domain—a domain of invisible ideals and beliefs—there is little hope for political initiatives to prioritize it. And given that principles transcending time and physicality provide order to our lives, their dissolution heralds an age of confusion and lawlessness, be it the breakdown of castes that Hinduism describes as a signature of the Kali Yuga, or a shattering of ties of kinship and boundaries between human and beast foretold in the poems of Norse mythology.

The only immaterialities valued by modernism are unbounded immaterialities: ideals deemed valid everywhere and to everyone. Their names are individualism, equality, democracy, liberty—all the cornerstones of the America-as-idea concept that Steve Bannon so despises.

What counts, then, as an authentic binding principle or ideal? Religion and faith are prime examples, especially in their ability to infuse the material world with symbolic meaning and inspire people to organize and limit their actions. Traditionalists would add that practicing loyalty toward a deity—indeed, practicing loyalty toward any intangible ideal beyond oneself—is anti-modern behavior. That would include the institution of a family or a tribe, in part because they themselves are unintelligible from a materialist perspective and find their signatures in the symbolic and the unquantifiable (a family is more than the sum of its material parts). But if honoring the bonds of blood and history is too abstract a concept for modernity, so are social principles that would regulate primal materialistic and bodily desires. Prohibitions of sexual activity based on an ideal—say, monogamous heterosexual relationships bound by marriage—rely on remaining loyal to the abstract and intangible and deprioritizing the physical desires of the moment.

If you cannot motivate people to observe intangible and spiritual principles, the effects are manifold. From the moment those principles fail to advance a materialistic agenda—the creation of wealth, the satisfaction of bodily desires—they will be dispensed of, and doing so in one setting will invite an assault on transcendent values in another. A loss of religious faith, a willingness to fracture communities large and small, the dispensing with established social norms—each move weakens the authority of the immaterial, making its defeat during the next confrontation more likely.

Correspondingly, if you manage to bolster the immaterial in one cause, you will have advanced it in others. Treat humans as if they are more than bodies. Treat them like souls shaped by history and dreams and embedded in a spiritual lineage, the products of a deep context rather than a universal blank slate to be relocated without consequence. Do that, and perhaps it will be easier to awaken others to the boundaries that move invisibly through the universe, to see even how physical space holds metaphysical properties to which we owe our obedience. As if there were a long, coiling neon light that sliced and organized our world, outlining nations, separating men from women, families from tribes or religious communities, right from wrong. As if it all had the same power source, and it was either on or off as one.

ON FRIDAY, APRIL 6, 2018, less than a year before Steve's rally in Tucson, a member of the Trump administration had issued this statement: "Attorney General Jeff Sessions today notified all U.S. Attorney's Offices along the Southwest Border of a new 'zero-tolerance policy' for offenses under 8 U.S.C. § 1325(a), which prohibits both attempted illegal entry and illegal entry into the United States by an alien."

The attorney general followed up and clarified the statement: "To those who wish to challenge the Trump Administration's commitment to public safety, national security, and the rule of law, I warn you: illegally entering this country will not be rewarded, but will instead be met with the full prosecutorial powers of the Department of Justice."

Surging violence and poverty in Central and South America had been fueling an uptick in migrants approaching the border, including illegal entries. And while the new policy announced on this day was directed officially at halting the efforts of those choosing to cross the border, it also had a hidden appeal to the administration, one never mentioned in the attorney general's statement.

Since at least March of the previous year, members of the Trump White House had been contemplating separating children from their parents at the border. Each would be sent to different detention centers while their cases were processed. It wasn't the first occurrence of family separations at the border. This had taken place during the previous Obama presidency, too. But something was different now. The trauma children would withstand during such an experience was not incidental or collateral damage in the minds of administration officials. Trauma inflicted upon children was the very goal: multiple White House officials described separation as a strategy to "deter" illegal border crossings. Family bonds mattered—for those not fully modernized, those from the global south—and through those bonds, perhaps the U.S. border could be made to matter to them as well.

The new "zero-tolerance policy" of the administration now provided a legal pretext to do this on a larger scale. All attempts of illegal border crossing would now be investigated as criminal offenses. The U.S. government would regard the adults involved as criminal defendants rather than asylum seekers. And as criminal defendants, they could not be housed with their children.

The policy had led to the detentions of over two thousand children within little more than a month, and more than two thousand a month after that. When confronted by a reporter on June 14, 2018, about the practices, the attorney general referenced Romans 13 to make his point: "Let everyone be subject to the governing authorities, for there is no authority except that which God has established. The authorities that exist have been established by God. Consequently, whoever rebels against the authority is rebelling against what God has instituted, and those who do so will bring judgment on themselves."

His words did little. As national and international outcry reached a fevered pitch, the president abruptly ended the separations on June 20, 2018, by means of an executive order. An unnecessary surrender, Bannon later told me. Had Trump held on only a few days longer, public attention to the topic would have withered and moved on, and the separations could have continued.

BACK AT THE SMOKEHOUSE in Tucson, I am thinking about space and time, red lines and synergies, as well as inconsistencies.

*Is Bannon the Traditionalist trying to advance or reverse time? Does he have a plan or is he just flip-flopping from one direction to the other, like a hamster on a spinning wheel?* Meanwhile, our night is drawing to a close. Darren Beattie and I are chatting. Prior to his days in the Trump administration, he was a philosophy professor, and we are talking about obscure authors we knew about.

"Do you know Michael Millerman? A Heidegger scholar, into Aleksandr Dugin," Darren asked.

I replied. "Yeah, yeah. I've read his stuff. Another guy I know from my research, his name is Jason Jorjani, he's—"

A clatter. Did Steve just drop his silverware? That's what it sounded like, but my eyes were turned away at that moment.

"How . . ." Steve is suddenly in our exchange, staring at me with a new intensity. "How do you know who Jason Jorjani is?"

"I know him from my past research," I say, taken aback. "I know a lot of those guys."

Bannon says nothing and turns back to peek at his cell phones. How does *he* know who Jason Jorjani is—an obscure intellectual moving in the darker corners of the far-right and associated with Arktos? Then I remember a moment from last year. A book, a request, an inscription; I never followed up.

The story I had been following about Bannon, Dugin, and Olavo had become serious and foreboding in ways I hadn't anticipated. Now it was about to get weird.

# 16

# THE DISINTEGRATION OF THE WORLD

IT WAS MAY 2019 AND I WAS BACK HOME IN COLO-
rado, standing outside the library in my small town, next to
its swollen springtime creek. I decided to check in with Jason
Jorjani.

"Jason? This is Ben Teitelbaum. I know, it's really been a
while. And I'm sorry I haven't been able to deliver the book to
Steve. But I am curious about what this is all about, this inscription. What were you wanting to say to him?"

My focus throughout the past months had been on the major
power brokers—Dugin, Olavo, and Bannon—and on the fact
that these Traditionalist-inspired men had become serious influences on executives in large nations at roughly the same time.
But I hadn't considered what this state of affairs meant for the
underground Traditionalist radical right. And that's exactly what
Jason could shed light on. As it turns out, it is an equally unlikely
story, about that underground's effort to capitalize.

Jason Reza Jorjani is the son of an American mother of Scandinavian and Irish ancestry and an Iranian exile father, and he
grew up wealthy in New York. Most people who meet Jason

comment on how young he looks for his thirty-eight years. His eyes are bright; his hair is full and youthful. His face is evidence of a gentle life.

But Jason had a vision, and he was willing to sacrifice for it. You could call it an Iranian nationalist vision, but that wouldn't capture its fervor or eccentricity. He dreamed of a unified Aryan world where societies with Indo-European spiritual roots would mobilize as one to assume leadership in a new global order. This would include Buddhists in Japan; Hindus in India in the East; Europe and its satellites in North America; and Iranians—the fount of Zoroastrianism and its Shia Islamic incarnations—at the center. These are the great peoples, the superior civilizations best positioned to handle the challenges facing humanity and the world. The unification begins, Jason believes, with a cultural and political revolution in Iran aimed at returning the nation to its own roots and throwing off its allegiances toward Islamic counterparts in the Sunni world, followed by integration with its true spiritual brethren, the other Aryan states, including the U.S.

Jason talks big. At times it sounds fanciful and unserious, especially considering his background and lack of direct contacts with government. He was a humanities professor at the New Jersey Institute of Technology and a philosopher (he earned his doctorate in philosophy in 2013). He's a writer, in other words, not an official policy maker. However, his was a Traditionalist, Evolian vision, one that seeks to base state formation and geopolitics on historical essences and spiritual roots, with not always veiled allusions to racial determinism (Jason has discussed using eugenics programs to rid Iran's population of its Mongol genetic traces), not to mention a specific celebration of Indo-European spirituality and the hierarchical exaltation of "Aryans." And this approach had a chance to be implemented in the brave new world that emerged following the rise of Trump and the arrival of a Traditionalist in the White House. At least Jason thought it had a chance. That is why he attempted a daring campaign that would bring him into partnership with parapsychological terrorists and international money launderers, transform organized white nationalism, and eventually present a public relations hurdle for the Trump administration.

On the phone, Jason began to tell me the story. He explained that in February 2016, well before the presidential election in the United States, he had published a book arguing for the West to embrace the spiritual archetypes of its pre-Christian Greek heritage: *Prometheus and Atlas*—the same book that Jason later asked me to give to Steve Bannon. In it, Jason claimed that reviving ancient spiritualities would allow the West to not only escape dry rational modernism but even unleash repressed ways of thinking and knowing—most specifically ESP and psychokinesis. He published the book through an outlet he had just recently come to know: Arktos. Arktos was not only a controversial outlet but an unstable one. Its then editor in chief John Morgan warned him during the production phase of the book that interpersonal conflicts at Arktos were flaring and that his own ouster appeared imminent. Still, Arktos was open to his commentary on psychic and telekinetic powers, and it turned out that this was a plus for both author and publisher. *Prometheus and Atlas* garnered an award from the American Parapsychological Association.

However, you write a book on topics like these, and freaks of all kinds come out of the woodwork. By mid-spring 2016, Jason was receiving emails hard and fast from people making outrageous claims about their psychic abilities, professing to have unlocked secrets of the universe and to be representatives of hidden orders. Some even threatened to attack Jason through parapsychological means.

One of these figures stood out. Not because his initial presentation diverged from the standard, but because he eventually showed himself to be a person of considerable resources. "Who is this guy?" I asked. Jason replied only that he is a man from London, a regular reader of Arktos's books, and that he has moved in Traditionalist circles surrounding the late Martin Lings. I asked if I could contact him, but Jason discouraged me from doing this. Jason eventually learned that this man—let's call him the Londoner—was involved in Satanism, occultism, and Nazism and was known throughout European radical right circles as productive, charismatic, and shockingly well connected. His network had somehow expanded to include wealthy Iranians and possibly members of the British government. My first thought upon hearing all this was that this figure sounded like a law enforcement plant. Governments in Britain and Germany are particularly aggressive about sending undercover spies into far-right circles, sometimes with tragic results.

Regardless, the Londoner started giving Jason advice. He knew about the administrative turmoil at Arktos. Maybe Jason would like to take John Morgan's position—after all, he was a native English speaker with scholarly training. Jason thought that a compelling possibility. In fact he had been speaking to the company's Swedish CEO, Daniel Friberg, about it. As the rift between John and Daniel grew larger, Jason was there to fill the void, accepting the offer in September 2016.

Further, what separated the Londoner from the other email stalkers was his offer to help advance Jason's current interests—not just parapsychology but also the implementation of his vision for Iran, namely, supporting a nationalist revolution and (re)uniting Iranians with their Aryan kin. The Londoner's claim was provocative: he might have a plan for getting Jason's messages into Iran and even into the White House. And the Londoner was ready to move on all this immediately. He told Jason, "We work with Michael Bagley at Jellyfish, and they can help you. Here is his number. I'll tell him you are going to call."

I remembered the inscription in the book Jason asked me to

give to Steve and the mysterious reference to Jellyfish. I asked, "So this is what you were referring to in your note to Steve, the whole thing about Jellyfish trying to set up a meeting between you two?"

According to the plan as I understood it, Michael Bagley, remarkably, was a link between this murky Traditionalist underground and the halls of power in Washington, D.C. And even at this early date—in the spring and summer of 2016, still ahead of the presidential election—he seemed to know of a potentially receptive and sympathetic target for a lobbying campaign: Steve Bannon. Jason wouldn't talk to me about the Londoner. But who was this other guy—the link?

MICHAEL BAGLEY IS PRESIDENT of Jellyfish Partners. Once characterized by *Mother Jones* magazine as seeming "ripped from the pages of a spy novel," the firm described its mission as one of acquiring and selling political intelligence to corporate clients. However, Bagley launched a surprisingly effective publicity campaign that portrayed Jellyfish as an agent intervening in and shaping global affairs in addition to studying them. That is not surprising, considering its roots. Jellyfish was founded in 2011 with Keith Mahoney serving as CEO and Michael Yorio serving as executive vice president. Both men were veterans of the infamous private security firm Blackwater. The U.S. military and the Central Intelligence Agency (CIA) had intermittently used Blackwater to protect assets, provide combat training, and assassinate people. The assassinations didn't come to public attention until 2009, two years after a series of scandals involving murders of Iraqi citizens by employees were already cementing perceptions that Blackwater was a racket of armed goons given a license to kill by the U.S. government. Bad publicity and legal woes caused the organization's various divisions to splinter into new independent entities, and Jellyfish was one such initiative. Its founders had worked with Blackwater's intelligence division called Total Intelligence Solutions; Keith Mahoney had been its director. Jellyfish represented their attempt to preserve and expand that formidable network of contacts and know-how.

Michael Bagley came to Jellyfish with experience. Once a legislative aide for Democratic senator Patty Murray, he was tapped to be CEO after having in 2009 founded a nearly identical firm called the OSINT Group (OSINT being shorthand for *open source intelligence*), staffed by individuals with a background in covert, legally dubious intelligence work. Practically speaking, Jellyfish absorbed this organization along with Michael during its debut.

And what a debut it was. In addition to boasting about its roots in Blackwater, Jellyfish claimed in a 2011 press document to have over two hundred "intelligence assets" throughout the world, "including within the Muslim Brotherhood in Egypt, clerical circles in Iran, and tribal leaderships on the Pakistani side of the [Afghanistan-Pakistan] border region." As *Washington Examiner* journalist Shane Harris noted, in what could be construed as an exceptional gift of PR, this would make Jellyfish a private sector rival of the CIA. The money appeared to be there: Michael Bagley claimed during a media interview that the firm's list of clients included giant Philip Morris.

Something wasn't right with Jellyfish, though. Michael Bagley talked big and seemed to have some treacherous ways about him, his colleagues thought, and they noticed that he was unable to get a security clearance from the U.S. government. Founder Keith Mahoney couldn't really put his finger on it. Bagley not only clashed personally with him but also made the hairs on his neck stand. He seemed dangerous. Within a month, Mahoney was out, as well as most of the others. Jellyfish was soon a one-man operation—at least in the United States.

By summer of 2016, at the time Jason called him, Michael

Bagley was pursuing radical political change in Iran. Or rather, he was working for people pursuing radical political change in Iran; Jason came to think that Bagley was following the directives of the Londoner, among others. Maybe the Londoner was a corporate client of Jellyfish's? Perhaps the two of them worked for another entity? Or maybe Jellyfish was just a front for something larger? Jason wondered. Regardless, in phone calls and emails Michael and the Londoner had presented their visions as broadly aligning with his own. They sought the destruction of the Islamic Republic in Iran and its replacement with a government detached from its current network of alliances—Turkey and China as well as Venezuela—and integrated with the West.

They wanted to achieve this through a campaign of domestic lobbying initiatives as well as attempts at geopolitical maneuvering. The details Jason was learning about all this were startling. The Londoner, Jason believed, had mediated contact with Fethullah Gülen—a Turkish political refugee living in the United States whom Turkey's government accused of helping organize a failed coup against its president in 2016. He would later learn that the Londoner also sought and was preparing for governmental turmoil in Venezuela. Regimes in both places maintained a favorable relationship with Iran's Islamist government.

But where did Jason—a professor and an editor at an obscure publishing house—fit in with all of this? The answer: Jellyfish saw him as a propaganda and lobbying asset whose unique resources were just about to come into vogue with the rise of Steve Bannon.

IN SEPTEMBER 2016, Jason and Michael Bagley met for lunch at the Persepolis Persian restaurant on Manhattan's Upper East Side.

"You know, I had a Persian girlfriend once. I got to know the culture . . . I love chelo kebab," Bagley declared. Jason was dressed in his standard ensemble: a suit with a white shirt and a tie, the only flourish being a gold lapel pin of the eagle-like Zoroastrian Faravahar. The burly, goateed Michael, in contrast, looked like he had just emerged from a sports bar—an untucked button-down shirt over jeans, with a dress coat. *But never mind looks,* Jorjani thought. This was about business.

Bagley and company claimed to have access to a radio facility well within range of Iran, in Croatia, and planned to broadcast anti-government propaganda into the country. Could Jason help with that, supply content for the broadcasts? You bet. Jason said he could even draw assistance from a sympathetic organization to which he belonged, Iranian Renaissance. He could have content for Michael by the end of the month.

That timeline sounded fine. Bagley said that they planned to launch their media platforms by mid- to late January. Funds for it would come, via a windy path, from the U.S. government. This would only be possible, however, once stickler bureaucrats from the Obama administration were replaced by others with a laxer grip on finances.

Yes, Bagley was confident, a month before the presidential election, that Donald Trump would win, and this was the basis for the second request.

It wasn't enough to push their agenda within Iran and among its allies—Jellyfish wanted to shift policy toward Iran closer to home. To this end, Bagley and his colleagues were already studying the future Trump administration before it had come into existence. They knew, for instance, that the president's son-in-law Jared Kushner would be the key party responsible for policy toward Israel. And they said that Trump's new campaign manager, a man named Steve Bannon, whom few in Washington were acquainted with, was certain to remain in the administration as a powerful influence on the president. Any effort to shift U.S. policy toward Iran—to turn away from the entrenched duality of either acquiescing to the mullahs or marching off to war, of working instead toward sparking a nationalistic revolution—would receive a major boost were Bannon to support it. Bagley already had channels into these circles, he would claim publicly. In order to lobby Bannon, however, they wanted a more dynamic approach—to speak to him from his preexisting interests. Jellyfish, months ahead of the American media, knew not only that Bannon associated himself with the white nationalist alt-right movement but that he was also a reader of Arktos's texts and a Traditionalist.

Bagley wasn't acquainted with that stuff, but the Londoner sure was, and they saw an opening through Jason. Not only was Jason now the editor in chief of Arktos, the largest producer and retailer of Traditionalist literature in English, but the geopolitical realignment he was advocating was Traditionalist in nature. An Iran that returned to its roots and let its essential spiritual signatures define its place in the world would turn to the West. Furthermore, a West that embraced Iran would likely be prioritizing its spiritual identity as well, and its historic embeddedness within the Indo-European community. That the ramifications of a repositioned Iran would also include further isolation of China—known even then to be a key agenda for Bannon—made the plan seem even more auspicious.

Jason began to suspect that the possibility of an in with Bannon might have been part of the reason that the Londoner encouraged him to seek the position of editor in chief at Arktos months earlier. He would probably need an even larger profile and status if he wanted the ear of people within the White House. The Jellyfish guys had a thought. Why not play the alt-right angle more, create a hub organization for that movement with Jason at its top—something with a forceful media component but also something that would appeal to Bannon's intellectualism? Just make sure that you, Jason, are on top, so that if a connection with Bannon and the White House becomes possible, the message about Iran gets through.

JASON HAD BEEN telling me about the launch of an effort to gain influence, to lobby the executive branch of the American government for a change in foreign policy, based on Traditionalism. Had I not been aware of Dugin's, Bannon's, and Olavo's recent activities, I probably would have dismissed what Jason was saying. Instead I found myself curious and believing that he was describing his experiences honestly. But as I pondered his tale, some of the background facts didn't jibe. Could Bagley and the Londoner actually be real, serious people well connected to the world of intelligence and power *and* be foolish enough to think that the hapless world of far-right activism could be useful for more than hooliganism? Something seemed wrong. Then again, this was a new age and a new far right, and Jason was an unusual character.

A few months after his lunch with Bagley, Jason would again be sitting in Persepolis restaurant. This time, however, he was meeting with white nationalist Richard Spencer.

Jason had just returned from a trip to London, where he spoke before an Iranian nationalist crowd and met the Londoner for the first time. The Londoner received a full report about his and Bagley's meeting, and he wanted to help develop the idea that the two had hatched, that of building a new organization. It should be a "think tank," the Londoner insisted, one that combined the best resources in the radical right these days. Arktos could cover the deeper intellectual stuff, but Red Ice—another Sweden-based outfit headed by a man named Henrik Palmgren and specializing in slick radio and video shows—could serve as a media outlet. And perhaps an American organization could be involved, too, like Richard Spencer's National Policy Institute, which had been hosting large white nationalist seminars and conferences for years. They could call the umbrella organization the AltRight Corporation. And, the Londoner added, he could make sure it was well funded.

That was the conversation that brought Jason back to Persepolis. He was here to solidify the American wing of this new project. Spencer had been catapulted into the public eye as the face of the alt-right movement, amid claims by journalists, pundits, and Hillary Clinton herself that the alt-right was deeply involved in Donald Trump's then floundering campaign for the U.S. presidency. Spencer wasn't sure that those allegations were true. Steve Bannon had publically referred to his media company Breitbart as a platform for the alt-right, but it was unclear what he meant by that (the term *alt-right* was still new and its meaning a matter of debate). Still, during the campaign, Trump had been slow to reject the endorsement he received from former Ku Klux Klan leader David Duke, though he eventually issued a condemnation. Small stuff, but even the slightest hint of receptiveness from a major presidential candidate was cause for elation among the likes of Spencer. It was something they had only dreamed of—namely, momentum, and the potential that the most maligned and rejected political cause in the post–World War II West might have made an inch of progress toward the goal of relevance, maybe even influence. Further, it was a position they achieved not by camouflage or clandestine infiltration of the mainstream, but as themselves—as unapologetic white nationalists. The radical right saw this as an age of possibilities, a time for innovation and ambition.

Perhaps that is why Richard was so eager to say yes to Jason— yes to a new three-way partnership among Red Ice, Arktos, and his own organization, the National Policy Institute. Their partnership would mark the unification of the major transatlantic cultural and intellectual platforms associated with white nationalism today. The AltRight Corporation was going to be a reality.

The lunch at Persepolis was just the after-party. Jason and Richard had reached their agreement the day before and had then headed to a private club for a night of booze and celebration. During the wee hours of the morning the two posed for a picture. Against a wall behind them stood a statue of Hermes—the Greek god of trickery. Jason had included Hermes in the picture on purpose.

# 17

# ALT-RIGHT, INC.

BY LATE SPRING 2019, BANNON'S FORTUNES WERE shifting. His plans to start a school in Italy had received a potentially fatal blow: after months of public outcry, the monastery where he planned to house the school outside of Rome had decided to evict him and his partners. However, at the same time, his collaboration with Olavo seemed to be bearing fruit. The two were meeting frequently, Bannon was sponsoring events in Olavo's honor, and Bannon was continuing to be invited to official Brazilian government functions, especially those associated with Brazil's foreign minister, Ernesto Araújo, Olavo's former student and a Traditionalist. Dugin, however, wasn't in the mix. He hadn't met a second time with Steve, and he hadn't been responding to my requests for more interviews after I let him know that I had learned of the infamous meeting in Rome.

This gave me time to delve deeper into Jason's story. I wasn't sure yet what to make of it. It could be seen as a tale of tragicomic fools spinning their wheels while thinking their moment for power had just about come. Or alternatively it could represent a compelling link between the White House and the far-right underground.

Jason had told me about the Londoner and Bagley and their efforts to help him take over Arktos publishing and thereafter form the AltRight Corporation with Richard Spencer in order to reach Bannon, to lobby him on the basis of his Traditionalism for a change in U.S.-Iran policy. All of this was going to be made possible, in part, by infusions of money that would strengthen the publishing and media channels themselves, and allow Jason to assume leadership positions in both. This would allow him to deliver *his* message, not the boilerplate white nationalism of his partners—a message for Bannon to help unite the Aryan world by bringing Iran back into alignment with its true spiritual brethren in the West.

But in the wake of Trump's 2016 election, almost immediately after Jason, Richard Spencer, and Swedes Daniel Friberg and Henrik Palmgren of Red Ice formed their partnership, the plans began to falter.

THE ALTRIGHT CORPORATION had become a reality on January 16, 2017 (coincidentally, Jason insists, on Martin Luther King Jr. Day), with a slick website in whites and blues. The organization was supposed to be run equally by all the leaders—a Knights of the Round Table model. However, Richard was the outward face of the organization, whether they liked it or not. He had become famous as an icon of the new white nationalism. Both he and his ideology were constructions of the media, Jason believed. But Spencer's persona was a liability. In late January, he was punched in the face during a filmed interview outside on the street, and the video of the attack was spread virally by liberal

America. Richard, meanwhile, had taken to carrying weapons, even to work. A mythos seemed to be forming around him. This presented a major branding problem, because thanks in part to Richard's antics, their name was starting to mean something other than what Jason wanted.

*Alt-right.* The term was originally coined not by Spencer as the media kept saying, but by a renegade philosopher and professor named Paul Gottfried who published books with Arktos. Its rise to public attention during the 2016 presidential election came in part when Steve Bannon was quoted describing Breitbart News as a "platform for the alt-right." The term was further solidified about a week after Bannon took over Trump's campaign, when Hillary Clinton devoted a speech in Reno, Nevada, to exposing the alt-right as a white nationalist cause that—via Bannon and Breitbart News—had "effectively taken over the Republican Party." Alt-rightists themselves were thrilled by the attention, although they also knew that the characterizations were somewhat inaccurate. *Alt-right* was being used internally as a catchall for a wide range of actors and ideologies, some of them ideologically irreconcilable. What they shared was a strong opposition to immigration, hostility toward the established conservatism in the Republican Party (hence the *alt*, or alternative right), and—the main innovation meriting a new moniker—a methodological focus on internet activism. All that, plus a relative lack of squeamishness about sharing space with white nationalists. Political extremes are dens of sectarianism, but this new term was uniting a broad coalition.

Now Richard had taken it over, and this made Hillary Clinton retroactively correct in her characterizations—*alt-right* was becoming synonymous with old-fashioned white nationalism. Daniel Friberg was basically in that camp; the Traditionalism that Arktos published seemed like a side interest of his. Jason was now swept up in it, too. Shortly after Trump's election, Richard held a gathering for white nationalists in Washington—a victory rally, basically—and toward its conclusion held a press conference. Jason was invited to the stage and he obliged, saying nothing and appearing less than comfortable with this degree of visibility, sitting between famous American white nationalist ideologues like Kevin MacDonald and Jared Taylor before a sea of international cameras and journalists.

Jason wished the term *alt-right* had retained its more open definition—he bet Bannon did, too—if only because association with the movement was becoming riskier to him professionally. Already in late 2016, his faculty colleagues at the New Jersey Institute of Technology were beginning to take notice of his emerging public profile. But Jason was willing to sacrifice: the alt-right was offering him a megaphone.

What a novel concept: gaining mainstream political influence in a Western democracy through the far-right underground. This would have been unthinkable just a few years earlier. But the advance of European nationalists, Brexit, and Trump had changed things, and people inside the scene could feel it. They had watched as Trump was hit with the usual attacks in public, being labeled a racist and a Nazi and so on. Trump didn't even make an effort to conform to liberal standards, and he won anyway. *They* won. It scared some of them, and they struggled to believe it: in a poignant analogy, one white nationalist writer compared the sensation to that of an unattractive young man who grandly rejects future romance rather than be rejected himself, only to cower when against all odds opportunity knocks on his door one day.

Could it really be true, the end of the liberal world order— the dying gasps of the tiger? Dare they open themselves up to hope? Might the radical right have become attractive instead of a pariah—a milieu that serious, powerful people want to be on good terms with and treat as an asset? Michael Bagley seemed to think so. He knocked; Jason planned to answer.

ON JANUARY 2, 2017, Bagley sent an email to Jason from his Jellyfish address:

> The USG [US government] funds for Jellyfish Media activities should be allocated in mid/late January but certainly by/ before February 1, and that is the target date to set up the administrative and media platforms. We are really only waiting on the official hand-off from Obama to Trump, and that is 20/21 January, of course.

It was signed, "With kind regards from Washington, Michael." Jason was reassured.

But here it was February, and nothing had come through. Nothing. And this was no small matter, because that money was key to Jason's entire plan. Money and influence would, to quote the Londoner, "lubricate" challenging social relations within the AltRight Corporation, and it would empower Jason to seize leadership of the organization, change its outward profile, and catch Bannon's attention.

Meanwhile, Jason was learning more about how all of this was supposed to work. Bagley was pursuing a project to create a series of "micro-cities" in North Africa. I would later learn that he had tried to do something similar during the Obama administration with an eye toward the U.S.-Mexico border, but was rebuked. These "micro-cities" were designed to contain migrants headed north. They supposedly weren't refugee camps but "resettlement towns," which in North Africa would be outfitted with job opportunities in the oil industry. It was a multibillion-dollar project that would require investment from various governments and private actors. But it was a solution for the refugee crisis in Europe. A humanitarian effort. *That,* I thought as I learned about the initiatives, *or a clever barrier to southern migration into the global north. A border wall of a different kind.*

Michael claimed that under the Trump administration, money for this could be freed up as a "black budget" operation— that is to say, through funds allocated for national security purposes whose purpose and use are classified. Was there any reason to think that Trump would allocate those funds for Michael Bagley's experiment? Well, there was a general impression that the flow of money might not be as closely monitored under this new administration. Some—it wouldn't take much—could "slip through the cracks" to Jellyfish and thereafter be funneled to Jason for his work with the Iranian Renaissance and for the AltRight Corporation. Yes, they were going to use government money to lobby the government.

Meanwhile, Michael explained to Jason, Jellyfish was making important contacts with relevant people inside the administration who could direct funds deliberately. Indeed, on February 2, 2017, a pro-Putin Israeli political commentator, Avigdor Eskin, published an op-ed in Russia's RIA Novosti news agency, claiming to know that Jellyfish employees had met with incoming Trump national security adviser General Michael Flynn to present the "micro-cities" proposal. "The idea was accepted by General Flynn as fully compliant with the policies of the current administration," Eskin added. "A detailed work plan was presented to Flynn and approved by him." Bannon, Jason came to think, must have been aware of the plan, too.

But signs of trouble came early. On February 13, General Flynn resigned from the Trump administration amid accusations that he was serving the interests of Russia and Turkey. The fact that the FBI had been monitoring and recording Flynn's conversations made the situation perilous for Bagley, Jason thought. And indeed, Bagley hadn't been replying to his emails throughout the month of February. Bumps in the road. *Surely the money will still come through*, Jason thought, and he had plenty to keep himself occupied while he waited.

It was during this time of optimism and anxiety that I met Jason for the first time. He and I had crossed paths in Stockholm on February 25, 2017, in the lobby of the SAS Radisson Blu hotel overlooking Stockholm's harbor. He had been waiting to meet Arktos's CEO, Daniel Friberg, and so had I. I was in town to observe that year's Identitarian Ideas conference—the same conference where I had met Aleksandr Dugin years earlier. I was especially interested to see how that year's conference would be different, given Trump's victory, the news of Bannon, the alt-right, and whatnot. I assumed it would be a full-blown jamboree, and it was. I had no clue what Jason was really up to at the time. He was trying to take over the AltRight Corporation in anticipation of gaining access to Bannon.

Jason gave a well-received speech on the ills of liberal democracy, and afterward all the guests—it was the largest Identitarian Ideas ever—partied until dawn. Jason was jovial. But all that ended when on March 8, 2017, he flew back to the United States from Sweden and once again confronted an empty email inbox.

Jason emailed Bagley again.

We need to move on the plan that emerged this winter in the course of conversations with yourself in Washington and, much more extensively with [the Londoner] and one of his associates in London, to sideline Richard Spencer and install me as the leader of the AltRight Corporation. You may recall our conversation regarding my being able to approach Steve Bannon in a way that Richard cannot. [. . .]

He elaborated in great detail about why he needed money and just how he would use it to take over financial leadership of Arktos and thereafter leadership of the AltRight Corporation. He concluded:

> My apologies, for putting all of this into writing, but I am sure that you can appreciate the urgency of these matters [. . .] Richard Spencer, Daniel Friberg, and Henrik Palmgren are not people that you play around with.

Jason never heard back from Bagley. But before long he finally received a sign of life, a communication from the Londoner.

"WE ARE GOING to overthrow the government of Venezuela."

There was nothing special going on in Venezuela as far as Jason knew. An oppressive socialist government in bed with the Iranian mullahs, yes. But that was it.

"And we need to get into the oil industry before we do that."

There had been no movement on the black budget/microcities front, but the Londoner had gotten back to Jason with a new plan for funds. It began with a thirty-three-page document written by and addressed to names Jason didn't know, outlining a range of business plans—investment and contract work opportunities—most related to development of oil in the Orinoco Belt region in the heart of Venezuela, home to what is thought to be the largest petroleum deposit in the world. Jason happened to know a petroleum engineer at one of the world's largest oil companies. "Ask him if his company was willing to take on this project."

The Londoner revealed that there was a sizable commission for the person brokering the deal. This meant that if Jason pulled off such a feat, if his contact was interested in taking on the work or investment, then Jason would have a right to some portion of the commission. It would be plenty for Arktos and the AltRight Corporation.

Jason still had the document in 2019, and he allowed me to review it. Its main pitch was to find financiers and partners to re-vitalize Venezuela's state-owned oil company (PDVSA), which had fallen into debt because its basic oil production operations were being mismanaged and its resources were being tapped to support the struggling Venezuelan economy as a whole. PDVSA sought rehabilitation of 1,200 oil wells, along with 550 additions.

The plan called for increased infrastructural support to exploit the region's reserves in general, and contained a more specific proposal to make Venezuela's oil more competitive on the global market by mixing its output of primarily heavy oil with medium or light oil, which could be produced domestically, or, the document suggests, imported from abroad. Room for international cooperation was built into the offer, in other words, along with the suggestion that the investor could place its investment "in a bank of its own confidence"—an oblique reference to the instability of Venezuela's economy. "Funds do not have to enter the country."

It was an odd document. A bit scattered, with sloppy English throughout. But the names were real, and the companies—PDVSA and its subsidiaries—were real, too. Jason didn't know how the Londoner had gained access to this, but after Jason received it, he decided he would give it a shot and approach his contact in the industry. At least the Jellyfish guys were finally responding to him.

※

I SHARED JASON'S DOCUMENT with an industry insider I know. This insider read it not as pieces of a contract, but instead as a business plan, and a legitimate-looking one at that.

That left me curious as to what else was happening in the world of politics and oil trade at the time. On March 29, 2017, just after the Londoner approached Jason with the oil trade proposal, Venezuela's highest court seized the powers of the country's main legislative body. It was an effective power grab limiting the influence of opposition voices and strengthening Hugo Chávez's heir, President Nicolás Maduro.

This action prompted condemnation from other Latin American and Western governments, as well as an eruption of protests domestically. What was at stake, according to critics, was the continued existence of democracy in Venezuela, and by late April the country appeared in crisis as the number of demonstrations on the streets began to match that of the country's last crisis in 2014. By midsummer, protests were taking place daily.

It was surprising, therefore, when in May, international media began reporting that American investment bank Goldman Sachs had purchased $2.8 billion of bonds in the Venezuelan state oil company. PDVSA was a malfunctioning tool of a government that was not only oppressive but also unstable, and whose future appeared increasingly uncertain. Commentators questioned the moral and economic wisdom of the move. Goldman Sachs was mostly quiet in response, though a spokesperson offered a brief reply that seemed coyly directed to both camps of critics. "We agree that life there has to get better, and we made the investment in part because we believe it will."

The statement implied that Goldman Sachs anticipated some kind of change in Venezuela. Could the company have had some insider information indicating upcoming political transformation? Perhaps the same information that Jason's Londoner had accessed? Possibilities like that kept me wondering. Perhaps,

even though many of the elements of Jason's story sounded ludi-
crous, the people he was working with might actually have had
real resources, a real hope of reaching power.

To learn more, I would need to explore the story from the
other side. I asked Steve Bannon to tell me about his activities
during this same period of time—during the first months of the
Trump presidency in spring of 2017. And it turns out that while
Jason was struggling to launch his campaign, Bannon was busy
attempting to implement Traditionalism-inspired geopolitics.

# 18

## BANNON AGAINST THE WORLD

JUST BEFORE 5:00 A.M. ON APRIL 7, 2017, MISSILES fell from the sky in the desert outside of Homs, Syria. Homs, a city more than two thousand years old, had already been bombed beyond recognition between 2011 and 2014 during the Syrian civil war. Forces opposing Syrian president Bashar al-Assad had entrenched themselves in the city, and the government—backed by Russia and Iran—responded by turning Homs into a hollowed-out shell.

This morning, however, the fire came from the Mediterranean. They were Tomahawk cruise missiles shot from an American destroyer, retaliation for the Syrian government's alleged use of chemical weapons and the resulting gruesome deaths of children just days before. President Obama had warned Syria that the United States would not tolerate the use of chemical weapons in any conflict on account of their indiscriminate and uncontrollable nature. Now that Trump believed these weapons were being used on his watch, he opted to enforce the rule.

The target was Shayrat Airbase, a place of operation for Russian and Iranian forces as well as Syrian. Syria was attacking the rebels by air, so, the reasoning in Washington went, it would be appropriate to weaken their ability to fly.

U.S. destroyers in the Mediterranean fired off fifty-nine missiles. They fell on runways, parked fighter jets, fuel tankers, and hangars. And a handful of people died, too. How many depends on which government is telling the story.

THE DAY BEFORE, April 6, 2017, things were in a bad way for Steve Bannon. At least that's how he described it to me years later. He, the chief adviser to the president, had just been removed from his controversial appointment on the National Security Council. Steve had been in open conflict with Trump's daughter Ivanka and son-in-law Jared Kushner. That was hardly an auspicious position to be in. The administration had already experienced an exceptional amount of staff turnover. But Trump's family members weren't going anywhere. Everyone was dispensable except for them.

And nowhere was Steve's conflict with Jared and Ivanka more pronounced than in foreign policy and the question of interventionism. They were establishment types politically—Jared had been a centrist Democrat for most of his life. Their instincts leaned more toward maintaining the status quo, whereas Steve argued for a dramatic drawback of U.S. military involvement around the globe. Steve saw his role in the White House as one of holding the president to his earlier campaign promises, and putting an end to gratuitous war-making had been a pillar of their pitch to voters. It was part of Trump's pledge to American workers that his administration would start prioritizing them, making decisions based on whether or not their interests were being served. Spending their money and lives in wars that didn't directly involve them and their welfare was antithetical to that cause, the reasoning went.

America first.

But like many of Steve's principles, the one surrounding nonintervention had layers of justification. Being a nationalist for one's self must involve, he would tell you, being a nationalist on behalf of others. That is the Westphalian system of governance that he idolizes. It's about respect for the sovereignty of the nation-state as a transcendent principle. And it's about respecting the right of other nations to preside over their own affairs: only an anti-nationalist approach would grant one state license to intervene in another's internal dealings. The supranational forces that would violate the principle of independence? Communism, radical Islam, empires like China, as well as universalist democracy, human rights, and capitalism untethered from their Judeo-Christian context. Globalisms, all of them. A threat to the sovereignty of average people everywhere, for while citizens can shape the fate of a nation, they cannot control the nebulous international entities above.

That's his case—the nationalistic populist version, that is. It always struck me as curious, how much of it happens to overlap with recent incarnations of Traditionalism as well.

A UNIVERSE WHERE NOBODY is allowed to be unlike another person: homogenization. That is the dystopia of the Kali Yuga. The point is easy to miss, but think about it. Original Traditionalists celebrated hierarchy and typically did not want to see the upper castes assimilate the lower ones to create a mass society of warriors or priests. Homogenization and evangelism are features of modernity, not Tradition. Whenever all members of a society melted into the same caste, order had gone awry. As the Traditionalists saw it, assimilation occurs only in a downward direction: everyone becomes enslaved to materialism with time. Under the best set of circumstances, people are allowed to vary from one another in their lifestyles, dreams, and destinies. Social variation, here in the form of hierachy, is a hallmark of a healthy society. Sameness is not.

Traditionalists and Traditionalist-inspired thinkers played with this idea generations later, taking the concept of a hierarchy and tipping it over on its side. What's most important, they maintain, is not that the best people be prioritized over others, but rather that differences among potential equals be allowed to prevail. Not hierarchy per se, but pluralism; difference not vertically, but horizontally; the pyramid cut in lines side to side rather than layers top to bottom. This was a rendering of Traditionalism that could resonate with generations coming of age after World War II, Vietnam, and Afghanistan—among dissident anti-imperialists in the west.

The forces threatening each type of difference—hierarchy and pluralism—are more alike than not. The enemies of difference are universalisms—values or systems deemed true for all of humanity rather than for a specific group. Democracy is often understood in these terms, framed even in the founding documents of liberal nation-states as part of a set of self-evident and God-given rights, along with the attendant concept of universal equality. Once we cease to understand an idea as being embedded in a distinct society with its own history, character, and destiny, it will then tend to be applied universally—to break boundaries and deny difference.

For some, like thinkers of the French New Right, Christianity was the great precursor to the proliferation of universalisms in modernity. Pre-Christian polytheistic faiths weren't always evangelistic, and they were often tolerant of different religious practices, even different deities, for different peoples. Christianity, however, claimed to be a universal truth superseding local beliefs. It guided people to disdain and abandon their roots through its assertion that the past was sin and the future will bring salvation. Especially in its Protestant incarnations, Christianity would unite all humans in the pursuit of a unified goal at the end of history: communion with God. Marxism and capitalism adopted a lot of these ideas, each claiming to be an absolute truth for all people, regardless of blood or creed, and attempting to funnel all toward a unified goal in the future rather than the past—be it earthly communist utopia, personal wealth, or mere social "progress" instead of a union with the divine. The result? Wherever you turn in the modern Westernized world, regardless of whether the mainstream left or right is in power, you will come into conflict with doctrines hostile to anything that could make one community meaningfully different from another.

In religion, universalisms lead to evangelism. In geopolitics, they lead to interventionism and imperialism.

THE MEETINGS in Washington ahead of the bombings in Syria had been contentious. They took place in the West Wing of the White House, downstairs in the John F. Kennedy Conference Room—the Situation Room, as it's known. And they were lopsided, according to Steve. "With little exception, it was always me against the world."

Ivanka Trump and her ally in the administration, National Security Adviser Dina Powell, had led a charge to convince the president to respond. The deciding factor was not an argument about the ideological pros and cons of intervention, about the status of Trump's campaign promises, but rather visual aids. Trump was presented with photographs of gassed children, showcased by a child of his own.

Steve was exasperated. Why were the lives of these children worth more than others? Why did the method by which they were killed really matter? Were they really sure that the Syrian government did this? It was hard to imagine their motive. And what are we, the United States, really thinking we are going to do with cruise missiles?

He had been close to cruise missile strikes in the past, during his days in the Navy. Cruise missiles were, well, okay, but they wouldn't do anything substantial. This would be nothing but a token strike, for optics. It would cost money, and it would unnecessarily agitate others, notably the Russians.

There was no support for his protests. He had already been identified as a problem. Steve Bannon disagrees with something? Great! Let's do it. It was even reported that Jared was particularly repulsed after having learned of Steve's ideas about the necessity and unavoidability of destruction in the world. Bannon's Traditionalism, that is, in unnamed form.

But unbeknownst to Bannon at the time, his was not the only Traditionalist hand in the conflict in Syria. Back in November 2015, Turkey—a nominal U.S. ally in the conflict—shot down a Russian fighter jet after it crossed into Turkish air space along the border and ignored repeated warnings to exit. Rebel forces on the ground then shot and killed the pilot as he descended by parachute, as well as a member of the Russian search-and-rescue force on the ground. Tensions ran high afterward. Would Russia retaliate by attacking a NATO state and unleash direct conflict between itself and Western forces compelled to come to Turkey's defense?

Amid public denunciations and publicity stunts by politicians in Ankara and Moscow, channels of communication had been

opened between security forces in both places. By summer of the
following year, Turkish prime minister Recep Tayyip Erdoğan
would submit a letter to Vladimir Putin stating his sympathy
for the families of the deceased Russian fighters. He later had
the Turkish soldiers who had fired upon the plane arrested for
suspected links to his domestic political rival Fethullah Gülen.
Turkey and Russia were cool now.

The man behind this reconciliation was none other than
Aleksandr Dugin. He was the one who had the connections in
both governments, contacts forged as an unofficial emissary of
Moscow abroad. He arranged the back-channel communications and secret meetings, and made the suggestion that Turkey
at least investigate the fighters who downed the plane. The work
must have been a pleasure for him, for by smoothing over the
Russian/Turkish relationship, he was keeping the United States
from greater involvement in Syria, keeping the conflict in Russia's hands, and thereby showing the world that there was no one
force that could impose its will everywhere, at all times, with
impunity. As was the case when Dugin attempted to steer nationalism in Europe, his agenda in Syria had an ally in Bannon.

DIVERSITY, VARIATION, PLURALISM. All virtues in the
eyes of Traditionalists opposite uniformity and globalization.
Aleksandr Dugin looms large as a figure who derived multiple
lessons from these principles. For him, difference matters most
in groups' ability to maintain their own myths, spiritual beliefs,
foods, aesthetics, rituals, habits—ways of existing, or Dasein.
Others whom Dugin has partnered with on intellectual projects,
notably Alain de Benoist of the French New Right, placed more
emphasis on biologically inherited features like race and ethnicity
in a related concept of ethnic separatism called ethnopluralism.

Dugin, like de Benoist, could be much more philosophical in his elaboration of the idea, however, maintaining the importance of a group's ability to retain its own sense of knowledge and truth, its own epistemology. Just as he drew on the thinking of (generally left-leaning) early Anglo-American anthropologists to argue that no culture—no particular Dasein—was objectively better than another, so, too, did he use leftist postmodern philosophers to argue that truth was relative. In a world of difference, no society would claim to know "the truth" for anyone but themselves. The opposite claim, that an objective reality exists beyond culture, was nothing but a Trojan horse for epistemological colonialism. If one culture claimed to have accessed knowledge that wasn't specific to them but was instead true for everybody, it was then justified in invading and erasing the thinking of others, taking what once was a world with a vast array of knowledge systems and replacing it with one. And it so happens the culture bringing this scourge of epistemological uniformity on the world is—surprise—the modern West with its scientific method.

A Traditionalist has a right to push back against this. Indeed, a BBC reporter once asked Dugin about the conflict in Syria and whether he believed in the information being pushed by Russia state media. Dugin responded with a monologue citing Western postmodern philosophers and assailing the concept of "facts." He said that truth is relative. The United States has a right to its sense of truth about Syria, but meanwhile, "we have our special Russian truth."

Dugin's thoughts on geopolitics seem just another expression of this hyper-pluralist ideal formulated in terms of static, eternal civilizational and cultural divides. The Christian evangelist, the diplomat agitating for universal human rights, the global capitalist, the empiricist scientist, the investigative journalist seeking to uncover "the facts," Western state militaries enforcing supposed international law—they were all versions of the same thing, all enemies of difference. And the values that support the right of tribal societies to maintain their lifeways and visions of history, nature, and the divine also underpin the resistance to uniformity in global power relations. Multipolarity, the emergence of various power centers, prevents any one from dominating.

The step from there to doctrines of noninterventionism is small. Multipolarity also leads to visions of a world of nations where all agreed to respect the sovereignty of one another and pursue interests limited to their own sphere and the interests of their own people. Hence America first. It needn't be at odds with other world powers—quite the opposite. At least according to Steve, the Christian zealot who hates evangelism, a member—for a time—of a presidential administration that proclaimed "alternative facts."

ACROSS THE SPAN of multiple years, and before they would first meet, Bannon and Dugin had been working toward similar ends in Syria. That wasn't enough to propel Bannon to success in the White House. His efforts during April 2017 to prevent American military intervention had been a failure. And this was a skirmish in a larger battle. Bannon versus Jared: nationalism versus globalism, disruption versus the status quo, Trump's grassroots agenda versus establishment Washington.

When he thinks back on the exchanges in the Situation Room, Steve wishes he had been more adamant. He told me he regretted having acted uncharacteristically reserved, in part because he was sensing that the power dynamics in the administration were not in his favor. "Trying to be polite," that was his strategy, but deference didn't work.

And in hindsight, if you ask him, he was "right, as usual.

Right?" Jared, Ivanka, H. R. McMaster, "all these people were just wrong. I hate to say it, they're wrong and they're not even close. These are not close calls.

"The globalists—all they want to do, and it's all phony, it's all lies—what they want to do is they want to get up and they want to get a cheap shot at the Russians. 'Have something happen!' And we're shooting at each other. That's what the purpose of this is." There was still no proof that the Syrian government had used the chemical weapons. And the effectiveness of the bombing? Shayrat Airbase was launching missions again that same evening, and it had no noticeable impact on the course of events in the region.

Smug observations weren't going to help Steve, though. The administration was moving away from his populist nationalist agenda. He still had his office, though. He was down, but not out. Yet.

# 19

## UNITE THE RIGHT

THE WORLD SHIFTED DURING SPRING AND SUMMER of 2017. At least this period of time increasingly appeared to be a watershed in the histories of a number of figures I was following. It was the dawn of their dark age.

Steve Bannon was losing his status and by early summer seemed destined to leave the Trump administration altogether. The loss of his controversial appointment to the National Security Council on April 5 and his impotence in the fight over what to do in Syria was just one thing. Chief of staff General John F. Kelly didn't like him and suspected him of leaking salacious stories about opponents in the White House and of creating a shadow organization within. The president was increasingly resentful of a growing number of media narratives identifying Bannon, not Trump himself, as the architect of his electoral victory and the driving force behind the administration's initiatives. Meanwhile, Bannon's feud with Trump's son-in-law was so highly exposed in American media that it was even dramatized on leading satire television programs like *Saturday Night Live*. Things were not looking good for Steve.

It would take a sensational event, however, to push him out. The exact same event would also prove pivotal for Jason Jorjani and the alt-right.

THEY MET in McIntire Park in Charlottesville, Virginia, on Saturday, August 12, 2017, a little before eleven A.M. Daniel Friberg, Richard Spencer, and Henrik Palmgren—three of the four leaders from the AltRight Corporation—joined hundreds of other protesters assembling for the Unite the Right rally, its official purpose being to contest the removal of a local public statue of Civil War Confederate general Robert E. Lee. But as its name indicates, this rally was also intended to bring together actors who identified with the alt-right.

The most colorful attendees were masses of militant white nationalists, swastika-toting neo-Nazis, and Ku Klux Klan members. There were plenty of Confederate flags, too, of course. Marchers even seemed to have studied, rehearsed, and performed renditions of the Civil War Confederate war cry, the Rebel yell. They did these things while also adopting new symbolism specific to the online world that had given their cause a cultural and strategic rebirth. Icons of the alt-right cartoon meme Pepe the Frog appeared on signs and T-shirts, while marchers also flashed the "okay" hand signal meant to resemble the letters $W$ and $P$, standing for white pride. Many also wore red MAGA hats. Notably absent were organized groups from the so-called alt-lite, who oppose immigration and multiculturalism while claiming to disavow racism and anti-Semitism. What emerged was a gnarly mob explicitly championing white identity, emboldened by what they saw as the encroaching marginalization of their position in society and a simultaneous opening of support in the White House.

There had been a dramatic gathering the night before, when protesters surrounded the disputed statue with tiki torches and marched while chanting, alternately, "You will not replace us" and "Jews will not replace us": anxiety surrounding demographic change and the upward social and economic mobility of non-whites was a central protest theme as well.

Daniel and Richard missed all that. They arrived the following day dressed not for street warfare but in formal attire—in Daniel's case, a three-piece suit. Both were scheduled to speak. But whereas the night before, protesters had been able to move freely throughout the city, today a massive crowd of counterprotesters was poised to prevent the entire demonstration. Daniel could hear their calls as soon as he entered McIntire Park. "The fascist Richard Spencer is here! The fascist Richard Spencer is here!" He was glad that Richard's entourage included private former military security guards, but neither they nor the combined force of city police, state troopers, and U.S. National Guard could defend them against everything. Counterprotesters lined the march pathway from McIntire Park to Lee Park with its namesake statue. And as the procession advanced, tear gas and pepper spray rained down on them—literally. The counterprotesters sprayed up in the air, allowing the contents to fall down and coat faces, shoulders, hands, and hair. It was hot, and in his outfit, Daniel was sweating. He could wipe the spray off his face. But as he sweated, new doses of irritant dripped into his eyes.

At eleven, before the entire procession arrived at Lee Park for the scheduled speeches, the city of Charlottesville and later the governor of Virginia called a state of emergency, immediately canceling the event on the grounds that the safety of participants and spectators could not be guaranteed. Protesters were directed to vacate the area by walking back through the path of counterprotesters they had just come through. Richard, Daniel, and their nearest associates at first defied the order, but chaos ensued as protesters and authorities scattered in multiple directions. After some initial confrontations with police, Richard Spencer ran to his getaway car and left the scene. On his way out, he happened to see his informal predecessor walking the streets—the last man to emerge in American popular culture as an outspoken white nationalist, former Ku Klux Klan leader David Duke, who jumped to safety in their car.

The rest of the city remained in turmoil as protesters and counterprotesters met one another in open conflict. Words, gestures, and blows were exchanged and dozens were rushed to local hospitals. Around 1:45, a white nationalist from Ohio, James Alex Fields Jr., sat behind the wheel of his 2010 Dodge Challenger and turned onto 4th Street just blocks from Lee Park. Seeing a crowd of counterprotesters ahead blocking the street, he slammed his foot on the gas pedal and plowed forward. A few seconds later he shifted his car into reverse and sped backward. The police officer who stopped the car a mile away noted damage from baseball bats on the vehicle's exterior, as well as blood and human flesh. Back at the scene, a thirty-two-year-old counterprotester, Heather D. Heyer, lay dead on the ground.

ILL-FATED, TRAGIC, CATASTROPHIC—these were the words being used by the white nationalist intelligentsia during the immediate aftermath of Charlottesville. The menacing tiki-torch gathering, the militarized garb, the Nazi sloganeering, and of course the violence would wipe out any potential that the alt-right movement had to rebrand white nationalism and anti-liberal activism. Far from a display of ingenuity and innovation, the people marching in Charlottesville surely looked all too familiar to onlookers. Even participants voiced their reservations. Richard Spencer denounced the event organizer's response to the death of Heather D. Heyer online. And in the wake of an op-ed I wrote in the *Wall Street Journal* highlighting Daniel Friberg's uncharacteristic willingness to march alongside visible Nazis and Klansmen, he clarified to the Scandinavian media that he was unsettled by the presence of those actors and would have prohibited their participation had he been an organizer. He and another associate from Sweden were notified shortly thereafter that their visas for travel to the United States had been indefinitely revoked. But then an outside voice joined the public conversation, and in a most unexpected way.

"We condemn in the strongest possible terms this egregious display of hatred, bigotry, and violence on many sides—on many sides." President Donald Trump's statement came from his golf club in Bedminster, New Jersey, shortly after the events in Charlottesville unfolded. And instead of focusing his criticism on the white nationalist protesters, he widened the lens to also condemn leftist counterprotesters, Black Lives Matter and Antifa (Anti-Fascist Action) in particular. That was more than people like Richard Spencer would have hoped to hear from previous presidents. It was unbelievable. And after a period of near silence amid heated outcry over the weekend, Trump offered extended commentary the following Tuesday during a press conference held in Trump Tower in Manhattan. He launched into this remarkable reply after a reporter asked whether the attacks were prompted by the alt-right:

> When you say the alt-right, define alt-right to me. You define it. Go ahead. Define it for me, come on, let's go . . . what about the alt-left that came charging at [indiscernible]—excuse me—what about the alt-left that came charging at the, as you say, the alt-right? Do they have any semblance of guilt? What about this? What about the fact that they came charging—they came

charging with clubs in their hands swinging clubs? Do they have any problem? I think they do. As far as I'm concerned, that was a horrible, horrible day—wait a minute, I'm not finished, I'm not finished, fake news—that was a horrible day. I will tell you something. I watched those very closely, much more closely than you people watched it. And you had, you had a group on one side that was bad. And you had a group on the other side that was also very violent. And nobody wants to say that, but I'll say it right now. You had a group—you had a group on the other side that came charging in without a permit, and they were very, very violent.

Trump went on to argue in favor of the protesters' official message, that of resisting efforts to dismantle the Robert E. Lee statue. Do that, he argued, and you establish a precedent for removing statues of historic figures, including America's first president, George Washington, who was a slave owner.

The press conference prompted condemnation from both Republicans and Democrats as well as resignations from high-profile business leaders participating in reform initiatives with the White House. But not everyone was outraged.

Bannon was thrilled with Trump's response. Despite the fact that he had been isolated in the administration for months, the *New York Times* reported that he consulted with Trump about the response to Charlottesville. Indeed, all public communications from the White House following the rally aligned with Bannon's reported long-standing advice to the president, as the *Times* reported it, "not to criticize far-right activists too severely for fear of antagonizing a small but energetic part of his base." The president's behavior at the press conference marked a breathtaking stand in Bannon's eyes—a stand for the importance of history, a stand on behalf of who he believed were righteous people on the streets made invisible by the Nazis next to them, and a courageous refusal to bow to media pressure.

Being in step with the president at this particular moment turned out to be a liability, however. When the president received blowback for his remarks, critics blamed the incident on Bannon's influence, meaning that his dismissal could palliate to the ongoing outcry. They could attribute Trump's racism to the presence in the White House of a man who had presided over a news organization—Breitbart—that produced consistently positive coverage of European identitarian groups and seemed obsessed with crime committed by African Americans; a man who had allegedly developed ways to stir racial animus as vice president of Cambridge Analytica; who had celebrated the online world of the alt-right; and who had a tendency to be drawn to racialist culture and literature, from the Nazi war-era films of Leni Riefenstahl to the writings of Jean Raspail, Charles Murray, and of course, Julius Evola.

Three days after Trump's second press conference, Steve Bannon resigned, under pressure.

On the same day that Trump gave the press conference, August 15, Jason Jorjani left both the AltRight Corporation and Arktos. Ask him why and he'll tell you that he left in part because his original vision for a more dynamic and encompassing alt-right movement seemed dead. He was especially sobered by user comments on his own AltRight site. "Iranians is brown poopoo people," rang one. The alt-right was a narrow white nationalist initiative after all, just as its most vocal critics alleged. There wasn't room for his cause there. The "Charlottesville disaster," as he referred to it, solidified those impressions in spectacular fashion.

That was all just part of the reason for his departure, however. For by this time, he had lost the confidence of his colleagues after months of promising them funding. No, the money from Bagley and the Londoner never came through. As far as he knew, there had been no progress with Jellyfish's micro-cities project and the black budget it was supposed to access. And as for the oil contract strategy? The petroleum engineer returned the document to him and said the job was outside of their competence. This man worked for one of the largest oil companies in the world, but it was outside of their competence.

The silence from Jellyfish afterward resounded. There would be no AltRight Corporation pumping out media and intellectualism with Jason at its helm. There would, in fact, be no alt-right lobbying effort worth the name in Washington, and no Traditionalist in the White House to lobby.

As he reflected on the past year, Jason grew suspicious that Michael Bagley and the Londoner had been deceiving and manipulating him from the beginning. He wondered whether the Londoner encouraged him to seek out the leadership of Arktos in order to implant him as an agent in an underhanded power play against Daniel Friberg; he speculated that perhaps the oil contract could have been a ploy to implicate him and his industry contact in an attempt to overthrow the Venezuelan government; and when he learned that the Trump administration was not interested in his visions of a future ultra-nationalist Iran, he wondered whether he wasn't deliberately mislead into thinking otherwise.

*In order to understand the motive behind an action, look at its effects*, Jason thought. This premature centralization of the alt-right without proper capital investment—this attempt to bring together the likes of Richard Spencer, Daniel Friberg, and Henrik Palmgren—destroyed the AltRight Corporation. It also destroyed his career.

I thought back to my early suspicions when he first told me about the Londoner, that the figure sounded too sensational to be true, and that he might have been a law enforcement plant and spy. A conspiracy, perhaps, targeting the alt-right and Jason.

JASON AND I SAT in Persepolis, the same New York restaurant where he had his ill-fated meetings with Michael Bagley and Richard Spencer. We were talking about everything that had happened that summer. The story he had told me had been unusual in the stakes involved and the aspirations, but it was in other respects the norm for the radical right. It was a story about infighting, the impossibility of controlling a message, and—after an unusual burst of optimism—failure.

But what about the Londoner, what about the promised connections to Bannon? What about the things that made Jason think that this time things might be different—was it all just a lie? Well, as he was about to tell me, the story doesn't end in Charlottesville. Things would get worse for him.

About a month after the Unite the Right rally, on September 19, 2017, the *New York Times* published an article featuring Jason. He had met a young Swedish man named Erik Hellberg earlier that spring at a gathering called the London Forum. And later, in June, the two reconnected for a drink at an Irish pub close to the Empire State Building. What Jason didn't know was that "Erik Hellberg" was really Patrik Hermansson, an anti-racist activist who had infiltrated rightist circles in Europe and the United States. He was wearing a hidden camera during their conversation at the pub, and quotes from that conversation—to his horror—were now appearing in one of the largest newspapers in the world.

"It's going to end with the expulsion of the majority of the migrants, including citizens who are of Muslim descent. That's how it's going to end. It's going to end with concentration camps, expulsions, and war, that's how it's going to end. At a cost of a few hundred million people," Jason had told the undercover activist. He had been characteristically articulate in form and grand in content. But in print this didn't sound good either: "We will have a Europe, in 2050, where the bank notes have Adolf Hitler, Napoleon Bonaparte, Alexander the Great. And Hitler will be seen like that: like Napoleon, like Alexander, not like some weird monster who is unique in his own category—no, he is just going to be seen as a great European leader. You know like we say in English, you don't make an omelet without breaking a few eggs."

Jason contended that he was describing a "nightmarish prediction of a future that would follow from Western policy makers' failure to address the Muslim migrant crisis" rather than his own ideals. He said further that the reference to "a few million people" described a potential war between India and Pakistan, and that reference to "eggs" described Richard Spencer's need to expel unserious actors from the alt-right. How could he have meant all those things? Jason argued that the recording of his conversation posted online and cited in the article was clipped and rearranged to alter the meaning of his statements. The audio/video posted online was indeed clipped together, and neither Hermansson—whom I managed to reach via a strong contact—nor the author of the *Times* article responded to my requests for an unedited version of the file.

When Jason wasn't appearing to endorse a genocide, he also spoke in vague terms about his plan with Jellyfish, which at that point, by midsummer, he knew was faltering.

"Let me tell you, I had contacts with the Trump administration. This AltRight Corporation was not just—like I came up with some harebrained idea by myself, like 'Oh, I'm just gonna . . .' No, no, no, no, no. The alt-right would become like a policy group for the Trump administration. And the guy who was the interface was Steve Bannon," Jason told the activist.

The *New York Times* contacted the White House for a reply to Jason's claims. A spokeswoman said, "We have no knowledge of any conversations or contact with this person."

Jason wasn't just out of the AltRight Corporation, which would soon be dormant. His university in New Jersey would eventually fire him, too.

LEAVING NEW YORK to fly home after dinner with Jason, I had my doubts as to whether he was ever on the brink of gaining a hearing with Steve Bannon. Along the way, I flipped through files on my computer, stopping at the end of the email correspondence that Jason had forwarded to me months ago. The last one from Jason was dated September 26, 2017. "Dear Michael," it read. "This past week has been the worst of my life." Jason's letter was a recounting of his downfall, of the weakening of his position with his alt-right business partners due to the failed promise of money, and of the devastating *New York Times* exposé. And it was accompanied by both threats and a request for help. He must have been seething, and also feeling vulnerable, when he wrote it. A bit grandiose, too. He concluded,

> It is not in your interest, or for that matter in the interests of
> the Trump Administration, for me to be put in a position where
> I am not only defamed but destitute. In that event, I am sure
> that [ ] could cover the cost of taking this whole matter to
> the courts—possibly even as high as the Supreme Court. You
> do not want me reduced to poverty and testifying under oath
> there. You and [ ] need to figure out how I am going to be
> honorably extricated from this miserable situation . . .

Michael Bagley responded in a brief message just a few days later, on September 29, 2017.

> Jason . . . I am just receiving your Skype message. I'm sorry for the developments on your side, but my group was never able to get our project off the ground. To this day, we never received any funding.

It seemed quite likely that Bagley and the Londoner had not taken Jason as seriously as he had taken them. And Jason seemed to have suffered from naiveté. There are a lot of Michael Bagleys running around Washington, guys (mostly) who exaggerate their influence and promise a lot. It takes an experienced hand to spot them, and Jason didn't have that experience.

I closed the email messages and opened up and played a recording I had on my computer. It was taped just a few days before Michael Bagley wrote that last reply to Jason. Bagley was being interviewed for an online radio show hosted by New York billionaire John Catsimatidis. Bagley, representing Jellyfish, was the main guest. The subject? Micro-cities. Bagley claimed, "We've come up with a design that we've talked with the White House about. In fact, President Trump alluded to 'refugee resettlements' in his UN speech. So we've been working with and talking to the State Department, the Department of Defense, and various countries including Niger, Somalia, and Jordan."

I didn't think Jason was lying to me about his experiences. But Bagley? I had my doubts about him, and I was ready to wrap up the story. It was a just a standard case of clumsiness and debacle in the far-right underground. But a few days after returning home, I received a startling message, a reply to a request I had almost forgotten. Months ago, I had asked a contact, an old-guard anti-racist activist, for some help identifying this Londoner figure. He hadn't heard of him, but said he would work his networks. I didn't elaborate on my work, but I told him I was writing a book about Bannon.

He explained that he now had a report from his network. He wouldn't share any details with me at this point, because what he had read left him concerned—about me. This was due to "the seriousness" of the subject—the Londoner, that is—and the possibility that he might have a real connection to Bannon or other power brokers. The prospect of the two of them collaborating seemed to him both plausible and worrying; it was the kind of scenario that would attract governmental oversight and intervention. My contact was now wondering about my motivations and allegiances. He inquired directly: Was I working on behalf of the U.S. government? Was I a secret agent?

I didn't know how to respond to that, nor what to think of the fact that it was the second time someone had suspected me of this in the past year. Perhaps the explanation I gave of myself—that I was just a music professor—didn't fly.

Regardless, after having learned that the organizational hub of the infamous alt-right movement was created to lobby the U.S. government on Iran policy, after having followed this story of collapse, I wanted to turn back to an ongoing collaboration that seemed to be advancing. I pulled out my recordings to listen to an interview I had conducted days ago, in rural Virginia, ahead of coming to New York.

## 20

# DEEP STATES

"HE WRITES IN . . . IN THE STYLE OF KINGS." OLAVO reclined in his chair and took a puff from his pipe before continuing his reverie on Traditionalism's patriarch, René Guénon. Olavo continued, "He is one of the most efficient critics of Western civilization."

How bizarre it is to hear the name Guénon in this place, at the end of a country road in rural Virginia, nestled among pines thrashing in a violent spring thunderstorm, in what neighbors must have assumed to be a massive garage abutting a modest one-level country home. That's where I sat with Olavo de Carvalho in the spring of 2019. It took this long, including being stood up on a trip from Colorado once before, and crossing paths once in the lobby of the Trump hotel in D.C., to reconnect with him after that memorable dinner at Bannon's Breitbart embassy.

What we were sitting in tonight wasn't in fact a garage, though I'm not sure what to call it. A white-painted vaulted ceiling lined with fluorescent lighting shone down on it all: monumental shelves of meticulously organized books consumed most of the interior space and framed the perimeter. A wooden crucifix loomed above everything, hung at the architectural focus, at the apex of the pointed wall. Beneath it, where one might expect to see a pulpit, stood a broad wooden desk. Olavo sat behind, and his guests would sit facing him. You could have called the place a library, an office, a cathedral, or even a studio. It was here where he filmed his YouTube videos which, along with his ferocious tweets, articles, books, and radio podcasts, now reached hundreds of thousands in his homeland.

Olavo's routines had been fundamentally transformed after populist Jair Bolsonaro was elected in Brazil. The media had described Olavo as the new administration's mastermind, and journalists and governmental officials had been calling incessantly and streaming to his Virginia property. "Our lives became hell," he lamented to me, explaining why it had taken so long to respond to my requests for a visit.

This newfound fame had not quashed his penchant for conflict, however. He had recently lashed out against Brazilian government officials surrounding the president, including high-ranking members of the military as well as the vice president, Hamilton Mourão, all of whom he accused of seeking to undermine Bolsonaro. He feared in particular they were maintaining the country's China connection even as the president was working to reorient Brazil toward the West. The exchanges signaled the sharpening of a divide in Brazilian politics, with the country's military establishment and the vice president on one side, and the president, Olavo, and Olavo-friendly ministers (Ricardo Vélez Rodríguez and Ernesto Araújo)—all of whom were associating with Steve Bannon—on the other. Recently a body of high-ranking generals met to discuss the "Olavo problem," and during a public press conference, Vice President Mourão stated that the philosopher should stay out of politics and "return to being an astrologer."

These days Olavo's interest in the esoteric was most often invoked as an insult against him. Perhaps that explained his reluctance to attach himself to Traditionalism: why, when I had asked about Guénon's influence on him—the central question I sought answers to—he named simply Guénon's criticism of science, a peripheral rather than a signature feature of Guénon's thought. Olavo kept the Traditionalists at arm's length even when speaking in general terms. Many philosophers, he explained, "are right in everything they affirm, and wrong in everything they deny. Guénon is the opposite. He is correct in everything he denies and wrong in everything he affirms."

I struggled to think of Olavo's responses to me as mere strategy, however, if only because he had less and less reason to fear and accommodate critics. In the aftermath of the vice president's attack on him, a blistering social media response ensued in Olavo's defense, headed by none other than Bolsonaro's sons, with the apparent tacit permission of their father. Indeed, in the midst of the calamity, on May 1, 2019, Jair Bolsonaro awarded Olavo the Order of the Rio Branco—Brazil's highest diplomatic honor. When Olavo had come into conflict with Brazil's vice president, the president took *Olavo's* side. Such was his status in Brazilian politics. But Olavo's greatest weapon was less formal. As he and I spoke, his wife, Roxane, came to us and opened her laptop to a video filmed days earlier, on May 26. The scene was a square in a major Brazilian city filled with thousands clad in blue, yellow, and green, waving Brazilian flags and chanting, "Olavo, Brazil loves you!"

This bizarre cyberspace dialogue between the streets of São Paulo and gritty rural America had given Olavo something powerful, an amuletic mass of public support allowing him to harry Brazil's entrenched power structure at will. Critics could call him a loony and a weirdo, but a sizable portion of the Brazilian population wasn't listening to them, and for this reason they were struggling to control the conversation. Reportedly, the vice president was considering resigning over the controversy. Still, Olavo's fatalistic pessimism remained. "I'm not interested in Brazil's political future," he insisted to me with a chuckle in his voice. "Because it will be bad. There is nothing we can do."

I wanted to inquire further, but was diverted. Roxane returned to the room, purse hung over her shoulder. "We're ready to roll." It was time for ice cream. "We can continue talking along the way," Olavo said, so we made for the door.

OLAVO TOOK SHOTGUN in the minivan with me sitting behind. Roxane drove, and behind her, to my left, sat an assistant—along, it seemed, for the primary purpose of recording me. Olavo doubts the ability of journalists and scholars to write about him fairly, and their parallel surveillance seemed to be a precautionary measure to contest a false quotation. That was the most logical explanation. But perhaps he was planning to write about me as well, or at least to give himself the option to do so in colorful terms should some form of retaliation be warranted. Mutually assured destruction: I had experienced it before as an ethnographer, and it often yielded the best interviews. When "subjects" know they can fight back, they often speak more freely.

I rested my recorder on the back shoulder of his seat during the ride. His assistant sat with her recorder in hand, the receiver pointed at me as we headed east to a shopping mall complex at the edge of Petersburg. Circling through the empty parking lot—it was nearly ten P.M.—we pulled to the front of an IHOP restaurant. As we stepped out and began walking toward the restaurant, I noticed the bumper stickers on the back of the minivan, a heart-shaped American flag symbol and a yellow-

and-black "don't tread on me" decal, the hallmark of the Tea Party movement that mobilized in response to the election of Barack Obama.

We ordered a round of late-night breakfast food: omelets and bacon for them, lingonberry pancakes for me. Olavo was the only one following through with the plan for ice cream as well, asking for an ornate sundae. His mind seemed focused on geopolitics, so we continued. "I believe it would be good if Brazil was sided with the United States, but this will not happen, because all of the military are for Chinese—they love China and they hate the United States. And most of the politicians, too. So Brazil is an ally of China. An instrument of China."

"And you don't think that will ever change?" I asked.

"If the United States gave them more money! Ha! [. . .] All those people, they only think of money." There was melancholy in his voice, a hint that he had learned to relish his sorrow and disappointment when he talked about Brazil. "It's a funny, tragic country."

We were interrupted by the waitress. "Would you like your sundae before or after, sir?" Olavo shrugs and smiled at her, saying with a look what he didn't want to say aloud. "Well then, I'll bring it right out." Roxane cast him a disapproving glance.

Meanwhile, I was pondering how the scenario he just explained would square with Bannon and other Traditionalists. If Brazil's unity with the United States was to occur based solely on the quantitative results of a global game of monetary one-upmanship, would that really satisfy those yearning for a spiritual reorganization of the world?

Such an outcome wasn't likely in Brazil's case, but it could be possible in America and in parts of Europe, he said. "Things aren't going so bad there. People are waking up—many people, in Poland, and Hungary, and Romania. [. . .] Realizing the spiritual basis of civilization. Now they know that society cannot be based in what they call money, science, and technology. It's absurd. If you don't have any contact with God, we're lost."

I was still grappling with his pessimism and interjected. "But you don't see that happening in Brazil? An interest in spiritual . . ."

Our server walked by and Roxane caught her attention. "Can you bring the sundae after his meal?"

"Yes, ma'am."

Olavo looked a bit disappointed but kept on speaking. "The people of Brazil—the poor people, the simple people. They understand things much better than the intellectuals. Brazilian people have a kind of instinct of reality." Why is that? "I believe it is because their life is very hard. They don't have time to fantasize." But then Olavo clarified that it was more than just realism that gave this population a chance. "The Brazilian people, they're very Christian. The poor people. Under the middle class. Some are Catholic, some are Protestant, but they really believe in Jesus Christ."

That was Deep Brazil, as he also called it, an obvious analogue to the rural Real America that he had come to love in his new home. But the two weren't equivalent in their commitment to spiritual values. Whereas in the United States, society had been formed around the church, in Brazil, society had coalesced around the military infrastructure. The legacy was that even the rural poor—even Deep Brazil—continued to trust the military above all, and Olavo didn't think he could change that, as urgently as he felt change was needed and as urgently as the military ought to be labeled a failure in its own mission to advance the interests of the nation.

And the problem of institutions and institutional trust didn't end there. Olavo took glee in telling me, "if I were to show you pictures of Brazilian universities, you would only see naked people having sex. They go to the university to have sex, and if you try to stop them they revolt, they start crying, they say you are an oppressor."

The Bolsonaro administration had planned to reduce funding for education and culture, but Olavo anticipated that the reforms would be minor. If the administration cut what he considered to be an appropriate amount, say 2 percent, the protests would be devastating. So there wasn't going to be any fundamental change. The universities would continue to be a front like all institutions in Brazil—in this instance, a front for fornication. "It's absurd," Olavo concluded, "everything is fake. No reality. We live in another world." *A world of simulations*, I thought, hearing echoes of Steve Bannon as Olavo spoke.

Guénon's writings, in Olavo's mind, had a limited ability to explain what was happening in Brazil. "The problem is, Guénon takes all this in a very material sense. For example, he believes in a doctrine of cycles. I don't believe in cycles. When many things are going downwards, other things are going upwards—there is no cycle of decadence. It is impossible that everything decays at the same time. History is full of contradictions and opposite movements. And this is the most interesting part."

As our food arrived, he continued: "Cycles don't exist in the material sense. 'The cycle' is an interpretation."

Materialism, for Olavo, seemed tantamount with those facts about the universe that were knowable to humans, such that by claiming to understand the currents of time, Guénon was treating time as something material. Olavo, with what he was saying, seemed to be wanting to out-spirit Traditionalism's patriarch by invoking time's mystery. "You know, when someone asked Jesus Christ, 'When is the end of the world?' he said, 'I don't know, only God the father knows.' If even Jesus doesn't know, how would I, or René Guénon . . . ha! I believe most of these philosophers and spiritual masters, they are very presumptuous. They don't respect God."

Olavo cuts into his bacon and spots the waitress walking by again. "The ice cream sundae, please."

"Yes, sir."

Roxane rolls her eyes—accepting defeat, it seems—as we move on to a new topic, the resurgence of Traditionalism in the world today, and why he does not feel inspired by it.

"The whole of the Traditionalist school is falling under the power of the Russians." He thought that much of this was based on the idea, propagated by international exchanges of Traditionalists, that Russia was the pinnacle of a spiritual hierarchy consecrated by the pope. "All this is fake. It's only political power." It seemed he considered his efforts to defrock Russia during his exchanges with Dugin a failure.

Still, Bannon's initiative was one he couldn't help but support. He explained: "Bannon believes in an alliance between the United States and Russia. I hope he's right, but I believe he's not. It would be a great thing. And of course if he asks me to help him, I will. I will say, 'It will not work, but I will help you.'" It seemed Bannon had at least briefed Olavo on his current activities, which, as regards Russia, had no other fronts I knew of other than the courtship of Dugin. Perhaps pressure from two Traditionalists—rather than one—was what it would take to move the Russian philosopher.

Olavo's stated willingness to participate didn't make sense to me. In his mind, the spiritual credentials of Russia were lacking, but apparently not so much that they couldn't participate in the crafting of a more virtuous geopolitical order. A contradiction? I asked. Perhaps, but that didn't bother Olavo. He explained in terms that had me feeling lost at first.

"In this kind of studies"—by *studies,* he meant ways of

thinking—"and in life in general, the most important thing is to learn to admit contradictions. We will never solve them. Only God knows the point of unity. We never know. So we have to cope with contradictions of reality all the time. And also at many levels of reality—things that are opposed at a certain level can be together at another level."

He went on: "In certain aspects, this alliance between the United States and Russia is possible; in others, not. So we have to cope with this contradiction, and I pray to God to solve it, because we can't . . ."

The waitress came with the sundae, and Olavo's eyes lit up like a child's.

"Is it China that you fear, or Islam?" I asked, wanting to know what benefit he saw in a potential U.S.-Russia partnership.

"I believe China is the most dangerous. Because they don't have a real sense of humanity. They think people are things. [. . .] They believe you can substitute one person for another one. They are not good people." Lure Russia toward the United States, and China is isolated.

ROXANE PAID for my meal, against my protests, and we made our way back to the minivan and on home. Shortly thereafter we said our goodbyes. "God bless you," they said to me as I walked out the door, and I replied in kind.

I wondered, as I traveled north, about Bannon's interest in Olavo. Both to varying degrees were seen as ideologues of populist governments. And Olavo's reputation as a Traditionalist separated him, in Bannon's eyes, from the vast sea of conservative and populist thinkers throughout the world. But was that characterization still valid? Was it ever?

Olavo was unique, he would proudly tell you—a philosopher,

but not a disciple. As he wrote to Aleksandr Dugin years earlier, this gave him the right and the ability to change his opinion as often and in whatever ways he wanted to. It also made him an enigma to others, including to me. Set against the grid of formulaic ideological divisions, Olavo's individuality and the eccentricity of his background rendered him a trickster figure of uncertain origin and species, belonging and beholden to no one. An ideal position for a scholar and a commentator, I've long thought, for figures of this kind often gain insight, speak truths, and prompt action in ways others cannot, just as the tricksters of Indo-European mythology did.

And yet as his words ran through my head during my drive, I began to see an internal consistency to his thinking, as if the once-confusing ensemble of his philosophical, spiritual, and political engagements was in fact delivering a unified message. At the same time, it showed why Traditionalism, of all lenses through which to view society, was surfacing in the new right-wing populism.

Olavo's criticism of Brazilian society is essentially a criticism of its materialism. Sex and money—bodies and goods—constitute the core pursuits of his home society. All of it, even those sectors forged in aspiration of transcendent values—patriotism, culture, and spirit—are infected with materialism, with the mind-set of the slave and of the merchant. University sages have become pimps. Warriors in the military, simple tradesmen. And the Catholic Church, all of the above. That is the dark age of Brazil, modernism's Kali Yuga in the tropics, where a faux Traditionalist hierarchy is leveled to the institution of the military, which is in turn a simulated front for promoting humanity's lowest values. A society of the slave lurking behind a mirage of the warrior.

I was beginning to understand why a reader of Guénon would become a champion of Bolsonaro. Olavo's focus on Traditionalism's opposition to modern science, though seemingly an apolitical subject, may have been more relevant to his analysis of political and social life than I first thought. In writing and in conversation he waxes seamlessly from criticisms of the scientific process to critiques of modern knowledge to criticism of the institutions whose authority rests obliquely on modernist knowledge. It is in that final step when Traditionalism and populism can come together, when we can draw a line between astrology, alchemy, and the president. Not only are Brazil's media, education system, and government corrupted by money and self-interests in his mind, but they are purveyors of ignorance, too, because of their blind investment in modern science and its inability to account for, let alone value, spirituality. The only immateriality they will admit is the abstractions of mathematics, which themselves serve to confuse as well, Olavo contends. Like Bannon, Olavo finds a trace of solace among the poor and uneducated, those most distanced from institutionalized education and knowledge production. In Brazil as in the United States, they are the keepers of spirit, those who have achieved a measure of community and context otherwise elusive in modernity. They are neither mathematical abstractions nor the bearers of hollow titles granted by hollow modern institutions. They are reality. They are the core.

There were more parallels to be found. Rightist populism speaks of an opposition between a cosmopolitan establishment and a rooted people. Traditionalism sees the same divide, but could label it as one where technocratic mercantilists confront lay priests who have transcended time. Further, they share the conviction that the standard divisions of contemporary politics are an illusion: populists on the grounds that all politicians are corrupt; Traditionalists on the claim that the left and the right in the modern West are both progressive and materialist.

How bizarre was the notion that the worlds of Traditionalism and right-wing populism infused each other. I thought first of the cultures surrounding each that appear so distant from one another—hicks and rednecks, as Olavo affectionately calls them, and the bizarre occultists of Traditionalism. But stylistic and social differences might just be superficial wrapping for deeper commonality.

Thinking in these terms changed the way I looked at Olavo. It made his ostensible journey seem like no journey at all: his activities since discovering Traditionalism in the 1970s would instead appear variations on a theme rather than a dilettantish succession of gimmicks and reinventions. The leader of the tariqa and the gun-toting cowboy of rural Virginia—they were not only the same person but perhaps the same persona. Like the Native American and Muslim outfits of his old shaykh Frithjof Schuon, they were wrappings of a single core. There were likely very few individuals in the world with whom he could identify extensively, people who were both unvarnished populists and airy esotericists. People like Steve.

# 21

## THE RECKONING

ON JULY 25, 2019, I TRAVELED TO A CORDONED-OFF compound just west of El Paso where Texas, New Mexico, and Mexico meet. It is here where the We Build the Wall organization managed to construct nearly a mile of border wall on privately owned land with private money—over $20 million was raised on GoFundMe. The structure was impressive. Diamond-shaped posts of eighty-year steel stretching about twenty feet up in the air, buried in seven feet of cement that extend a considerable distance off on the north side, allowing for patrol vehicles to drive alongside and discouraging simple tunneling. The path of the wall shot up the steppe side of a mountain. It was the very kind of terrain that critics said was unconducive to a wall—jagged, gnarly land that seemed to constitute a border in itself, but which could still be traversed by the bold and the desperate. The idea with this structure was to cover an expanse that the U.S. government was likely to pass over, citing logistical concerns. We'll take the hard stuff, the builders reasoned. Hopefully Trump will cover the rest.

Steve was proud of the wall. He'd had his share of setbacks in recent years. Hardly anything in Europe was working: his plans for a school in Trisulti were in legal limbo, collaborators in his anti-papal campaign had dropped off, and the Movement—his umbrella organization for bolstering Europe's nationalists—had flopped. But the wall stood out as a victory—small, nascent—in the face of doubters. A few hundred local donors, as well as national anti-immigration dignitaries like Kris Kobach, Tom Tancredo, Candace Owens, Donald Trump Jr., and Steve himself, had gathered at this spot for a symposium on borders, walls, and the future of the United States. The assembly was giddy at times; this was a rally more than a symposium. And some of the organizers were wondering aloud whether it shouldn't be made into an annual event. The jovial mood aside, I couldn't understand their thinking. They were staging this in the worst place and time imaginable, in the desert during the hottest part of the summer. Attendees had already been transported to the hospital for heat exhaustion.

Steve and I found time to speak in the midst of his packed schedule. I was there not to probe into the activities of We Build the Wall, but with a question I had delayed asking for months.

"Have you met Michael Bagley?"

It was a loaded question if there ever was one, a trial inquiry into a far larger topic. I wanted to know whether he was aware of or participated in a formal attempt to link the world of the alt-right to the White House; whether he knew that his own Traditionalism had been identified as a potential avenue for outsiders to influence President Donald Trump and advance a geopolitical agenda.

"Michael Bagley . . . how do you spell it?"

No, he said he didn't know the name. Not Jellyfish, either. He switched into inquisitor mode, peppering me with queries, which did not portend well for the fate of the interview: when he gets like this, I have little chance of guiding the conversation. I gave him my best quick overview, starting with Bagley's past as a staffer for Senator Patty Murray, his joining Jellyfish in 2011 with former Blackwater intelligence figures. Then I told him about Bagley's initiatives: the micro-cities concept for Northern Africa and the push to refashion Iran with a new regime and a geopolitical perspective that counted it as part of the West. Steve was quick to interject.

"This Bagley, he sounds like a visionary."

I got to the point. "They claimed that they were in touch with the White House about the micro-city idea."

Steve shrugged. "People are always making pitches to the Department of Defense and the State Department, and thing-umajig. And [micro-cities], it's not a crazy idea. There was a lot of interest in airbases in southern Libya for the simple reason to interdict the migrants there and give them some sort of ac-commodation that then could sort this thing out before they got to the coastline. The reason the micro-cities doesn't sound that robust is that most of the things I've heard of, most of the things people have talked about is, don't let migrants get—if the mi-grants get to the coast, they are getting to Europe. And so the key is—maybe a micro-city works. I just don't know. I've never heard the pitch before. And I haven't heard Bagley's name."

Time to update him. "Bagley's in jail right now."

I HAD FOLLOWED the whole thing through legal documents that were being updated daily. On April 16, 2019, Michael Bagley had laundered $50,000 in cash that he had received from two men with whom he had been meeting in and around his hometown of Alexandria, Virginia. The funds they gave to him, he understood, was drug money from Mexican cartels, and if he managed to securely transfer it into a safe American bank account, he could keep 10 percent. Bagley did just that, using a complicated scheme involving crowdfunding sites like GoFundMe. After completing that task, he was given a larger sum to launder, $100,000, on May 13. Cleared again—Bagley was good at this. On June 10, he and one of the men met again for an additional handoff of $101,000. These were all smaller installments of the larger sum they had agreed upon: $20 million. As they parted ways, Bagley said, "I want to let you know that I'm also moving [laundering money] for El Mayo in Mexico City as well." Ismael "El Mayo" Zambada García is the suspected leader of the infamous Sinaloa Cartel.

One month later, on July 10, in a parking lot by an office and apartment building at 300 North Lee Street, in Old Town Alexandria—just a block away from Founders Park and the shore of the Potomac River—Michael Bagley was invited into a car. Inside sat Bryce Oleski, special agent of the FBI, and two associates. The whole thing had been a sting operation: the men Bagley had been laundering money for during the past months were both FBI informants. Special Agent Oleski and his team advised Bagley of his rights.

Sitting in the car, Bagley described the whole thing as a "rabbit hole," and added he was lying when earlier he claimed to work for El Mayo of the Sinaloa Cartel. When the FBI agents asked him why he did it, Bagley said it was to fund his business. He was the sole account holder for Jellyfish Partners, likewise its sole employee on record, the FBI thought. But he told the agents about a plan to make something called "micro-cities" for migrants in Mexico, and claimed to have spoken with Mexican government officials and U.S. diplomatic staff about the idea. He even said he had met with President Andrés Manuel López Obrador's staff and the Mexican president himself for a handful of minutes. The agents presented a copy of a text-message photo showing Bagley and President Obrador taking a selfie together.

Yes, Bagley said to the agents, the Mexican government liked the micro-cities idea. But there were no tangible contracts or agreements resulting from these efforts. An agent listening to it all in the car wrote, "Bagley has never gotten past the discussion phase on his proposed micro-cities projects." At the time of his arraignment, Bagley was being represented by a public defender, facing up to twenty years in prison.

I relayed all this to Steve. He was amused with the story, but made a point of distancing himself from it all.

"You are telling me a staffer, a Democratic staffer, on a milk-toast staff"—Senator Patty Murray is arguably one of the least controversial figures in the U.S. Congress—"ends up getting some Blackwater guys together, trying to build cities in North Africa to help migrants, and to get money for it he starts laundering money for Mexican drug cartels?"

I nodded. And he elaborated. "Some guy, not altruistically, is trying to build micro-cities for migrants to 'keep them safe' and laundering money for Mexican drug cartels—that's the worst thing in the world, and a guy that the Mexican drug cartels would think has expertise, it's a guy who really knows what he is doing. So my point is, if you know money laundering, you're a bad guy by definition." He was giving me the signal to move on to other questions. "I don't want to hear about no micro-cities. The guy's a fuckin' bad guy."

I SHIFT TOPICS, kind of. "Have you heard of Jason Jorjani?" I knew the answer to that one, but was still surprised by Steve's response.

"I know the name."

Just know the name? I continued, without mentioning the last time we had an exchange about Jason. "A pretty complicated guy, he gave me a book to give to you, *Prometheus and Atlas*." I didn't feel great about serving as a courier for the people I was studying. But I did make a commitment to Jason. Steve seemed interested.

"*Prometheus and Atlas*. Sounds cool. Is he on a [university] faculty somewhere?"

"Yes, but he got booted—"

"I've heard about this guy."

"He took over Arktos, the publishing company."

"Ahhh! Arktos." Evola, Dugin, he had gone through their stuff. Sophisticated. But he had never remarked on Arktos before when I mentioned it. Strange.

"But he got in cahoots with Richard Spencer."

"Oh, is he a white nationalist?"

My face contorted as I started in on a series of *well*s and *um*s until I worked my way to an answer. "He founded an organization called the AltRight Corporation, and he was thinking early on—"

"He thought he was going to brand it? Ha." The alt-right, that is.

"Yes, he thought it was going to be branded in a different way. He wanted to gather all of the anti-establishment, anti-Republican party, but he's also a Traditional—"

"But that is what alt-right started as!"

"Yes, but . . ."—perhaps I was just not presenting Jason clearly—"he also is a Traditionalist who was open to working with Richard Spencer, who branded the term."

"Well, he didn't brand it. It was the mainstream media who wanted to brand it."

Steve was poised to sympathize. After all, he, too, had initially understood the term as meaning something other than shorthand for organized white nationalism. He took a sip from his water bottle, and that gave me a moment to expand on Jason.

I explained that Jason is a Traditionalist, a Zoroastrian as well, and an Iranian nationalist. And that was how he got hooked up with Bagley, based initially on the belief that "Persia used to be part of the West. And that was Jason Jorjani's interest to see that Persia would work its way back to being part of the West. And—"

"Were they part of the West?" I couldn't finish my sentence before Steve jumped in to question what he just heard. Forget about Jason. "I would actually say Persia has been the representative of orientalism to the West. I wouldn't say they are part of the West. I think in Roman history they have been the great enemy of Rome, right? If you look back two thousand years, it's China, Rome, and Persia, you know."

Sounds like Steve would have needed considerable convincing to be receptive to Jason's message. And Steve didn't see much novelty in someone trying to lobby the White House on Iran policy with an agenda opposing the Islamic Republic and the mullahs that run it. "There are guys who have been running around on Iran for twenty, thirty years. Iran is a lifestyle for some people. They're obsessed with Iran. Though they're not into Zoroastrianism. They're into mullahs that are lit on fire."

After he spoke, I could see him pondering Jason a bit more. Would a Traditionalist foreign policy not entail the union of Iran as much as Russia with the West? I was ready to ask. "But why does a guy who is that sophisticated get hooked up with Richard Spencer?" Something about Jason's story as I presented it made him sound suspect. "Richard Spencer is a goofball, and you can't get in business with goofballs like that."

Steve was hurrying me along, signaling that it was time for the interview to end. I, meanwhile, was struggling to explain the broader significance of this story: that the most encompassing alt-right organization was designed as a ploy to get to him, ignited not only by his political advance, not only by his perceived openness toward white nationalists, but also and especially on account of the novelty of his having been a Traditionalist in power.

I took his hint to wrap up, though, and began to pack my recorder. As we departed, he asked about my plans for later. "You've got to go out booming." Juárez, of course, was within walking distance.

I RETURNED HOME from El Paso on July 28, 2019. The Rocky Mountain aspens were in full summer bloom. It was just past lunch and I waited until my toddlers had gone down for a nap. I tiptoed to the back door, slipped out onto the porch, and called Jason.

I explained what Steve had said—that he knew Jason's name, but not Bagley's. I added, "For what it's worth, I believe him."

Jason wasn't moved by my words. "Well, somebody is lying. Either Bannon or the guy who is sitting in jail right now for dealing with Mexican drug cartels." Bagley and the Londoner told Jason explicitly that they had contacts with Bannon.

I was growing impatient. The Jellyfish guys were phonies. Reality had caught up with Bagley in the back seat of an FBI car. He confronted the fact that he had been tricked; Jason was due for a similar reckoning. "Jason," I said with audible exasperation, "the guy is being represented by a public defender. He doesn't have any money. He's ruined. And he just spilled everything to the FBI."

"He definitely could be a fake, Ben. I've said that all along. But I have to admit something doesn't make sense about all this. First, the FBI seems to think that Jellyfish is based in Washington, D.C., and that it has no employees and is bankrupt and so on. No, Jellyfish is based in Europe, and its Washington branch was just a tentacle. And like I said to you earlier, Michael Bagley is not in its leadership. He is an underling, expendable. He might have been thrown under the bus by the people above."

I took a deep breath, but paused. In fact, I had lingering questions about the whole affair, too. Namely, why would Bagley be so desperate to get money for this micro-cities project? And why would the FBI have invested so many resources to catch him? There was as of yet no evidence that he had laundered money for an actual drug cartel, just the fake one created by the FBI. So what had he done to get on their radar in the first place? I also didn't understand how Jellyfish, according to the FBI, still existed as a legal business entity. I had spoken to baffled former employees who claimed to have opened and closed the company twice: once in Delaware, once in Wyoming. How could Bagley have reopened it? Jellyfish was a strange entity. Indeed, I believe I had been near to receiving an interview with General Michael Flynn. But when his handler asked for the name of the intelligence firm I was interested in speaking about, and I replied, "Jellyfish," I received a quick and blunt no. I tried following up for weeks: they would never respond to me again.

There was even more I could have said to Jason. I was fairly certain I had learned the identity of his Londoner. I had found a guy long involved in occultists and paranormal circles—he directed an association on the paranormal during the early 1990s. He had also participated in New Rightist and Traditionalist circles in London for years and was an enthusiast for Aleksandr Dugin's Eurasianism and National Bolshevism. He had creepy social media profiles: he often posted a bizarre combination of skull and chaos-sign icons along with articles about Steve Bannon and Michael Flynn. His connections with wealthy Muslims were real. They included the former emir of Qatar and, of equal note, a wealthy, well-known rabble-rouser—a half-Iranian Iranian nationalist from the UK named Darius Guppy. Guppy, like Michael Bagley, had been caught in elaborate illegal schemes to raise money for unclear purposes, and had once conspired with his friend and fellow Old Etonian British prime minister Boris Johnson to have a journalist physically beaten.

Those were the connections that had so worried the anti-fascist activist who had helped me investigate this Londoner, for the information outlined the possibility that Jason had been contacted by someone with channels to power. His and Bagley's circle of contacts also included the CEO of a media company who moved between Mexico and London and who published a website tracking oil prices and trading—that's probably where the Venezuela documents (for yet another money raising scheme) came from. And this Londoner figure was also registered from 2013 until the present as the director of Jellyfish Europe Limited. If nothing else, that information corroborated a bit of what Jason had just told me—namely, that Michael Bagley seemed not to be Jellyfish's sole employee, claims of the FBI aside.

I also had contact information now, a handful of ways to reach out to the Londoner directly. But the number of informed individuals who had warned me against doing that had now reached three, two of them mentioning the fact that I had children. In another life I would have ignored the warnings, but not now. I'm a music professor.

A FEW WEEKS LATER, on September 1, I was in Budapest.

"The Vaishnavas here have surely made an offering of the food, which means that Krishna has come into the food. The food is 'non-different from Krishna,' which means we just ate Krishna." I thought to myself of Steve Bannon's favorite of Guénon's books, *Man and His Becoming According to the Vedanta*, which stresses divine infusion of everything in the world, and thus the constant presence of the spiritual.

John Morgan and I were at Govinda's, the Hare Krishna restaurant in Budapest on Vigyázó Ferenc street, nestled between
the banks of the Danube and the increasingly vacant Central
European University. John was on a return visit, both to the city
and to the world of Hare Krishna. Perhaps for that reason there
was a mood of reminiscence in the air.

He remained a writer and book editor for the white nationalist online portal Counter-Currents, and he did freelance editing
and authorship for a range of global interests on the "dissident
right," as he puts it. Some of the people I had been studying
for this book came into my life only recently—Bannon, for example, only a year and a half ago. John? I had been following his
career and talking with him for close to a decade. I'd seen him
move between organizations and roles, watched as opportunities
and fortunes waxed and waned. And it was clear that the person
I encountered today had a different outlook than he did a few
years earlier. In the wake of Trump's election, he was overcome
by a wave of optimism, even a sense of responsibility, as a long-
standing intellectual agent in the scene. The True Right's time of
exile had ended; the tiger's knees had grown weak.

How did he look back on those days now? Naive indulgence
in a fantasy. It died, the fantasy—maybe with Trump's bombing
of Syria, maybe with Charlottesville, maybe with Bannon's departure from the White House, or with the news that Bannon's
Traditionalism was less doctrinaire than he might have hoped.
He should never have forsaken the pessimism that was once such
a fundamental piece of his worldview.

We finished our meal, headed up from the cavernous dining
room of Govinda and up onto Budapest's sparkling pedestrian
thoroughfares. We walked toward St. Stephen's Basilica just to
the east. It houses what is said to be the right hand of St. Stephen,
the first king of Hungary. What I like about it most, though, is
in its north tower—a bell with an astonishingly pure overtone se-

ries. As we made our way, I briefed him on the story I had to tell
about Dugin, Olavo, and Steve; about Jason and Bagley; about its
precedents, oddities, mysteries; as well as about my musings on
the meaning of it all. John works at a white nationalist blog portal, yes. But he's also an irreplaceable resource on matters dealing
with Traditionalism and the contemporary right.

Here and there he interjected a thought or a correction to
keep me honest, but he mainly just listened. The basilica came
into sight. "You want to know the strange thing?" John said.
"Back when we formed Arktos, we agreed specifically that we
would never be connected to a political party or movement. Because we knew it wouldn't work. You just can't combine Traditionalism, philosophy, and ideas of that kind with politics."

Can't combine Traditionalism with politics *easily*, I imagined
Bannon replying. Take the actions of the right people, at the right
time, with reckless ambition and industry—by virtue of the absurd, as Kierkegaard would put it—and you can advance the currents of time and revive eternity. If you are the type of person who
understands, if you see above time and have the will to act, you
have to make the transition: you have to try.

# 22

# WAR FOR ETERNITY

IT'S SEVEN-THIRTY IN THE MORNING, EARLY FALL 2019—the last time I would meet Steve—and he and I were at the dining room table in his D.C. townhouse. The flashy space in pastels where he continues to host world leaders for lavish dinners looked gray, with only a dim cloud-covered sunrise filtering through the windows. Steve cast himself in the same color palette this morning, with a weathered blue button-down shirt and a day-old beard of silver. The townhouse was sleepy, and so was I. Steve, however, was bursting with energy. Coffee would have given me a chance of keeping up with him as he spoke a mile a minute, but I had come to expect more austere receptions when I met him alone like this. Caffeine would have to wait.

During the year and a half that I had spent speaking with him, I had seen his fortunes shift back and forth without any discernible direction or current. Journalists labeling him "irrelevant" have come and gone throughout 2018. He may have overcome such commentary based on his overall persistence rather than through any major accomplishments.

He had a drive, like nothing I've ever seen before, but also a sense of his own importance to go with it. My research assistant Kelsey has a theory about his code name, the one he asked me to give to hotel reception desks when coming to see him: Alec Guinness. She thought Steve used the name to associate himself with one of the British actor's most beloved characters: Obi-Wan Kenobi from *Star Wars*. Obi-Wan, who was a master teacher, the torchbearer of a warrior-scholar tradition; who channels an immaterial and intangible power—the Force—which no longer has an institutional home after the Jedi council is destroyed, but which nonetheless is omnipresent and accessible to those who search for it; Obi-Wan, who becomes more powerful after he is killed and becomes a spirit rather than a material body; Obi-Wan, who finds and promotes a farmer, a peasant—Luke Skywalker—to destroy the technocratic Empire.

*Self-aggrandizing* wouldn't be a strong enough word. Still, I could attest to the fact that Bannon continues to be swarmed by people demanding his time—not only media but also politicians and influencers of various ideological persuasions, within the United States and abroad. They ask his advice in punditry, publishing, and parliamentarianism. Some of that activity has been leaked to media, some hasn't. Meanwhile, writer Michael Wolff was speculating that Steve and President Trump were moving toward collaborating again. Steve was frequently appearing on television as a pundit, often as a defender of Trump, and within a few months' time he would even launch a radio show from the basement below us to propagandize against the efforts to impeach the president. He had put Europe behind him, so most of his public commentary these days dealt either with Trump or with China, and that is what we were talking about.

I wanted a final update on his interactions with Dugin, and there was relatively little to report. The two had not spoken since their meeting in November 2018. That wasn't a sign of disinterest or hostility. Dugin had a deadline for finishing a book on Iranian civilization and spirituality for a Russian publisher. There were reports of personal problems, too. I had spoken with Dugin a few weeks ago, on August 10, 2019. He still refused to discuss—even confirm or disconfirm—his meeting with Bannon, though it was clear in our conversations that he was responding to positions and ideas from their earlier exchange. During our August interview, and the one I was having with Steve today, I realized that I was playing a role of mediator between them: my interviews were allowing their conversation to continue.

Steve's coordination with Olavo's people, in contrast, continued apace. Steve would be hosting Brazil's foreign minister Ernesto Araújo in a few days, ahead of a highly unconventional speech for the Heritage Foundation in which the Brazilian would argue that the West needed to regain its trust in "symbolism." All of that reflection on Westernness coming from Brazilians was in line with Bannon's aim to pull Brazil away from its key trade partner, China, and toward the United States, primarily on cultural and spiritual, rather than economic, grounds.

And as for Russia's integration with China, Steve thought it had only gotten worse since his first meeting with Dugin in November 2018. The result will not be the emergence of a "multipolar world," Steve asserted to me, but instead the rule of the Eurasian landmass by a single coalition of forces—unipolarity within that key geopolitical sphere. And the reason for all of this mess, according to Bannon, "is the secular order's rejection of Russia"—that is to say, the liberal West's opposition to Putin on the grounds of democracy and human rights. "We have forced what should be one of our most important allies into this."

The most urgent solution, Steve said, was not trade deals, military treaties, high-level meetings between Trump and Putin and Xi Jinping and the like. No, it was getting to Dugin. "Dugin is key," he said. But from Steve's perspective, getting Dugin to change his stance—ideally to begin agitating intellectually for ties between the United States and Russia in ways he had with Turkey years ago—would be a daunting task. Steve said in a sober assessment of Dugin that "if he's living in Shanghai, the CPC—he's an agent, they got him. A hundred percent signed off. You don't understand—these guys are the—they fucking roll . . ." If Steve was correct in that assessment—if Dugin was also formally tasked with shaping opinion and policy related to the Communist Party of China—well then, that would make two: two Traditionalists working for opposite sides in a debate over the Chinese government. It would indeed foretell bleak prospects for his campaign to change Dugin's mind.

But Steve felt he had to try. Not the political leader, but the spiritual guide, the strategist, the guru. Call it metapolitics.

Steve turned to his phone.

I THANKED STEVE for his time and walked down the steep stairs of the Breitbart embassy and headed down the street, rounding the United States Supreme Court to the south and proceeding past the Capitol Building, which peered out across the National Mall and its towering obelisk to the west.

Feeling discontent with aspects of "modern life" is commonplace in societies like this one. What sets Traditionalism apart is the full-scale nature of its opposition. It strives to destroy all of modernity's values and rally behind their opposite. That few Traditionalists seem able to imagine, much less plausibly claim to want to live in, a genuinely premodern society, is beside the point: their rising prominence is a dramatic expression of widespread dissatisfaction with political and social life throughout liberal democracies. Traditionalism, perhaps ironically, is providing Bannon, Olavo, and Dugin ideological space and divine sanction to imagine wholly new political systems.

Traditionalism declares modern society meaningless on the grounds that our states and communities are increasingly based only on economics or bureaucratic formality rather than culture and spirit. Its theories of inversion provide theological, eschatological justifications for rejecting the institutions that provide us with knowledge about the world we live in, whether they be universities or the media. It implores us to consider how the liberal project of progress might have been degrading our lives under the guise of social advance; to view artificial intelligence as a late stage of secularization and the removal of spirit from the world; to regard the emancipation of women as a step toward loneliness and confusion born of the death of given social roles; to view support for mass immigration as an outgrowth of an instinct to view people as mere quantifiable material; to envision the loss of community, diversity, and sovereignty when we hear talk of universal democracy.

It can inspire racism as well, though one can make few assumptions about how Traditionalists today—including those I studied—deal with that legacy. While it is true that even avid followers of Julius Evola have found ways to excise the Italian thinker's views on race, it also is no accident that when Traditionalism has made inroads into politics, it has almost always done so in or near the company of race ideologues and anti-Semites. The reasons for this may run deeper than you think, and may speak to the fact that Traditionalism comes from a common conceptual source of those other pathologies.

Consider *The Protocols of the Elders of Zion*, the late nineteenth- and early twentieth-century bible for organized anti-Semitism. In it, Jews were portrayed as globalists operating against the nation-state, both communists and bankers—the differences between those personae didn't matter. Jews were confessing a non-Christian faith but were also agents of secularism; they were always cast as urbanites, a stark contrast with the good folks in the country. They were avatars of modernity. That's what mattered, more so than talk of culpability for Christ's death.

Racism can be just a smaller, even peripheral piece of the full-scale opposition to modernity that Traditionalism tries to encompass. But when I consider the stories that I followed, and the prospect that individuals inspired by Traditionalism may have a say in shaping the future of world politics, it isn't any one issue—race, gender, religion—that most unsettles me, but rather one of Traditionalism's overarching features.

The time cycle. The will to fight on behalf of eternity rather than to imagine a better, brighter future. That's how you tell a real Traditionalist apart from someone who is merely conservative— merely a traditionalist, small *t*. It's the difference between someone who believes we live in a time of destruction, who maintains that the crumbling of monuments is something to be celebrated and that the will to build something grand is the cause of a wicked fool, as opposed to someone who is merely pessimistic. What does it mean if a critical mass of world leaders have been advised by thinkers with a goal of disassembling everything, who value stillness over progress, who want our universe brought into alignment with what we were rather than what we dream we could become?

Perhaps part of the unease we might feel in the face of this situation is that of the unknown. Many of the ideological and spiritual beliefs voiced by these figures are unspecific. And this is not because they have a common secret understanding—more specific and pointed—that I never gained access to. Traditionalists today have vastly different notions of what Traditionalism is and what it asks of its followers, of if and how it dictates a particular geopolitics. Indeed, when I asked Steve Bannon to describe what Traditionalism *supports* rather than what it rejects, he named things like *immanence* and *transcendence*—concepts that aren't completely void of meaning, but which nonetheless are more form than content; they are picture frames surrounding a blank canvas. I've wondered if the airy vagueness of Traditionalism wasn't itself Steve's way of riding the tiger—of adding mystery and a sheen of the sacrosanct to agendas too offensive to enunciate.

Still, we can characterize aspects of their ideal world in broad terms. It is a world of reduced scales, of shrunken political spheres, and of radically different goals. No empires, no domineering transnational entities plotting beyond the view and control of average people. Instead, a world of nations or civilizations; of bounded enclaves—that's what's important—each based on something that ought to align with its robust borders: its people. And what is a people? A people is distinct from other peoples; a people share a past as well as a future, holding allegiances toward both. They possess an essence, a spiritual and cultural way of being, that transcends time. Don't we envoke the idea of race to encapsulate all this? Sometimes, but the Traditionalists' concept of a people extends further yet. They claim that these days, the individuals most likely to embody a people's essence are those most distanced from modernity itself, from secular institutional training and cosmopolitanisms and from time. The working class, the peasantry, that is. They're the ones first in line to access eternity, and it is the duty of the state to pursue their well-being. Secure the peasantry's existence and you will have made possible the greatest virtue—namely, allowing people to journey through their distinct essence toward the spiritual core, to follow your distinct beam of light back to the sun.

An ideal political unit is not one based on an ostensibly universal secular political principle like democracy or human rights, principles that would fold limitless numbers of other peoples into the nation's destiny and cause it to stretch its sphere outward through military incursion, market expansion, or immigration justified by the notion that someone *there* is deprived of our rights *here*—our rights that in fact apply everywhere. To behave in this way is to treat secular political values as being the central motivation for geopolitics. An alternate model would prioritize economics and the formation of trade partnerships. But in these Traditionalists' minds, spirituality should be the central motivation, meaning that a given nation's primary alliances are to be with nations who belong to and can complement its spiritual destiny. It's radical but also a de-emphasis of the role that human rights and democracy play in the world.

But as we consider how someone would make practical politics out of this, all of the vagaries come to play a larger role. What exactly is this essence, and who gets to decide? If a people is defined by its history, what happens to citizens whose personal background diverges from the norm? What to make of Brazilians, Americans, and Russians who are not, and have never been, Judeo-Christians?

Certain answers to these questions have a legacy in flames, and not only because Traditionalism in its original forms offers little incentive to be concerned about material inequalities and inequities. When its perceived edict to rally populations around archaic spiritual essence is combined with an ideology that maintains its own brand of apocalyptica—like the messianism of evangelical Christians with the added belief that earthly destruction is necessary for an *earthly*, rather than heavenly, utopia—there may be cause for alarm. Indeed, in the case of a number of our characters—Dugin, Bannon, the figures in Hungary—the philosophy provided the pretext not for apathy, as might be expected from those riding the tiger, but paradoxically for the exact opposite: for rash transformative action in the belief that the world is about to change, and therefore bold measures are justified. Traditionalism sees no reason to subordinate itself to politics.

Then again, these new Traditionalists may not really be contributing new practical innovations. As I reflected on my interviews and observations, I noticed again the many ways in which a principle from Traditionalism resonated closely with unrefined populist rallying cries. The critique of reason, the opposition to globalism, the disinclination toward movements of social progressivism, celebration of nationalism and localism, contempt for professionalization and institutionalization—perhaps the function of Traditionalism is that it allows people like Bannon, Dugin, and Olavo to be their eccentric highbrow selves while participating in a political cause that they might otherwise find socially and intellectually alienating. The impact, in that case, would be that it brought figures with exceptional resources and daring ambition to the helm of populist causes.

But for all the overlap between Traditionalism, populism, and nationalism, the doctrines also clash. Populism and democracy are able to coexist, even nourish each other, so long as populism doesn't actually come to power: fulfilling its agenda often requires undemocratic actions. Likewise, I wonder if Traditionalism could share space with a right-wing populism that wasn't oppositional but instead functioned as the establishment in metapolitical and formal political venues (which, in the United States and Brazil, it isn't yet). Would Traditionalism's pessimism and hostility toward official intellectual authority allow it to endorse such a society? And will the fact that it ultimately must (and often does) condemn the nation-state as a modernist construct—as a tool for leveling and homogenizing a population—lead it into conflict with nationalism?

Conflicts like these would prompt figures like Bannon,

Dugin, and Olavo to take sides: to show whether they saw Traditionalism as a means to an end or an end in itself.

I WAS FINISHED with my interviews, finished chasing Steve
and Olavo around the globe and hounding Dugin for interviews.
Perhaps I would hear from Steve again, though. He had called
me out of the blue one day, on July 31, 2019, encouraging me
to write a column about spiritualist and momentary Democratic
presidential candidate Marianne Williamson. Why, I couldn't
really figure, and he didn't give me an opportunity to ask. (Steve
initiates and concludes calls without salutations.) Maybe it was a
ploy to prime me in my writing, to lead me away from the standard media allegations against him by suggesting that he was
some kind of fan of a left-wing candidate advocating a "politics
of love."

However, I could imagine Steve being roused by a candidate
who criticized dry wonkishness and claimed that "dark spiritual
forces" beckoned, even if she was referring specifically to him and
the candidates he bolstered. She was speaking beyond materialism, thinking about politics as a matter of zeitgeist and spirituality, and that alone must have counted as an advance in his eyes.

It reminded me of something a Swedish nationalist politician said to me in 2018 after socialists and free-market capitalists aligned in his country to blunt the influence of his far-right
party. He was thrilled with the arrangement, he said to my
surprise. It meant that economic issues were becoming less important. Socialists and capitalists could work together because
disagreements about wealth distribution and taxes didn't matter that much anymore. Now the definitive political battles were
about unquantifiable, intangible, immaterial things like culture
and identity. Everyone had to pick sides: were they for openness

and freedom or continuity and security? All else was secondary. And by prioritizing these spiritual concerns, politics had become unmodern again, leaving technocrats and systematizers of all stripes—modernists on the left and the right—without a home.

Yes, the Steve Bannons of our times can find victories where others see defeat. With weapons and armies sometimes manifest, sometimes invisible, they view the world through radically different sets of eyes—witnessing chaos in structure, order in ruins, and the past in the future.

# ACKNOWLEDGMENTS

PROFESSORS ARE ACCUSTOMED TO BOOK PROJECTS with prolonged gestation periods. This was no such project. The timeliness of the topic and the urgency of bringing it to press meant that it had to be researched and written in a dash. I would have had no chance of doing this as an untenured professor and father of two toddlers without sacrifices and support from others in both my professional and my personal life.

A grant from the Center for the Arts and Humanities at the University of Colorado Boulder enabled my preliminary research. I am especially grateful to the College of Music at the University of Colorado Boulder—notably Dean Robert Shay and my dear colleagues in the Department of Musicology—for allowing me to take teaching leave to write. Though music hardly appears in this book, my research methods and drive to listen come from my work as an ethnomusicologist, and I hope that the final product channels the same commitment to excellence that leads me and others to take distinct pride in our institution.

It was thanks to another university colleague, violinist and author Edward Dusinberre, that I came in contact with a brilliant transatlantic agent duo: Melissa Flashman and Rebecca Carter of Janklow & Nesbit. I am yet to feel qualified for their expert counsel on matters professional and intellectual. Similarly, a team of editors—Alessandra Bastagli, Casiana Ionita, and Jeff Alexander—were skilled critical readers of my text, and the production teams at HarperCollins and Penguin UK were reliably talented and professional.

Beyond industry professionals, I benefited from the advice, assistance, and expertise of various friends, colleagues, and mentors. I must mention in particular Thomas Zeiler, Marc Perlman, Sherrill Harbison, David Josephson, Reihan Salam, Elektra Greer, Guillermo José Estrada-Rivera, Mathias Nordvig, Kajsa Norman, Jessica Vansteenburg, Leonard Fisher, Matthew Teitelbaum, and Anton Shekhovtsov. To Patrick Sutton: it is a rare privilege to have a friend with such a sharp mind, and such a gift for language, to turn to for frank feedback. Thanks to professor Mark Sedgwick of Aarhus University, whose combined qualities of generosity and unparalleled expertise on the history of Traditionalism made him an invaluable resource throughout my work.

Thanks to four anonymous sources.

I had student research assistants helping me throughout this process as well. Thanks to Pedro d'Avila for his skilled assistance with foreign language material (all mistakes in translation are my own). And a special thanks to Kelsey Fuller, who not only helped me with the grunt work of interview transcription but who also became nothing short of a consultant to me on the project as a whole. This book would never have been completed without her intelligent feedback from beginning to end.

Time for my students has been compromised throughout the project, and I am eager to return to my standard roles in the classroom and office hours. But it has been my family who has borne the brunt of my absence for travel and writing. This includes my extended family—my parents and stepparents in particular—who have intervened for more than their fair share of babysitting shifts with Signe and Liv. I must mention Deborah Voss, Ginger Johnson, the Sparks family, and Lynn Mizones Carroll in this context as well.

My foremost gratitude goes to my wife, Kajsa. It is with awe and not without guilt that I recall all of the sacrifices she has made throughout nearly two years of chaotic travel and writing schedules. She did this, not only while caring for our family, not only while maintaining her own career as an artist, but also while serving as editor, respondent, and therapist to me. I've done a lot of taking from our marriage. With this project behind us, I will do more giving.

# NOTES

## CHAPTER 1: PILLARS OF TRADITION

6 *philosophical and spiritual school:* Traditionalists have included professors, philosophers, even royalty in Europe today. Not all are associated with the radical right. See, for example, Charles Upton, *Dugin Against Dugin: A Traditionalist Critique of the Fourth Political Theory* (Sophia Perennis, 2018). My focus here, as explained in the next sentence, is on those combining Traditionalism and far-right politics.

9 *beyond fascism:* Mark Sedgwick, *Against the Modern World: Traditionalism and the Secret Intellectual History of the Twentieth Century* (Oxford: Oxford University Press, 2004). See also Elisabetta Cassini Wolff, "Evola's Interpretation of Fascism and Moral Responsibility," *Patterns of Prejudice* 50, no. 4–5 (2016): 478–94.

12 *"the underlying principle":* Julius Evola, *Metaphysics of War: Battle, Victory, and Death in the World of Tradition,* 3rd ed. (London: Arktos, 2011), 22.

## CHAPTER 2: POLLYWOG GONE NATIVE

20 *become a "shellback":* These details come not from my interview, but from recollections of his fellow sailors. See Mark D. Faram, "Steve Bannon and the National Security Council: What We Can Learn from His Navy Career," *Navy Times,* February 1, 2017.

22 *many valid paths:* During one of our interviews, Steve struggled to respond when I asked him if he could ever have imagined himself becoming a Sufi: BT: "Could you have ever seen yourself practicing Sufism? Becoming a Sufi?" SB: "You, you, it . . . it, it depends, it depends on where your journey takes you. Are there people, I know people are, that have gone totally to the Vedanta, or gone totally to the— It, it depends on what's your line of work, where your, where your journey takes you, right? And I don't, I don't um, um, before Christ, there was Christianity. Saint Augustine lays it out. Right, it's, it's— So look, for me, it's being a Christian. And I can get very comfortable with that, and in learning from these other great religions,

the process of understanding transcendence, and not just that, understanding being in the metanoia, and how these other practices help you in the, the, in, um, in perfecting your being, which to me is the journey."

24 *cultural dissidents in white American society:* Thomas A. Tweed, *The American Encounter with Buddhism: 1844–1912* (Chapel Hill: University of North Carolina Press, 2000). See also Philip Goldberg, *American Veda: From Emerson and the Beatles to Yoga and Meditation—How Indian Spirituality Changed the West* (New York: Harmony Books, 2013).

24 *Beat poet Gary Snyder famously wrote:* Gary Snyder, *Earth House Hold: Technical Notes & Queries to Fellow Dharma Revolutionaries* (New York: New Directions Books, 1969), 92.

25 *were a problem for leftists:* See Richard Hughes Seager, *Buddhism in America* (New York: Columbia University Press, 1999).

## CHAPTER 3: THE JEDI MASTER

30 *a sign of phoniness:* David Von Drehle, "Steve Bannon Is a Swiss-Cheese Philosopher," *Washington Post,* September 12, 2017, https://www.washingtonpost.com/opinions/steve-bannon-is-a-swiss-cheese-philosopher/2017/09/12/3a45f43c-97e7-11e7-82e4-f1076f6d6152_story.html.

35 *"an adviser who hearkens back to Julius Evola":* "Steve Bannon at DHI," Soundcloud (BuzzFeed News), 2014. https://soundcloud.com/buzzfeednews/steve-bannon-at-dhi.

## CHAPTER 4: KILLING TIME

42 *the hidden world of their own psyches:* See Natalya Tamruchi, "Bezumie kak oblast svobody," *NLO* 100 (2009), http://magazines.russ.ru/nlo/2009/100/ta33-pr.html.

42 *Third Reich uniforms and shout "Sieg Heil!":* Charles Clover, *Black Wind, White Snow: The Rise of Russia's New Nationalism* (New Haven, CT: Yale University Press), 2016.

43 *Arctic origin of the Aryans:* See Victor Shnirelman, "Hyperborea: The Arctic Myth of Contemporary Russian Radical Nationalists," *Journal of Ethnology and Folkloristics* 8, no. 2 (2014): 121–38.

46 *between a liberal "Atlantic" and an opposing "Eurasia":* These were ideas he adapted from German philosophers Carl Schmitt and Karl Haushofer, and British political theorist Halford Mackinder.

47 *"support isolationist tendencies in American politics":* Translated in

John B. Dunlop, "Aleksandr Dugin's Foundations of Geopolitics," *Demokratizatsiya* 12, no. 1 (2004).

47 *Dugin as a geopolitical expert:* Ibid. See also Stephen D. Shenfield, *Russian Fascism: Traditions, Tendencies, Movements* (London: Routledge, 2001), 199.

49 *a stream of other official meetings:* Clover, *Black Wind, White Snow.* See also Marlène Laruelle, *Russian Eurasianism: An Ideology of Empire* (Baltimore: Johns Hopkins University Press, 2008). See also Dugin's private Facebook page.

49 *a WikiLeaks release:* "PUTIN VISITS TURKEY: RUSSIA BIDS TO TURN TURKEY FROM WEST; TURKS KEEPING OPTIONS OPEN," WikiLeaks, https://wikileaks.org/plusd/cables/04 ANKARA6887_a.html.

49 *rewrote the introduction:* "PUTIN VISIT TO TURKEY SEPTEMBER 2–3," WikiLeaks, https://wikileaks.org/plusd/cables/04ANKA RA4887_a.html.

50 *a network of individuals:* Marlène Laruelle, "Alexander Dugin and Eurasianism." In ed. Mark Sedgwick, *Key Thinkers of the Radical Right: Behind the New Threat to Liberal Democracy* (Oxford: Oxford University Press, 2019), 155–79.

50 *Eurasianist Youth Union members climbed Mount Hoverla:* "'Gerbiamo' profesoriaus pasiūlymai: okupuoti Gruziją, padalyti Ukrainą, suvienyti buvusią," *Ekspertai.* http://www.ekspertai.eu/gerbiamo-pro fesoriaus-pasiulymai-okupuoti-gruzija-padalinti-ukraina-suvienyti -buvusia-sssr/.

51 *Separatist forces targeted:* Council of the European Union, Independent International Fact-Finding Mission on the Conflict in Georgia, Brussels, September 30, 2009.

51 *"Tanks to Tbilisi!":* "No Compromise—Tanks to Tblisi!" *Evrazia,* http://evrazia.org/article.php?id=571#english.

52 *spread throughout Russian media:* Anton Shekhovtsov, "Aleksandr Dugin's Neo-Eurasianism: The New Right *à la Russe*," *Religion Compass* 3, no. 4 (2009): 697–716.

52 *"like hell":* Peter Finn, "A Two-Sided Descent into Full-Scale War," *Washington Post,* August 17, 2008, https://www.washingtonpost.com /wp-dyn/content/article/2008/08/16/AR2008081600502_pf.html.

## CHAPTER 5: SOLAR EUROPE

57 *Vona made a baffling reversal:* "Vona: Kész vagyok bocsánatot kérni a zsidóságtól és a cigányságtól," *ATV,* http://www.atv.hu/belfold

/20170814-vona-kesz-vagyok-bocsanatot-kerni-a-zsidosagtol-es-a -ciganysagtol.

58 *a hard-core Traditionalist:* He not only established the only Traditionalist church I've ever heard of in his hometown of Debrecen but also published books through a company called Kvintesszencia he founded in 1996. He would eventually publish translations of Dugin's work, too.

58 *the distant past:* Marlène Laruelle et al., *Eurasianism and the European Far Right: Reshaping the Europe–Russia Relationship* (Lanham, MD: Lexington Books, 2015), 191; Éva Mikos, "Ablonczy Balázs: Keletre, magyar! A magyar turanizmus története. Jaffa Kiadó, Budapest, 2016," *Korall–Társadalomtörténeti folyóirat* 18 (2018): 201–206; Emel Akçalı and Umut Korkut, "Geographical Metanarratives in East-Central Europe: Neo-Turanism in Hungary," *Eurasian Geography and Economics* 53, no. 5 (2012): 596–614.

59 *unity between Greece and Russia:* Sonia Ephron, "Opinion: The Frightening Popularity of Golden Dawn's Anti-Semitism in Greece," *Los Angeles Times*, May 22, 2014, https://www.latimes.com/nation/la -ol-greece-elections-neo-nazi-golden-dawn-20140522-story.html.

61 *succeed in altering a society's culture:* The strategy of metapolitics has unlikely roots. It was brought into far-right activism by a Traditionalism-inspired ideological school called the French New Right, or Nouvelle Droite, who in turn adapted the idea from Sardinian neo-Marxist Antonio Gramsci, who died in Mussolini's prisons. Gramsci was trying to understand why communist revolution hadn't come to pre–World War II Italy when all the economic conditions for it seemed to be in place. His conclusion? Italy's culture stood in the way. Average people might have been suffering in a system that stole from them the fruits of their labor, but the values they took as common sense dissuaded them from revolting. Here, contrary to what Karl Marx predicted, culture was a more powerful driver of social behavior than economics. See Benjamin Teitelbaum, *Lions of the North: Sounds of the New Nordic Radical Nationalism* (Oxford: Oxford University Press, 2017).

62 *pull targeted individuals out of the mainstream:* Christopher Wylie, *Mindf•ck: Cambridge Analytica and the Plot to Break America* (New York: Random House, 2019).

62 *an organization called Leave.EU:* Peter Geoghegan, "Brexit Bankroller Arron Banks, Cambridge Analytica and Steve Bannon—Explosive Emails, Reveal Fresh Links," Open Democracy, November 17, 2018,

https://www.opendemocracy.net/en/dark-money-investigations
/brexit-bankroller-arron-banks-cambridge-analytica-and-steve
-bannon-expl/.

63 *channel money illegally:* Jamie Ross, "It's Official: The Brexit Campaign Cheated Its Way to Victory," Daily Beast, July 17, 2018, https://www.thedailybeast.com/its-official-the-brexit-campaign-cheated-its-way-to-victory?ref=author.

63 *key to the victory:* Joshua Green, *Devil's Bargain* (New York: Penguin, 2017), 207.

63 *he would be arrested on sight:* Nick Thorpe, "Far Right Holds Secret Congress in Hungary," BBC News, October 7, 2014, https://www.bbc.com/news/world-europe-29503378.

64 *schools of this kind:* See, for example, "Lega, al via la Scuola di Formazione Politica. Siri: 'Unici a puntare sulla competenza,'" *Il Populista*, http://www.ilpopulista.it/news/27-Ottobre-2017/19903/lega-al-via-la-scuola-di-formazione-politica-siri-unici-a-puntare-sulla-competenza.html.

66 *swing in his approval ratings:* Neil Buckley, "Orban's Hard Line on Migrants Proves a Ratings Winner at Home," *Financial Times*, September 20, 2015, https://www.ft.com/content/248dc176-5f8e-11e5-9846-de406ccb37f2.

66 *Hungarian language's links to Finnish:* "Unkarin pääministeri: Kielisukulaisuus on tosiasia," *Turun Sanomat*, May 13, 2013, https://www.ts.fi/uutiset/kotimaa/484810/Unkarin+paaministeri+Kielisukulaisuus+on+tosiasia.

66 *buy armored vehicles from Turkey:* "Hungary first in EU to buy Turkish armored vehicle," *Daily Sabah*, February 9, 2019, https://www.dailysabah.com/defense/2019/09/02/hungary-first-in-eu-to-buy-turkish-armored-vehicle.

67 *"spiritually sick Europe":* "Gábor Vona, leader of Jobbik: 'Hungary Is for Hungarians Until Our Final Breath!'" YouTube, https://www.youtube.com/watch?v=HqlraNaGipo.

69 *the birth of multipolarity:* "Brexit: Europe Is Falling into the Abyss | Alexander Dugin," *Fourth Revolutionary War*, June 27, 2016, https://4threvolutionarywar.wordpress.com/2016/06/27/brexit-europe-is-falling-into-the-abyss-alexander-dugin/. Transcript lightly edited.

70 *financial support from Putin's government:* Anton Shekhovtsov, *Russia and the Western Far Right: Tango Noire* (London: Routledge, 2017).

## CHAPTER 6: THE METAPHYSICS OF THE PEASANTRY

75 *Nadia Urbinati recently put it:* Nadia Urbinati, "Political Theory of Populism," *Annual Review of Political Science* 22 (2019): 111–27.

86 *"racially isolated communities":* Jonathan T. Rothwell and Pablo Diego-Rosell, "Explaining Nationalist Political Views: The Case of Donald Trump," Gallup, November 2, 2016, http://dx.doi.org/10.2139/ssrn.2822059.

## CHAPTER 7: STRANGLE THE TIGER

89 *marvelously decorated soldiers:* Evola presented this theory in 1935, in the article "Sulle forme dell'eroismo guerriero" in "Diorama mensile." *Il Regime Fascista.*

90 *"readjustment":* René Guénon, *Crisis of the Modern World,* rev. ed., trans. Marco Pallis et al. (Hillsdale, NY: Sophia Perennis, 2004).

91 *strangle it and thereby find freedom:* Julius Evola, *Ride the Tiger: A Survival Manual for the Aristocrats of the Soul,* trans. Joscelyn Godwin and Constance Fontana (Rochester, VT: Inner Traditions, 2003 [1961]). See also Paul Furlong, "Riding the Tiger: Crisis and Political Strategy in the Thought of Julius Evola," *Italianist* 31, no. 1 (2011): 25–40; Elisabetta C. Wolff, "Apolitìa and Tradition in Julius Evola as Reaction to Nihilism," *European Review* 22, no. 2 (2014): 258–73.

92 *"a future, formative action":* Evola, *Ride the Tiger,* 7.

93 *the Movement:* While Bannon was transitioning into the White House, on January 9, 2017, a Belgian lawyer named Mischaël Modrikamen founded the Movement. After exiting the White House later that same year, and thanks to intervention and introductions from Nigel Farage, Bannon would assume co-leadership of the Movement. See Nico Hines, "Inside Bannon's Plan to Hijack Europe for the Far-Right," Daily Beast, July 20, 2018, https://www.thedailybeast.com/inside-bannons-plan-to-hijack-europe-for-the-far-right.

94 *Steve wanted to participate:* Indeed, Marion Maréchal—granddaughter of National Rally founder Jean-Marie Le Pen and niece of party leader Marine Le Pen—was opening the Institute for Social, Economic, and Political Sciences (ISSEP) in Lyon, France, that same year, with an unorthodox curriculum blending training in business, politics, sports, ballroom dancing, and wilderness survival skills. See "Le Pen's Niece Opens Grad School to Train New Generation of Far-Right Leaders," Public Radio International, January 4, 2019, https://www.pri.org/stories/2019-01-04/le-pen-s-niece-opens-grad-school-train-new-generation-french-far-right-leaders.

94  **$1 million annually:** Jonathan Swan and Erica Pandey, "Exclusive: Steve Bannon's $1 Million Deal Linked to a Chinese Billionaire," Axios, October 29, 2019, https://www.axios.com/steve-bannon -contract-chinese-billionaire-guo-media-fa6bc244-6d7a-4a53-9f03 -1296d4fae5aa.html.

94  **"un-Christian":** Daniel Burke, "Pope Suggests Trump 'Is Not Christian,'" CNN, February 18, 2016, https://edition.cnn.com/2016/02 /18/politics/pope-francis-trump-christian-wall/. At this time Bannon was already partnering with anti-pope Cardinal Raymond Burke (though their partnership would eventually implode) on ways to cause scandals and weaken papal powers. For Bannon, this would ultimately include pursuing plans to make a film based on a book by leftist French journalist Frédéric Martel, titled *In the Closet of the Vatican: Power, Homosexuality, Hypocrisy,* with the hopes of dealing a death-blow to a besieged Catholic establishment who in Bannon's mind embodied a toxic brew of progressivism and sexual evils.

95  **secure Russian funding:** Alberto Nardelli, "Revealed: The Explosive Secret Recording That Shows How Russia Tried to Funnel Millions to the 'European Trump,'" BuzzFeed, July 10, 2019, https://www .buzzfeednews.com/article/albertonardelli/salvini-russia-oil-deal-se cret-recording.

95  **met with Aleksandr Dugin in 2016:** "Italy, EU and Trump," KATE-HON, November 24, 2016, https://katehon.com/article/italy-eu-and-trump.

95  **"Russians are white":** Quoted in John Lukacs, *A History of the Cold War* (New York: Doubleday, 1961), 268.

96  **"a fan of his writing":** Author James Heiser likely brought Dugin to Bannon's attention in 2014. After Heiser published a critical book on the Russian thinker, he wrote summary articles for *National Review* and *Breitbart.* Shortly thereafter, in 2014, Bannon asked to interview Heiser on his *Breitbart* radio program. Heifer later told me that Bannon's statements during their interview suggested he had little knowledge of Dugin at the time. Given the generally uninformed nature of Bannon's commentary on Evola in the Vatican speech that followed, and given the fact that Bannon later became interested in both Heidegger and Evola, I and others suspect that he learned of Evola and Arktos after having been exposed to Dugin via Heiser. For more on Heiser's commentary on Dugin, see James D. Heiser, *"The American Empire Should Be Destroyed": Alexander Dugin and the Perils of Immanentized Eschatology* (Malone, TX: Repristination Press, 2014).

## CHAPTER 8: THE RACE OF THE SPIRIT

101 *the historical extent of the Indo-European languages:* See Stefan Arvidsson, *Aryan Idols: Indo-European Mythology as Ideology and Science,* trans. Sonia Wichmann (Chicago: University of Chicago Press, 2006).

103 *could live on while bodies die:* This point was made by Evola admirer and white nationalist Tomislav Sunic in "Julius Evola on Race," *Occidental Observer,* May 1, 2010, https://www.theoccidentalobserver.net/2010/05/01/sunic-evola-on-race/.

104 *mysticism into their sense of race:* For more on mysticism, Evola, and conceptions of race in the Third Reich, see Nicholas Goodrick-Clarke, *Black Sun: Aryan Cults, Esoteric Nazism, and the Politics of Identity* (New York: NYU Press, 2003).

104 *recommended he be marginalized:* H. T. Hansen, "A Short Introduction to Julius Evola," in *Revolt Against the Modern World: Politics, Religion, and Social Order in the Kali Yuga* (Rochester, VT: Inner Traditions, 1995).

## CHAPTER 9: THE MAN AGAINST TIME

109 *"destroy all of today's establishment":* "Steve Bannon, Trump's Top Guy, Told Me He Was 'A Leninist,'" Daily Beast, https://www.thedailybeast.com/steve-bannon-trumps-top-guy-told-me-he-was-a-leninist?source=twitter&via=desktop.

110 *called* **The Fourth Turning:** William Strauss and Neil Howe, *The Fourth Turning: What the Cycles of History Tell Us About America's Next Rendezvous with Destiny* (New York: Three Rivers Press, 1997).

112 *private school of their choice:* "Opinion: DeVos: Families Don't Need DPS Retread," *Detroit News,* February 22, 2016, https://www.detroitnews.com/story/opinion/2016/02/22/devos-families-need-dps-retread/80788340/.

113 *"little safe territory":* "Dick and Betsy DeVos at The Gathering 2001," YouTube, February 23, 2015, https://www.youtube.com/watch?v=qJYFPMLuVRE.

113 *"advocate against the EPA's activist agenda":* Scott Detrow, "Scott Pruitt Confirmed to Lead Environmental Protection Agency," February 17, 2017, https://www.npr.org/2017/02/17/515802629/scott-pruitt-confirmed-to-lead-environmental-protection-agency.

114 *cut billions in foreign aid:* Dexter Filkins, "Rex Tillerson at the Breaking Point," *The New Yorker,* October 6, 2017, https://www.newyorker.com/magazine/2017/10/16/rex-tillerson-at-the-breaking-point.

115 *"would like to get rid of it":* "Rep. Mick Mulvaney: CFPB 'Sick, Sad Joke,'" September 10, 2014, YouTube.com.

116 *calls* **palingenesis***:* Griffin argues that it is the fundamental distinguishing ideological characteristic of fascism. See Roger Griffin, *The Nature of Fascism* (London: Routledge, 1993).

116 *expression of nostalgia:* The phrase could be seen as an example of what the late Harvard scholar Svetlana Boym described as "restorative nostalgia." See Svetlana Boym, *The Future of Nostalgia* (New York: Basic Books, 2008).

116 *"those who came before us":* He referenced Edmund Burke when making this case.

120 *so fast they can't focus:* See also "Zero Tolerance: Steve Bannon Interview | FRONTLINE," PBS, 2019, https://www.pbs.org/wgbh/front line/interview/steve-bannon-2/.

121 *the influence of Guénon and Evola:* Her explicit references to these Traditionalists appear in her book: Savitri Devi, *Souvenirs et réflexions d'une Aryenne* (N.P.: Éditions Contre le Temps, 1976). Note that these weren't the only factors making Savitri Devi an exceptional case. She is one of the only women I know to call herself a Traditionalist. Far-right nationalism has long valorized women, often through viewing them as vessels of antique national essence shielded from modernity thanks to their historical underrepresentation in cosmopolitanism, commerce, and formal education. Traditionalism, however, seldom includes such romanticizations. The ideology that, following Evola, theorized the subordination of women and femininity—which dismissed much feminism as a ploy to dissolve identity via the eradication of gender—had few female takers. That is not to say that Devi is the lone Traditionalist woman. During the 1980s an all-women group of Traditionalists formed in Oxford, England, under the name Aristasia. See Mark Sedgwick, *Against the Modern World: Traditionalism and the Secret Intellectual History of the Twentieth Century* (Oxford: Oxford University Press, 2004), 216–19.

121 *"exterminators without ideologies":* Savitri Devi, *The Lightning and the Sun* (Calcutta: Temple Press, 1958), 41.

122 *"Age of Truth'":* Ibid., 48.

## CHAPTER 10: ESOTERIC GATHERINGS

126 *his acceptance speech:* "Bolsonaro's Victory Speech with subtitles in English," YouTube, October 29, 2018, https://www.youtube.com /watch?v=blYxwdG8dBo. I have edited this translation of the speech.

127  *He had met with Eduardo Bolsonaro:* "Steve Bannon Endorses Far-Right Brazilian Presidential Candidate," Reuters, October 26, 2018, https://www.reuters.com/article/us-brazil-election-bannon/steve-bannon-endorses-far-right-brazilian-presidential-candidate-idUS KCN1N01S1.

127  *advising the Bolsonaro election campaign:* "Brazil: Steve Bannon to Advise Bolsonaro Presidential Campaign," Telesur, August 15, 2018, https://www.telesurenglish.net/news/Brazil-Steve-Bannon-to-Advise-Bolsonaro-Presidential-Campaign-20180815-0003.html.

129  *occultist magazine* **Planète:** This magazine was founded by Louis Pauwels, who later collaborated with Alain de Benoist of the French New Right.

130  *the man next to it wearing a horned headdress:* For his commentary on the symbolism of the dance, see Frithjof Schuon, *The Play of Masks* (Bloomington, IN: World Wisdom, 1992).

131  *Sun Dance of the Sioux:* Some Native Americans looked upon Schuon's use of their clothing and ritual as an embarrassing reminder of their need to safeguard their traditions. See the article by Avis Little Eagle in the *Lakota Times,* July 1992.

131  *circular dhikr dances of the Sufis:* Hugh B. Urban, "A Dance of Masks: The Esoteric Ethics of Frithjof Schuon," in eds. G. William Barnard and Jeffrey J. Kripal, *Crossing Boundaries: Essays on the Ethical Status of Mysticism* (New York: Seven Bridges, 2002).

132  *brainwashing, extortion, and abuse:* For an excellent academic treatment of power dynamics in these and similar settings, see Elizabeth Puttick, "Sexuality, Gender and the Abuse of Power in the Master–Disciple Relationship: The Case of the Rajneesh Movement," *Journal of Contemporary Religion* 10, no. 1 (1995): 29–40.

132  *they could claim followers:* Mark Sedgwick, *Against the Modern World: Traditionalism and the Secret Intellectual History of the Twentieth Century* (Oxford: Oxford University Press, 2004).

133  *"institutional" qualities:* I rely on Urban, "A Dance of Masks," for this information.

133  *"black," and "yellow" races:* Frithjof Schuon, *Language of the Self,* trans. Margo Pallis and Macleod Matheson (Madras: Vasanta Press, 1959). It should be noted that a significant portion of Schuon's followers viewed his as a message of universalism, one reinforcing tolerance and openness rather than any form of hierarchy and sectarianism. In doing so, however, they overlook the thinker's complexity in general and the presence of contradictory signals in particular. See Gregory A.

Lipton, "De-Semitizing Ibn ʿArabī: Aryanism and the Schuonian Discourse of Religious Authenticity," *Numen* 64, no. 2–3 (2017): 258–93; James S. Cutsinger, "Introduction," in ed. and trans. James S. Cutsinger, *Splendor of the True: A Frithjof Schuon Reader* (Albany: State University of New York Press, 2013).

135 *a tip from a friend:* Whom Olavo told me was Greek author-musician Marco Pallis.

135 *Lima, Peru:* One of Lings's visits to the area is documented by Mateus Soares de Azevedo in "Special Section: Tributes to Dr. Martin Lings (1909–2005)," *Sacred Web* 15 (2005).

136 *"a saint of first magnitude":* "Martin Lings speaks of his impressions on first meeting Frithjof Schuon," YouTube, August 5, 2013, https://www.youtube.com/watch?v=MB1w305x-hw.

136 *knowledge that has been rejected:* For a discussion of the academic definitions of esotericism, see Michael Bergunder, "What Is Esotericism? Cultural Studies Approaches and the Problems of Definition in Religious Studies," *Method & Theory in the Study of Religion* 22, no. 1 (2010): 9–36.

137 *"Primordial Gathering":* Some accounts treat the Primordial Gathering and the Sun Dance as the same event, but I have additional indication based on off-the-record conversations with witnesses that these were two separate occurrences.

138 *"her celestial prototype":* Frithjof Schuon, *Gnosis, Divine Wisdom* (Bloomington, IN: World Wisdom, 1957), 54.

138 *"be naked like her baby":* Frithjof Schuon, *Erinnerungen und Betrachtungen.* N.p.: n.p. (1974), 295.

138 *"to the celestial state":* "Frithjof Schuon's interest in the Plains Indians," World Wisdom, http://www.worldwisdom.com/public/slideshows/view.aspx?SlideShowID=44&SlideDetailID=403.

138 *age of the other participants:* Writing about this episode in Frithjof Schuon's life is exceptionally complicated and ethically fraught. He was accused of child molestation and indicted by an Indiana grand jury in the early 1990s for actions allegedly taken during these rituals. The case was eventually dropped for lack of evidence. Many of Schuon's followers noted that the most vocal public accuser was a former initiate named Mark Koslow, who held considerable animus toward Schuon over a separate matter and detailed his accusations in a memoir. Some of the same followers have also threatened, by legal means and otherwise, authors and scholars who have written about this history and endorsed the notion of Schuon's culpability. Mean-

while, the correspondence of ideological and social infrastructure for such encounters to have taken place in the community seems apparent to many commentators, including me. Authors have thus had to face the prospect of either contributing to a false accusation or inadvertently providing cover for the horror of sexual abuse. This footnote is my attempt at a balance.

## CHAPTER 11: LET US TRANSCEND MODERNITY

143 *"Unmodern thinkers gathering":* "Omoderna tänkare samlas i Stockholm," *Friatider,* July 27, 2012, https://www.friatider.se/omoderna -tankare-samlas-i-stockholm.

144 *Center for Conservative Studies:* Information on his curriculum at the time can be found at Aleksandr Dugin, "Biography," http://dugin.ru /biography.

144 *guest on Iranian state media:* Reza HaghighatNehad, "Putin's Brain, the Darling of Iranian Hardliners," Track Persia, http://www.track persia.com/putins-brain-darling-irans-hardliners/.

144 *Sergey Naryshkin:* Christoph Laug, "Prominent Right-Wing Figures in Russia," *Russian Analytical Digest* 135 (August 5, 2013), https://css .ethz.ch/content/dam/ethz/special-interest/gess/cis/center-for-securi ties-studies/pdfs/RAD-135-6-9.pdf.

145 *"All that is anti-liberal is good":* "Alexander Dugin (Introduction by Mark Sleboda) Identitär Idé 4 / Identitarian Ideas 4," YouTube, September 14, 2012, https://www.youtube.com/watch?v=7X-o_ndhSVA. Note that I lightly edit Dugin's English throughout these quotations, as I do in my interview with him.

146 *Francis Fukuyama:* Francis Fukuyama, "The End of History?" *The National Interest* 16 (Summer 1989).

147 *all three were modernist:* These ideas are more fully elaborated in Aleksandr Dugin, *The Fourth Political Theory* (London: Arktos, 2012), 17.

## CHAPTER 12: THE SUMMIT

153 *nobody seemed to notice:* Luca Steinmann, "The Illiberal Far-Right of Aleksandr Dugin. A conversation," *Reset DOC,* December 4, 2018, https://www.resetdoc.org/story/illiberal-far-right-aleksandr-dugin -conversation/.

156 *"Solar Putin":* Charles Clover, *Black Wind, White Snow: The Rise of Russia's New Nationalism* (New Haven, CT: Yale University Press, 2016), 327–28.

## CHAPTER 13: DINNER AT THE EMBASSY

168 *Seminário de Filosofia:* "Que É o Seminário de Filosofia?" *Seminário de Filosofia,* https://www.seminariodefilosofia.org/o-seminario/.

## CHAPTER 14: GLOBAL ALTERNATIVES

175 *"into the toilet":* Brian Winter, "Jair Bolsonaro's Guru," *Americas Quarterly,* December 17, 2018, https://www.americasquarterly.org/content /jair-bolsonaros-guru.

176 *Schuon's Traditionalism:* Mark Sedgwick, *Against the Modern World: Traditionalism and the Secret Intellectual History of the Twentieth Century* (Oxford: Oxford University Press, 2004), 271.

178 *Dugin opened the debate:* "The USA and the New World Order," March 7, 2011, http://debateolavodugin.blogspot.com/2011/03/alex ander-dugin-introduction.html.

182 *U.S. conservative language:* Dugin, six months later, would also make some friendly overtures to the American people. See "Alexander Dugin: Real Friend of the American People!" Green Star News, September 24, 2011, https://greenstarnews.wordpress.com/2011/09/24 /alexander-dugin-real-friend-to-the-american-people/.

183 *Seven Towers of the Devil:* Little on this subject is to be found in Guénon's texts translated into English. One exception is a passing remark made in René Guénon, *Insights into Islamic Esotericism and Taoism,* trans. Henry D. Fohr (Hillsdale, NY: Sophia Perennis, 2003 [1973]).

184 *located in California:* Unpublished letter, René Guénon to Vasile Lovinescu, Le Caire, May 19, 1936.

## CHAPTER 15: ENCHANTED BORDERS

187 *an age of wolves:* Jackson Crawford, trans., *The Poetic Edda: Stories of the Norse Gods and Heroes* (Indianapolis, IN: Hackett Publishing Company, 2015), 12.

193 *limp-dick motherfucker:* Joshua Green, *Devil's Bargain* (New York: Penguin, 2017), 188.

## CHAPTER 16: THE DISINTEGRATION OF THE WORLD

202 *Mongol genetic traces:* Jason Reza Jorjani, "Against Perennial Philosophy," AltRight.com, https://www.altright.com/2016/10/21/against -perennial-philosophy/.

205 *"a spy novel":* Tim Murphy, "The Fastest-Growing Washington Industry You've Never Heard Of," *Mother Jones,* November–December

2013, https://www.motherjones.com/politics/2013/11/political-intel
ligence-industry-jellyfish/.

206 *private sector rival of the CIA:* Shane Harris, "Former Blackwater Officials Form Global Intelligence Company," *Washington Examiner,*
May 12, 2011, https://www.washingtonian.com/2011/05/12/former
-blackwater-officials-form-global-intelligence-company/.

206 *Philip Morris:* Murphy, "The Fastest-Growing Washington Industry
You've Never Heard Of."

206 *He seemed dangerous:* Personal communication, Keith Mahoney, various dates, August 2019.

209 *Bagley already had channels:* John Catsimatidis, "Michael Bagley—
A refugee solution?" Catsimatidis, September 24, 2017, http://www
.catsimatidis.com/michael-bagley-refugee-solution/.

211 *platform for the alt-right:* Sarah Posner, "How Donald Trump's New
Campaign Chief Created an Online Haven for White Nationalists," *Mother Jones,* August 22, 2016, https://www.motherjones.com
/politics/2016/08/stephen-bannon-donald-trump-alt-right-breitbart
-news/.

### CHAPTER 17: ALT-RIGHT, INC.

216 *compared the sensation:* Jef Costello, "'That's It, We're Through!':
The Psychology of Breaking Up with Trump," *Counter-Currents,*
April 10, 2017, https://www.counter-currents.com/2017/04/thats-it
-were-through/.

218 *"A detailed work plan was presented to Flynn":* "Will Russia and the
USA Help Libya Together?" *RIA,* https://ria.ru/20170202/14870
43738.html.

220 *largest petroleum deposit in the world:* See World Petroleum Resources Project, "An Estimate of Recoverable Heavy Oil Resources
of the Orinoco Oil Belt, Venezuela," USGS, https://pubs.usgs.gov
/fs/2009/3028/pdf/FS09-3028.pdf.

222 *Goldman Sachs had purchased:* Landon Thomas Jr., "Goldman Buys
$2.8 Billion Worth of Venezuelan Bonds, and an Uproar Begins,"
*New York Times,* May 30, 2017, https://www.nytimes.com/2017/05/30
/business/dealbook/goldman-buys-2-8-billion-worth-of-venezuelan
-bonds-and-an-uproar-begins.html.

### CHAPTER 18: BANNON AGAINST THE WORLD

230 *unavoidability of destruction:* Michael Wolff, *Fire and Fury* (New
York: Holt, 2018).

231  *none other than Aleksandr Dugin:* Henry Meyer and Onur Ant, "Alexander Dugin—The one Russian linking Donald Trump, Vladimir Putin and Recep Tayyip Erdogan," *Independent,* February 3, 2017, https://www.independent.co.uk/news/world/americas/alexander-dugin-russian-academic-linking-us-president-donald-trump-vladimir-putin-turkey-president-a7560611.html.

232  *"special Russian truth":* "Aleksandr Dugin: 'We have our special Russian truth,'" *BBC Newsnight,* YouTube, October 28, 2016, https://www.youtube.com/watch?v=GGunRKWtWBs.

## CHAPTER 19: UNITE THE RIGHT

236  *Rebel yell:* Kyle Chattleton, presentation during roundtable, "Recognizing and Confronting White Supremacy Through Sound Scholarship," Annual Meeting of the Society for Ethnomusicology, Albuquerque, New Mexico, 2018.

237  *"The fascist Richard Spencer is here!":* This account comes from Daniel Friberg's partner, Chris Dulny, who also attended the rally. "Vita pillret—Avsnitt 9—Sanningen om Charlottesville och Unite the Right," YouTube, September 1, 2017, https://www.youtube.com/watch?v=iHxFE1h7r5w.

239  *he clarified to the Scandinavian media:* "Udklip fra min korrespondance med en global alt-right-leder," *Zetland,* https://www.zetland.dk/historie/soV7BpEX-aegXAYg6-57bae.

240  *"they were very, very violent":* "Full text: Trump's comments on white supremacists, 'alt-left' in Charlottesville," Politico, August 15, 2017, https://www.politico.com/story/2017/08/15/full-text-trump-comments-white-supremacists-alt-left-transcript-241662. I have lightly edited this transcript.

240  *condemnation from both Republicans and Democrats:* Michael D. Shear and Maggie Haberman, "Trump Defends Initial Remarks on Charlottesville; Again Blames 'Both Sides,'" *New York Times,* August 15, 2017, https://www.nytimes.com/2017/08/15/us/politics/trump-press-conference-charlottesville.html. See also Robin Eberhardt, "Fifth leader resigns from Trump's manufacturing council," The Hill, August 15, 2017, https://thehill.com/homenews/administration/346614-fifth-leader-resigns-from-trumps-manufacturing-jobs-council.

240  *"not to criticize far-right activists":* Maggie Haberman and Glenn Thrush, "Bannon in Limbo as Trump Faces Growing Calls for the Strategist's Ouster," *New York Times,* August 14, 2017, https://www

.nytimes.com/2017/08/14/us/politics/steve-bannon-trump-white
-house.html.

241 *courageous refusal to bow to media:* Jonathan Swan, "What Steve
Bannon Thinks About Charlottesville," Axios, August 16, 2017,
https://www.axios.com/what-steve-bannon-thinks-about-charlottes
ville-1513304895-7ee2c933-e6d5-4692-bc20-c1db88afe970.html.

241 *critics blamed the incident on Bannon's influence:* Michael D. Shear
and Maggie Haberman, "Trump Defends Initial Remarks on Charlottesville; Again Blames 'Both Sides,'" *New York Times,* August 15,
2017, https://www.nytimes.com/2017/08/15/us/politics/trump-press
-conference-charlottesville.html.

241 *world of the alt-right:* Steve once described Breitbart as being the platform of the alt-right, which Josh Green described as having been born
of a misunderstanding on Steve's part as to the meaning of the term.
*Alt-right* at the time had an unclear connotation in public discourse,
representing both the renegade white nationalist movement and wings
of conservatism opposed to the Republican Party establishment. Steve
seemed to refer to the latter when he used the term. However, employees of his have also referenced him being sympathetic to "much"
of the white nationalist alt-right ideology. Joshua Green, *Devil's Bargain* (New York: Penguin, 2017), 212. See also Joseph Bernstein,
"Here's How Breitbart and Milo Smuggled White Nationalism into
the Mainstream," BuzzFeed, October 5, 2017, https://www.buzzfeed
news.com/article/josephbernstein/heres-how-breitbart-and-milo
-smuggled-white-nationalism.

244 *"nightmarish prediction":* Jason Reza Jorjani, "Why I Left the Alt-
Right," September 20, 2017, https://jasonrezajorjani.com/blog/2017
/9/20/why-i-left-the-alt-right.

244 *video posted online was indeed clipped:* I emailed Hermansson on
July 24, 2019, and sent Singal a message through his website the same
day or the day before.

245 *"We have no knowledge":* Jesse Singal, "Undercover with the Alt-
Right," *New York Times,* September 19, 2017, https://www.nytimes
.com/2017/09/19/opinion/alt-right-white-supremacy-undercover
.html?mcubz=0.

246 *"we've been working with and talking to the State Department":* John
Catsimatidis, "Michael Bagley—A refugee solution?" Catsimatidis
.com, September 24, 2017, http://www.catsimatidis.com/michael
-bagley-refugee-solution/.

## CHAPTER 20: DEEP STATES

252 *vice president was considering resigning:* Guiherme Mazui, "Vice Mourão diz que Olavo de Carvalho deve se limitar à função de 'astrólogo,'" *Politica*, April 22, 2019, https://g1.globo.com/politica /noticia/2019/04/22/vice-mourao-diz-que-olavo-de-carvalho-deve -se-limitar-a-funcao-de-astrologo.ghtml.

255 *reduce funding for education and culture:* Shannon Sims, "Brazil Slashes Funding to Scientists. The Planet May Suffer," *National Geographic*, April 19, 2019, https://www.nationalgeographic.com /environment/2019/04/brazil-cuts-funding-scientists-grad-students -environment-suffers/.

## CHAPTER 21: THE RECKONING

265 *"Bagley has never gotten past the discussion phase":* This information is based on publicly available court documents from the U.S. District Court for the Eastern Division of Virginia, Alexandria division. Case number 1:19mj315.

270 *physically beaten:* Simon Murphy, "'A Couple of Black Eyes': Johnson and the Plot to Attack a Reporter," *Guardian*, https://www.theguard ian.com/politics/2019/jul/14/black-eyes-boris-johnson-plot-attack -reporter-darius-guppy.

# INDEX

# ABOUT THE AUTHOR

BENJAMIN R. TEITELBAUM is an award-winning expert on the radical right and a professor of ethnomusicology and international affairs at the University of Colorado, Boulder. He is the author of *Lions of the North: Sounds of the New Nordic Radical Nationalism* and has written on far-right politics for the *New York Times,* the *Wall Street Journal, Foreign Policy,* the *Los Angeles Review of Books,* and *The Atlantic.*